D1761095

CROSSING FIELDS IN MODERN SPANISH CULTURE

THE EUROPEAN HUMANITIES RESEARCH CENTRE

UNIVERSITY OF OXFORD

Director: Martin McLaughlin
Fiat-Serena Professor of Italian Studies

The European Humanities Research Centre of the University of Oxford organizes a range of academic activities, including conferences and workshops, and publishes scholarly works under its own imprint, LEGENDA. Within Oxford, the EHRC bridges, at the research level, the main humanities faculties: Modern Languages, English, Modern History, Classics and Philosophy, Music and Theology. The Centre stimulates interdisciplinary research collaboration throughout these subject areas and provides an Oxford base for advanced researchers in the humanities.

The Centre's publishing programme focuses on making available the results of advanced research in medieval and modern languages and related interdisciplinary areas. An Editorial Board, whose members are drawn from across the British university system, covers the principal European languages. Titles currently include works on Arabic, Catalan, Chinese, English, French, German, Italian, Portuguese, Russian, Spanish and Yiddish literature. In addition, the EHRC co-publishes with the Society for French Studies, the Modern Humanities Research Association and the British Comparative Literature Association. The Centre also publishes a Special Lecture Series under the LEGENDA imprint, and a journal, *Oxford German Studies*.

Further information:
Kareni Bannister, Senior Publications Officer
European Humanities Research Centre
University of Oxford
76 Woodstock Road, Oxford OX2 6HP
enquiries@ehrc.ox.ac.uk
www.ehrc.ox.ac.uk

LEGENDA

European Humanities Research Centre
University of Oxford

Crossing Fields in Modern Spanish Culture

EDITED BY

FEDERICO BONADDIO AND XON DE ROS

European Humanities Research Centre
University of Oxford
2003

Published by the
European Humanities Research Centre
of the University of Oxford
47 Wellington Square
Oxford OX1 2JF

LEGENDA is the publications imprint of the
European Humanities Research Centre

ISBN 1 900755 87 4

First published 2003

British Library Cataloguing in Publication Data
A CIP catalogue record for this book is available from the British Library

LEGENDA series designed by Cox Design Partnership, Witney, Oxon
Printed in Great Britain by Information Press, Eynsham, Oxford OX8 1JJ

Copy-Editor: Dr Jeffrey Dean

CONTENTS

PREFACE

Federico Bonaddio

The margins of a page have long ceased to be guarantors of the place where a literary work begins or ends. With respect to art, the same may be said of the borders of a canvas or a frame. Neither does the cinema screen contain the full picture, nor the musical score all its performances. Boundaries are the markers not of finitude but of the site of a plurality of crossings. Crossings between text and context (at the levels of production and reception), between text and intertext, between a multitude of discourses (aesthetic, economic, political and scientific), between subjectivity and objectivity, between different disciplines, between the life of texts and life itself. Such a view of the textual naturally privileges those modes of critical analysis that have abandoned idealistic and essentialist notions about the creators of texts and the texts they create, which are neither conceived of nor produced in isolation and whose meaning and effect can never be limited solely to an understanding of their internal organization. Yet it does not seek either to replace such notions with equally simplistic notions of causality that conceive of the text purely as the product of external influences. For it is important to bear in mind that the crossing always runs both ways and that the relation between texts, discourses, disciplines and so forth is necessarily dialogical.

The essays collected here deal variously with the dialogue and interrelation between different cultural fields in nineteenth- and twentieth-century Spain. Some essays bring more evidently into play other fields such as economics, politics and medical science, whilst others focus more specifically on the crossing between different disciplines in the arts.

The first three essays are linked not only by their coverage of nineteenth-century topics but, more significantly, by their concern with the way in which discourse is bound up with political, social and cultural identities as articulated through the processes of writing and painting, legal texts and literary criticism. Andrew Ginger, in his essay 'Identity and Dissociation in the Mid-Nineteenth-Century Paintings of Eugenio Lucas and Contemporaneous Fiction', identifies a concern in that period to undermine the direct expression of identity. Beginning with examples from the experimental literature of Antonio Ros de Olano and Rosalía de Castro, Ginger moves on to discuss the ways in which the little-known short-story writer, Agustín Bonnat, is overtly artistic in the creation of an identity for himself in works that are self-parodic and put the reader centre-stage. And what Bonnat achieves with words, the painter Eugenio Lucas, no doubt influenced by the writer, manages to achieve with paint, continually reinventing himself in paintings that rework the paintings of other artists. Only, unlike Bonnat, Lucas also has a political concern, aiming as he does to engage the viewer in the Republican re-creation of Spain by means of works that self-consciously depart from the models of identity offered by Romantic self-portraiture and its melancholy.

Stephen Jacobson's 'The Rise and Fall of the House of Fontanellas: Narrative, Class and Ideology in Nineteenth-Century Barcelona' focuses on a *cause célèbre* that took place in Barcelona from 1861 to 1864. Its central concern is the crossing from fictional narratives to real life and vice versa. Jacobson describes how, in respect of the Causa Fontanellas, comedy, tragedy and romance entered the discourse of defence and prosecution; in other words, how familiar literary narratives structured the very legal process seeking here to establish the identity of a man laying claim to an inheritance by allegedly falsifying his persona. What is more, Jacobson, in a more general commentary, alludes to a possible correlation between the construction of bourgeois identities and the status and success of narrative genres. Richard A. Cardwell, on the other hand, in his essay, 'Oscar Wilde and Spain: Medicine, Morals, Religion and Aesthetics in the *Fin de Siglo*', shows how a variety of discourses—moral and medical, as well as aesthetic—can inform the practice of literary criticism. Cardwell takes as his case study the reception of Oscar Wilde in *fin-de-siècle* Spain, with particular attention to the construction of identities for the writer that serve either to denigrate or idealize him. Central to the argument for or against Wilde were the theories on the relationship between mental degeneration, genius and criminality espoused by Cesare Lombroso, Professor of Mental Diseases at the University of Pavia, and taken up and adapted in turn by Max Nordau, one of the professor's most enthusiastic supporters. Both Lombroso and Nordau employed the discourses of new medical sciences in their critique of new artistic trends and their proponents, a critique that, despite its claims to scientific objectivity, was itself informed by a particular set of ethical and moral criteria. What Cardwell also points out is that even the defence articulated by supporters of Wilde—in the Spanish context, the Latin-American writers Enrique Gómez Carrillo and Rubén Darío—was coloured by the discourse of medicine, if only to reverse the binary oppositions of, for example, healthy/sick, sane/mad.

The next six essays concern themselves in different ways with the polyvalence of what may broadly be termed modernist production and consequently raise questions about the creative process against the background of the acute self-consciousness characteristic of early twentieth-century creativity. Roberta Quance's 'Norah Borges Illustrates Two Spanish Women Poets' makes a case for illustration being more than a mere accompaniment to texts. The texts in question are Concha Méndez's *Canciones de mar y tierra* and Carmen Conde's *Júbilos*. Quance discusses the relation of these women poets to the masculine character of the Spanish vanguard described by José Ortega y Gasset in his essay *La deshumanización del arte*. Each represented a different model of the woman poet, the former seeming to embrace the values of the vanguard, the latter depicting a world that could be regarded as more traditionally feminine. Yet despite these key differences, the elusive quality of Norah Borges's drawings of androgynous, angelic children at play succeeded in accommodating, enhancing even, the work of both women. Borges was a much-sought-after illustrator, and Quance suggests how her reputation may have shaped the critical evaluation of the works she illustrated. Reputation and criticism are also bound up in Jacqueline Cockburn's essay 'Gifts from the Poet to the Art Critic'. Cockburn argues that the poet Federico García Lorca, frustrated by the folkloricist tag that (wrongly, in his view) some of his first publications prompted, turned to drawing in order to enter a wider, contemporary debate about creativity. Working in the same artistic field allowed Lorca to get closer intellectually, and perhaps personally, to people he admired, like the artist Salvador Dalí or the art critic Sebastiá Gasch. Lorca's drawings thus became the site of an intellectual exchange, informed as they were by his discussions with Gasch on the subject of art.

Xon de Ros, in 'Ignacio Sánchez Mejías Blues', explores the burdens and tensions of the act of writing about loss, proposing a reading of Lorca's *Llanto por Ignacio Sánchez Mejías* that highlights the poem's metapoetic dimension and, by extension, the position it occupies in a wider socio-cultural context. De Ros demonstrates how

Lorca adopts the idiom and rhythm of the blues, a music the poet encountered in the jazz clubs of New York, and considers the way the poem dramatizes a conflict between this cultural tradition and the elegiac tradition to which it is tributary. Through the association of the elegy with melancholia and the blues with mourning, de Ros explores the workings of gender in Lorca's poem, suggesting that the poem's failure to effect a reconciliation between the two forms has ideological implications that give the loss it laments a socio-cultural significance. Continuing with Lorca and with music, D. Gareth Walters, in his essay, 'Parallel Trajectories in the Careers of Falla and Lorca', examines the influence of traditional Andalusian culture on the work of the poet and on that of the composer Manuel de Falla. Walters draws attention to the strikingly similar evolution of their respective Andalusian phases, the influence of clichéd, romantic notions of Andalusia giving way to attempts by both men to convey something more authentic.

In 'Angels, Art and Analysis: Alberti's *Sobre los ángeles*', Helen Laurenson-Shakibi describes how Rafael Alberti's well-known collection of poems replicates pictorial techniques. Indeed, Alberti, who trained as an artist, made no distinction between poetry and painting. Drawing parallels with Goya and Maruja Mallo, Laurenson argues that Alberti's work is informed by his pictorial heritage. Yet she also points to another visual source for the construction of his poems: the visions accompanying the mental disturbances that plagued the poet. All the more significant given that *Sobre los ángeles* emerged from the ruins of a nervous breakdown. In 'The Theory of Surrealist Collage through Image and Text: Angel Planells and José María Hinojosa', Jacqueline Rattray also focuses on the crossing of the boundary between poetry and the pictorial arts, a crossing that is facilitated by surrealism's particular conception of the collage process. Beginning with an explanation of the processes at work in one of the collage drawings by Planells that illustrate *La sangre en libertad*, Hinojosa's last book of poems, Rattray goes on to describe how 'Ya no me besas', a poem from the collection, is constructed according to the same principles and produces corresponding effects.

The final five essays cover, for the most part, subjects from the Francoist period to the beginning of the twenty-first century, and together they bear testimony not only to contemporary culture's fascination with the past and its appropriation of traditional archetypes but also to the ever-increasing need to view Spanish culture in a transnational context. Elizabeth Drayson, in 'The Cid Legend in Opera and Film: A Modern Afterlife for Epic and Ballad', examines the recreation of the Cid legend in nineteenth-century opera and in two film epics of the 1960s. If the medieval treatment of the Cid legend was itself varied, these modern adaptations are no less so. Intended as entertainment, they are shaped not only by the demands of genre and medium, but also by the effort to make the legend relevant to contemporary audiences. Drayson reflects on the claims to historical authenticity made by the films, which provide another point of comparison in so far as they are examples of European and Hollywood productions respectively. The subsequent essay, Jo Labanyi's 'Impossible Love and Spanishness: *Adventures of Don Juan* (Sherman, 1949) and *Don Juan* (Sáenz de Heredia, 1950)', also compares Hollywood and European films, its subject of investigation being a Spanish remake of a Warner Brothers production. Produced for Cifesa, José Luis Sáenz de Heredia's remake of Vincent Sherman's *Adventures of Don Juan* attempts to correct its predecessor's negative portrayal of the Spanish monarchy. However, Labanyi argues against readings of the film that would see it simply as exemplifying Nationalist values. Instead, she explores the film's ambivalent relation to the Hollywood production and reflects on the models of Europeanness constructed in both films via a discourse on romantic love.

In 'Why *Giselle*? Tusquets's Use of Ballet in *Siete miradas en un mismo paisaje*', Abigail Lee Six discusses the intertextual possibilities of Esther Tusquets's short story 'Giselle', which centres on its protagonist's infatuation with a foreign ballerina. Lee Six considers how the plot line of the ballet *Giselle* contributes to an understanding of Tusquets's protagonist. She explores both class and gender issues, the latter connected in part with the paradox inherent in the choreography of ballet which is dependent on the strength of its ballerinas in order to create the illusion of fragility. In addition, Lee Six reflects upon the reference to another ballet, *Scheherazade*. In '*Los dominios del lobo* by Javier Marías: Hollywood and *anticasticismo novísimo*', Alexis Grohmann describes how Javier Marías's novel, set in the United States and peopled by American characters, employs the idiolect of Hollywood cinema and in particular film noir. Grohmann also notes the foreign references in the poetry of the *novísimos*, along with its antirealist character. He argues that the fascination with the foreign and the tendency towards aestheticization and literariness represent a generational shift, a turning away by new writers from the localism and realism that characterized much literature written under Franco.

Finally, Paul Julian Smith's essay, 'From Brussels to Madrid: EU–US Audiovisual Relations and Spanish TV Production', moves us onto firmly twenty-first-century ground. It is in two parts. The first, in the context of a European Commission Trade Conference on EU–US Relations held in Brussels in 2000, touches upon the impact of globalization as well as competing economic and cultural discourses on audiovisual production. The second focuses more specifically on *Cine de barrio*, a low-budget and unashamedly nostalgic Spanish television show comprising studio chat with film stars of the Francoist period, documentary inserts and a screening of a film from that period. Smith argues that history is domesticated or banalized by the show, whose immense popularity is evidence not only of the national entertainment industry's neglect of a particular demographic but also of the way in which peculiarly local and transnational formats can sit side by side on our screens.

The essays in this collection, paying attention to cultural processes and strategies as well as to the poetics of texts defined by their formal hybridity, contribute to contemporary efforts to widen the boundaries of academic research and find a critical language to encompass different fields of study. In so doing, they respond to the demands of an academic readership that is more and more interested in culture in its broadest sense.

NOTES ON THE CONTRIBUTORS

Federico Bonaddio is Lecturer in Modern Spanish Studies at King's College London.

Richard A. Cardwell is Professor of Modern Spanish Literature at the University of Nottingham.

Jacqueline Cockburn is Head of History of Art at Westminster School and Lecturer in Spanish Art at Birkbeck College, University of London.

Elizabeth Drayson is College Lecturer in Spanish at Peterhouse and New Hall, University of Cambridge.

Andrew Ginger is Lecturer in Hispanic Studies at the University of Edinburgh.

Alexis Grohmann is Lecturer in Spanish at the University of St Andrews.

Stephen Jacobson is Lecturer in European Studies at King's College London.

Jo Labanyi is Professor of Spanish and Cultural Studies at the University of Southampton.

Helen Laurenson-Shakibi is Lecturer in Spanish at the University of Leeds.

Abigail Lee Six is Professor of Spanish at Royal Holloway, University of London.

Roberta Quance is Lecturer in Spanish at Queen's University, Belfast.

Jacqueline Rattray is Queen Sofía Research Fellow in Peninsular Spanish Literature at Exeter College, University of Oxford.

Xon de Ros is Senior Lecturer in Modern Spanish Studies at King's College London.

Paul Julian Smith is Professor of Spanish at the University of Cambridge.

D. Gareth Walters is Professor of Hispanic Studies at the University of Exeter.

ACKNOWLEDGEMENTS

Many of the essays in this volume were originally presented at a conference held at King's College London in September 2001 and sponsored by the Department of Spanish and Spanish-American Studies. We are indebted to all the participants in that event whose enthusiasm and encouragement accompanied the project from the outset. We would also like to thank the contributors to the volume for the work they have put into preparing and revising their essays. The publication of this volume has been possible thanks to the generous support of Professor Arthur Lucas, former Principal of King's College London. We are also grateful to the Cervantes Institute in London and to the Department of Spanish and Spanish-American Studies at King's for their contributions to its funding. We would also like to acknowledge our gratitude to Professor Barry Ife for his advice and guidance and, of course, to Kareni Bannister and all the staff in the European Humanities Research Centre (Oxford University) for their critical scrutiny of the manuscript and their editorial advice and expertise. Finally, we would like to thank Paloma Altolaguirre, Herederos de Federico García Lorca and Asunción Hinojosa Nagel for kindly providing print permissions.

Federico Bonaddio
Xon de Ros

CHAPTER 1

Identity and Dissociation in the Mid-Nineteenth-Century Paintings of Eugenio Lucas and Contemporaneous Fiction

Andrew Ginger

The most experimental works of art and literature of mid-nineteenth-century Spain were driven at least in part by an impulse to dissociation from direct communication of personal identity, but this was conceived by the Spanish nineteenth-century avant-garde across a number of fields as a means to some more authentic communication of identity. In the 1860s the prose works *El doctor Lañuela* (1863) by Antonio Ros de Olano and Rosalía de Castro's *El caballero de las botas azules* (1867) are indicative of this trend.[1] Ros's still neglected *El doctor Lañuela*, described by Menéndez Pelayo as an 'indecipherable word-puzzle',[2] tells how the orphan Josef falls in love with a magnetized ideal woman Luz, whilst being pursued by his former lover Camila, at the same time as seeking a cure for his Uncle's corns from Luz's captor, the quack Doctor Lañuela. *El caballero de las botas azules* recounts how a man is transformed by a transsexual muse into the mysterious Duque de la Gloria whose blue boots entrance Spanish society, and who promises redemption both of literature and society by bringing the Book of Books.

The details of *El doctor Lañuela* are less important to us here than are Ros's remarks about his authorial presence in Josef's first-person narrative and his comments on the autonomy of literary objects and the role of the reader. Ros takes as his starting point the well-established Romantic theory that fiction should transcend objectivity and subjectivity, or hold both in ironic, eternal transcendental play (*DL* 26). In so doing, it concedes significant roles to the reader, the writer and the autonomous text, the importance of which must be safeguarded. What Ros typically does, though, is to tip the balance significantly. He says that he appears in his little book as the shadow appears where light breaks against an obscure object (*DL* 27). This seems to be a significant reversal of the priorities in the famous allegory of Plato's Cave, for the true identity of the author is to be found, not by turning from the shadow to its God-like true source in the light, nor by seeing in the shadow faint traces of divine authorial light. Rather the author is to be found only where the shadow cast by his deliberately obscure work begins, as befits a text written after Luz, the light, has died. As a consequence, the author is no longer felt as so immanent within the text as before.

These ideas are reinforced by the narrator's claim that he is abandoned by his own book as it goes out into the world, asserting a more radical autonomy of the text (*DL* 281). As a result, the role of the reader is also greater than before. The text is described as oviparous rather than viviparous, born as an egg rather than as a fully alive mammalian creature, and readers are told they must sit upon the egg and gestate its meaning (*DL* 280–1). Whilst this view shares much of Romantic theory's insistence on the active participation of readers, it suggests that they must act in the relative absence of an internal dynamism driving the creature to growth, as would happen with mammalian animals in the womb. Ros claims, however, that the whole point of these changes is to provide a truer sincerity, and we are told to read the text thinking that he felt as he wrote (*DL* 26). This higher form of sincerity corresponds to the realities of a modern world and of an interior mental state, which are overwhelmed by loss of the Ideal. It relates too to Ros's claim that any more direct expression of subjectivity would in fact undermine an objective perspective.[3]

The concern to undermine direct expressions of identity in favour of something more remote and yet more authentic is central too to Castro's *El caballero de las botas azules*. It has been widely observed that the playful, ludic approach of the Knight's story is central to Castro's objectives as regards social change.[4] The point indeed is to provide an alternative to Romantic approaches to revolutionary change. Yet the most salient aspect of the Caballero's identity is less its mystery, even really its playful irony, than its vacuity, and it is in this respect that the

Knight is supposed to differ from his Romantic antecedents. In the place of the resonant Blue Flower of German Romanticism, we are presented with a fashion item, a pair of Blue Boots. The Book of Books that the Knight brings is judged only by its attractive cover— and by the fact that it costs nothing (*CBA* 343).[5] Though the Knight is linked to public art, both in panoramas and statues (*CBA* 107, 343–4), he fails to carry the charge of meaning that the nineteenth century expected. He himself tires and remarks, 'tu poder, querida Musa, sólo alcanza a añadir nuevas locuras y vanidades a las vanidades y locuras de los hombres' [your power, dear Muse, succeeds only in adding new follies and vanities to the vanities and follies of men] (*CBA* 301). Significantly, he has to destroy his own feelings for the woman Casimira (*CBA* 229) and feels the need to warn the innocent Mariquita of the danger he represents: 'Soy un duende inquieto y tornadizo que se complace en reírse de sí mismo y de los que se le parecen' [I am a restless, fickle little devil who delights in mocking himself and those who resemble him] (*CBA* 288).

The vacuity and self-parodic identity of the Caballero is, however, seriously intended as a means of understanding contemporary society, as critics like Charnon-Deutsch and Kirkpatrick have shown. Only through such a figure of infinitely inexplicable silliness and indefinition can so corrupt and desire-ridden a society be captivated as well as expressed. As the Muse of Novelty remarks (*CBA* 105–6):

Los espectadores devanarán los sesos por comprender su argumento, y te juro que no lo conseguirán, así como nadie comprende a ellos [...]. ¿Qué más puede ambicionar un hombre en el siglo de las caricaturas que hacer la suya y la de los demás ante un auditorio conmovido? [The audience will rack their brains trying to understand its plot, and I swear to you they will not manage to do so, just as no-one can understand them. What higher ambition could a man have in the century of caricatures than to caricature himself and everyone else before a thrilled public?]

The point of the Prologue quite simply is that the corrupt, self-deceiving, ambitious individual who seeks help from the Muse is transformed into the Knight of the Blue Boots because that caricature of himself, as the Muse puts it, is the supreme expression of the kind of person he is, and the logical extension of his ambitions. This is why throughout he laughs at himself as much as at others, and that hurts.

If the reader, however, thinks that the ending of the novel, with its apparent—but only apparent—transformation of the world, is what they should be reading towards as towards a revelation, they are falling precisely for the Muse of Novelty's trick. The point of the novel is rather that if we follow our desires towards that ending, we miss the most significant outcome, which was raised just before it in the tale of Mariquita and her admirer Melchor, both children of the poorest and most oppressed part of Madrid, living in the shadow of death. Mariquita needs to be corrected in her more Romantic outbursts, but equally, as the Knight says, is an admirable 'alma ardiente' [ardent soul] (*CBA* 288). Melchor, her unwanted lover, turns out to be an artist of genius, pointedly contrasted with the literary ambitions of the Knight, because, working in solitude, he has no ambitions or desire for glory. Melchor represents the true union of artistic *fantasía* and nature, and posseses genuine mystery in his 'misteriosa gruta' [mysterious grotto] (*CBA* 294–7). These two are lower-class repositories of values lost in the ludic approach necessary to understand and address wider contemporary society.[6]

Nonetheless, the novel remains open, and readers, if they have noticed (as many recent critics suggest) that the ending is not, as it were, the ending, are faced not with the ascent of the Knight and a definitive, revelatory termination,[7] however playful, but with the question of what will become of these two young people. The problem is that Melchor does not dress well or look very attractive, as the Caballero observes. What the Caballero offers is for Melchor to come with him to Madrid to aid him in his plan and thus gain the wealth, reputation and clothes that will impress Mariquita (*CBA* 297–9). We do not know what happens, but we are returned to a familiar difficulty both in Castro's fiction of the 1850s and '60s and in wider political literature, one that was central to the vacuous identity of the Knight. In order to be successful, one must deal in the ambitions and fashions of an essentially corrupt society. In order to triumph, the Knight became devoid of identity. The reader is left to ponder whether things can be any different for Melchor and Mariquita if they follow the Knight's advice.[8]

Thus, Castro centres our attention on a totally vacuous and dissociated version of identity in the ludic Knight, so as to understand and address a corrupt society, but her aim in so doing is for readers thereby to understand and see beyond it to a potential alternative. None the less, readers are tempted with a false conclusiveness in the ending of the novel, and must take up a new role attempting to think through the problematics of the untied thread of Melchor and Mariquita's tale.

Having seen how dissociation, and the increasingly active role of the reader, is intended to lead to a more authentic sense of identity, let us turn to the enigmatic figure of Eugenio Lucas, which has perplexed many critics. We do not know much about his life—a Court painter who was a left-wing militia member and a Republican, he lived in an extramarital relationship after abandoning his wife. Lucas rarely joined in public exhibitions and produced much of his work for private clients, who seem to have been eager consumers of his art.[9] For some time seen as an imitator or copyist of Goya, and then of several artists, Lucas's very personal and distinctive style is now widely recognized by critics, especially since Arnáiz's monographic study, but he remains a little known or understood painter.

One of Lucas's key concerns was the re-creation of paintings and painting styles from the past. He even marketed many of his works as such—paintings in the style of this or that painter. It is this that led to his being seen as a copyist or even forger. However, his re-creations of past works are often precisely that—they are not copies, nor are they simply hommages in the way that Goya's *Familia de Carlos IV*, for example, pays tribute to Velázquez's *Las meninas*. To take that particular example further, Lucas paints *Las meninas* but alters the expressions, the movements, the positions, the light, the colour, the application of paint, in short anything he feels like. Critics have, therefore, understandably compared his efforts to similar endeavours by Bacon and Picasso.[10] In other instances, Lucas creates scenes that, on the face of existing evidence might have been painted by a past painter—a bullfighting scene in the style of Goya, a genre landscape picture as might have been created by a seventeenth-century artist from the Low Countries—but markedly alters the way the paint is applied and the chosen colours.

As a result, in much of Lucas's *œuvre*, there seems to be what you might call a double alienation. On the one hand, there is a violation of any sense of identification with artists of the past, which the foremost Lucas critic, Arnáiz, describes as rather comic.[11] On the other, Lucas's own identity as a painter seems to exist, in these works at least, only in the donning of the successive (and distorted) masks of other, usually dead painters. Today Lucas is Velázquez, tomorrow Goya, now a seventeenth-century genre painter from the Low Countries, now, as sometimes occurs, a commercial artist from nineteenth-century Andalusia.[12] He seems to have taken to heart Larra's much earlier claim for his own use of alter-egos, that his true character was not to have one.[13] But more still than Larra, Lucas exists not just in self-created masks, but through other people, other times. The continuous underlying voice of Larra, projected beneath the masks and appearing in the act of doubling, seems to be replaced by a shattering of identity into multiple others.

This attitude is most dramatically summed up in Lucas's large painting, *Felipe IV, su corte y las meninas*, and in another, his *Fantasía sobre las meninas*. Both belong with a series of paintings that take genre scenes from the court of Felipe IV in such a way that we experience past time not as grandiose significance but as an anecdotal moment, merging (at its most striking in *Felipe IV, su corte y las meninas*) the scale of history painting (the work is 2.09 × 2.885 metres) with the relative insignificance of incident. In nearly all cases, the spectator is given, after the fashion of Velázquez's own *Las meninas*, the strange sense of having wandered into a scene in the past, as people turn and acknowledge our presence.

But at his most startling, Lucas does more than that. The reception we receive in *Fantasía sobre las meninas* is perplexingly hostile in a way that is not explained. In *Felipe IV, su corte y las meninas* (1858), the bizarrely massive gathering has no context to explain it: we seem to be being greeted by the court in a way never shown in seventeenth-century art. We as viewers are led to ask: Who are we? What are we doing here in the past? What is this court event we see before us? and, in the case of the angered faces of *Fantasía sobre las meninas*, What have we done? Our need to look further into these irresolvably enigmatic matters is reinforced by the repeated presence of spectacles: worn by Quevedo in a painting on the wall and in person in the foreground, and by the jester of *Las meninas*, who has been altered for the purpose. At the same time, Lucas asserts a problematic identity. Images on the wall at the back reappear as pastiche in the foreground, the paint of *Las meninas* on the wall dissolves into and merges with the image Lucas has created before it, graphically indicating the relationship and clash between past and present artist.

Pastiche techniques were readily used in the 1840s and '50s as a way of guaranteeing the authenticity of history plays—how better, after all, to make someone sound like Quevedo than to get him to speak in Quevedo-like verse? However, Lucas instead uses pastiche in a way that unsettles the viewer. In so doing, he makes a wider and more challenging point. Political and aesthetic ideology of the Spanish

Romantic period had rested to a significant extent on the recreation of the supposedly Liberal elements of the past in the present, adapting them smoothly and organically to the present day. That was what lay behind the techniques of many history plays about past writers.

Lucas seems to deny the possibility of such an organic rebirth of the nation, in particular through his choice of colours. Many Spanish art critics of the late 1850s, including Alarcón and the Progressive Regionalist Manuel Murguía, argued that the colour deployed by the French Romantics was a horrible violation of true Spanish colourism and urged a return to the sober palette of the seventeenth-century masters as part of a progressive national rebirth. In *Felipe IV, su corte y las meninas*, Lucas provocatively employs precisely that 'horrible colorido francés' [horrible French colour], as Murguía put it, to re-create the world and the art of the great Spanish master.[14] Even where his palette is marginally more subdued, as in the bleak *Fantasía sobre las meninas*, his characteristic nervous scraping and sculpting of thick impasto on the canvas (studied in depth by Arnáiz)[15] is far removed from the world of Velázquez. His work almost seems a joke on the widespread idea that artists should train by organically imitating the works of past artists.[16]

So, Lucas continually, enigmatically and even comically reinvents himself through other artists, in joint fusion and conflict with their identities, providing dissociation instead of identification, and, at his most extreme, leaving the viewer frankly perplexed. It is not entirely improbable that he does so under the influence (direct or indirect) of the writer Agustín Bonnat, which had spread like wildfire through much of the prose fiction of the mid 1850s. In Bonnat's obituary, written in 1858, his friend and collaborator Alarcón first refers to the style, not just the content, of Bonnat's work as part of the joke, as a kind of self-parody: 'aquel extravagante estilo, que era una humorada más de sus producciones' [that extravagant style, which was yet another joke in his work]. Secondly, he states that the reader was the main protagonist of Bonnat's work: 'El lector [...] desempeñó casi siempre el principal papel en sus novelas' [The reader almost always played the main part in his stories]. Thirdly (and with shades of dandyism here), Alarcón says that Bonnat's identity was literary, that is to say it was an artistic creation, and that this creation was disconcerting and deliberately bizarre: 'su saludo, su figura, sus costumbres, todo era en él literario, original, excéntrico' [his way of greeting you, his countenance, his behaviour, everything about him was literary, bizarre [or original], eccentric].[17]

It is not difficult to see how this might fit with Lucas's aims: putting the viewer awkwardly centre-stage, using a self-parodic style and, last but not least, being deliberately, overtly artistic in the creation of his own identity. Lucas, after all, forges his painterly identity out of physical works of art by other people. What is more, he is at pains to make clear that he does so too out of the physical material of the paint: one thinks here not just of the characteristic sculpted impasto that so evidently serves this purpose, but also that transitional area in *Felipe IV, su corte y las meninas* where paint flows, as it were, between Lucas and Velázquez. Lucas is a painter made out of paintings and paint.

However, whilst this formula works well for someone like Bonnat who, as Alarcón goes on to comment, was quintessentially apolitical,[18] it runs into complications with a painter like Lucas, who was highly politicized and who, when he felt like it, could take, at least apparently, a rather different approach. Lucas's own self-portraits in oils are monumentally sober with a dark, nondescript backdrop and very limited colours, seeming to follow in the steps of Velázquez. He produced other works that look far more similar to their seventeenth-century counterparts than his versions of *Las meninas*: *El santero del Escorial*, which features an image of a woman based on Ribera; *El cazador*, based on Velázquez's hunting paintings. Even in more fanciful works, he could use fantasy to pretty explicit ends: his allegory *La República guiando a España* on one level at least needs little exegesis, as do his fierce satires of Queen Isabel. The viewer in these latter cases quickly gets the point, and thus does not seem to be the protagonist in quite the same way as before.

It is not easy to reconcile the various elements here, and to some extent they doubtless respond to a playful reinvention of himself fuelled by his commercial endeavours: there would be one or other Eugenio Lucas for the buyer's taste, as Arnáiz's analysis of his sales of free imitations implies.[19] Doubtless, too, just as Goya used private patronage as an avenue to more independent work,[20] so Lucas goes further and makes commercial markets the *raison d'être* of his many faces. Yet it is possible we can get a little further than this. Let us turn for a moment to the most famous of the self-portraits. Lucas does not portray himself as self-absorbed or in a state of reverie, as did many of the Romantics before him, and as Courbet, for example, had done in the 1840s. Nor does he have dishevelled hair, or even interesting colours. He does not even portray himself at work. We have before us a fully paid-up member of the respectable middle classes: a man, it could be suggested, who sells paintings and has a decent job.

That latter element in itself is not an original guise: it had been used by Goya and by Lucas's immediate predecessor Alenza. However, what is especially noticeable is the lack of diffusion in the paint, and the lack of languor, melancholy or flights of emotion. Instead we have here, uncompromisingly portrayed, an aggressive look at the viewer, which surpasses in its violence the merely wry in comparison sidelong glance of Goya's frontispiece to *Los caprichos*, peeking out of the corner of his eye. The intensity of Romantic emotion, suggested in the ominous, looming darkness behind the figure and the shadowy brow, is turned outwards, not inwards, and projected against the viewer. Lucas raises his eyebrows and stares critically and rather amusedly at those of us looking at him. There is nothing uncertain or dissociated about this image, but it is very unsettling for the viewer, who seems to be taking up the position of a work of art to be examined somewhat harshly by the portrait. Whilst Lucas, then, asserts here a clearer identity and a stronger sense of national tradition, he does so whilst reaffirming a playfully critical outlook now detached from the melancholic inner world of someone like Larra.

If we turn from here to two appearances by Lucas in fantastic paintings (both identified by Arnáiz),[21] we learn more. Lucas appears bizarrely in *La república guiando a España* as a passing putto bearing a document that would appear to be the Constitution, as he flies beneath a turbulent fantastic crowd of Spain's ills, and above the Republic and Spain who stride before enslaved men in some Hellish landscape. In his second appearance, in a work known as *Mascarada*, which is created through pastiche from largely sexual imagery from *Los caprichos* (and elsewhere in Goya), Lucas takes on the guise of a dwarfish *bufón*. This may not, however, simply be a carnivalesque painting. A woman in a mask, supporting herself with two sticks (Goya's *Aún aprendo* comes to mind) is stopped by a tall figure with glasses wearing a carnival hat, who points her to where Lucas is heading. The rather twisted mouth and nose of this woman correspond to those of Lucas's portrait of Isabel II.

If this is so, then like many of the fantastic, apparently Goyesque works, this is a political satire of imprecise but resonant meaning. In both the allegory of the Republic and in *Mascarada*, the playful incarnation of Lucas has as his task the furthering of some political purpose, which in both cases requires an exit to the viewer's right, but, perhaps symbolically, the characters' left. Even in such evidently political works, the direction of the viewer's gaze thus becomes important. In the allegory, although we are led beyond the painting, neither the Republic nor Spain actually look ahead; rather both look backwards either to Lucas or to the scene behind them, perhaps underlining the problematic relationship of past, present and future for someone seeking to change the country. In the *Mascarada*, our gaze is directed beyond the painting to an unknown scene, in an echo of the last of Goya's *Desastres de la guerra*, entitled *Esto es lo verdadero*. This sort of playfulness would closely correspond to a strain of political satire in Spain in which fantastic political scenes are visited by the committed authors in some self-parodic guise. For example, the Republican polemicist and humourist Martínez Villergas appears in one leftist satirical fantasy of the 1840s as the chocolate-guzzling Fray Villergas.[22] Playful freedom becomes a means of enabling political and social criticism through laughter, in which the authors themselves must also be exempt from seriousness.

In that case, Lucas's disruptive responses to organicist ideas about a painter's identity, which we saw in his response to *Las meninas*, are part of a pattern of disruptive artistic activity rather than an end in themselves. One form of political and aesthetic organicism is subject to dissociation and confronted with the assertion of the painter's playful self-creation through paint and paintings, through the medium and its tradition. However, the emergent freedom is not supposed to end there, and nor is the relationship to the past. The new outward-looking creator, rather than the earlier melancholic, seeks to use his ability to fashion painterly materials, and to be fashioned in them, so as to stimulate the viewer to look in a more liberated way at the nation and its historical legacy. In so doing, viewers are to see in their own act of looking (sometimes, as we have seen, pointedly beyond the canvas) the grounds of action.

This more complex conception is perhaps underlined in the most striking of a series of paintings of 1858 depicting the opening of the water supply at Loyoza, an emblematic image of progress in mid-nineteenth-century Madrid. The painting perhaps looks fairly innocent and politically straightforward, emphasizing the populace over officialdom in a way not uncommon in painting of the Constitutional Period. However, the central figure before the fountain seems neither to be just a water-seller, nor in fact a contemporary person at all, but a reworking of seventeenth-century philosopher figures, and almost certainly of Velázquez's *Aesop*. If that is so, we have here a characteristically *luqueño* joke—Velázquez, and indeed Aesop, are *la fuente*, the source, in this case of Spain's material renewal as well as of the painter.

The choice of Aesop is not, it seems, coincidental. The genre of the fable enjoyed renewed popularity at the time, and had been in some cases updated for political and social purposes.[23] Velázquez's celebration of comico-serious philosophy with a practical edge is taken up by Lucas in a new form.[24] At the same time, Lucas invites us to see in the source of Velázquez a practical comico-serious philosophy that should be developed in an analogous spirit. Hence, rather than solemnly recreating the style of past masters, Lucas adopts Velázquez's enigmatic playfulness as a stimulus to the intelligence when treating *Las meninas*, for that is the true source.

At the same time, this view of the source in Velázquez helps explain some works more obviously related organically to the past—either in painting style, like *La Revolución* and *La ronda*, or even more directly, like *El santero del Escorial* and *El cazador*. These large-scale genre works in a sombre palette echo the efforts of Velázquez and other seventeenth-century Spanish painters to produce genre works on the scale of history painting, in a way that underlined the importance of practical and often popular experience.[25] But they do so in a startling new way. *El santero del Escorial*, based largely on Ribera's *Santa María Egipciaca*[26] and on Murillo's images of children, turns the saint into a beggar woman, accompanied by children. The inkpot beside her is a recurrent feature of Constitutional imagery, used to write the Constitution, and probably suggests on one level that this is Madre España, and that the children are the oft-referred-to *hijos de España* [Sons of Spain].[27] The torn paper on the ground (seen in other Lucas works) may well, therefore, represent the state of the Constitution. Behind her, we see middle-class and aristocratic crowds with whom comparison is invited, and beyond them, and with evident symbolism, El Escorial itself. The seventeenth-century use of genre figures on a large scale thus, perhaps, becomes a means to express the populace embodying national values rather than the ruling classes—thus echoing the appearance of Aesop.

That thought seems to be confirmed in *El cazador*, where the place of the King is taken by a gentleman insufficiently coiffed for higher society, whether out hunting or not, and quite possibly a poacher, behind whom we again see the upper-class crowds and a palace.[28] The playful reinvention of the seventeenth century for a symbolic realism thus now underlines the doctrine of popular sovereignty in the place of Royal and Church hierarchies. But matters are rather more complex still. Let us take the example of *El santero* (1862) to indicate this. In a triangular composition, two children look out at the viewer, whilst one looks only at his dog. There are two diagonals, one from the baby with a cross on his neck to the child looking out without one; the other to the child with a cross on his neck looking at the dog. The work seems to explore the merits on the one hand of the religious past (loyalty, fidelity) whilst underlining its lack of the *luqueño* virtue of aggressively staring out at the viewer. This new vision leaves the viewer, however, in a position where they must decide what attitude to take to the other beggar boy's direct gaze. The future is not just spelt out (though to some extent it is) but is generated by our reaction to the painting's aggressive stare (as was the case with *Felipe IV, su corte, y las meninas*).

And our reaction is not unproblematic, as the complex playing with imagery continues. The painting contains traditional sexual symbolism, reflecting Santa María Egipciaca's status as a former prostitute: a basket of fruits is tipped towards the viewer suggesting what is on offer.[29] What is more, no father is in sight. The painting thus becomes more resonant and less precise. Is the point that Mother Spain, like Isabel II (allegedly), has been prostituted (as contemporary satirists, including Lucas, often suggested)? Is the point that truly sacred values will only be found in this underclass driven to prostitution and looser morality? Such questions raise further issues. Births to single mothers and illegitimate children begging were matters of social, political and sexual anxiety. How will the viewer respond to them as the young Murillo-esque boy, apparently representing the future, tenders his empty cup?

Lucas's playful and enigmatic recreation of his identity through past artists disrupted organicist ideas and aimed to disconcert his viewers, asserting at the same time the primacy of the medium. Yet the ludic self-creating man of many faces was seeking a more authentic gaze, turning outwards from melancholic Romanticism, aggressively challenging the viewer. He hoped to direct our gaze towards a freer political perception and with it Republican values, but he did so by emphasizing the comico-serious legacy of the past to which we should respond rather than by a solemn attempt to fuse with it. Even when closest to the past, Lucas emphasized the provocations of his recreations, and sought to put the viewer on the spot, making them a protagonist in the recreation of Spain. In so doing, he expressed some of the central concerns of the mid-nineteenth-century avant-garde: to put dissociation in the place of earlier ideas of identity, to reinforce the role of the reader and viewer, but to do so in the quest for some higher understanding.

Notes to Chapter 1

1. Antonio Ros de Olano, *El doctor Lañuela: Episodio sacado de las memorias de un tal Josef* (Madrid: Manuel Galiano, 1863), abbreviated *DL* in text; Rosalía de Castro, *El caballero de las botas azules*, ed. Ana Rodríguez-Fisher (Madrid: Cátedra, 1995; first pubd 1867), *CBA* in text.

2. Marcelino Menéndez Pelayo, *Obras completas*, ed. Ángel González Palencia (Madrid: CSIC, 1948), xxvii: *Historia de la poesía hispanoamericana*, 395.

3. The points made here are discussed in rather greater depth in Andrew Ginger, *Antonio Ros de Olano's Experiments in Post-Romantic Prose (1857–1884): Between Romanticism and Modernism* (Lampeter: Edwin Mellen Press, 2000), 21–51, esp. 29–36.

4. E.g., in recent English-language criticism, Susan Kirkpatrick, 'Fantasy, Seduction, and the Woman Reader: Rosalía de Castro's Novels', *Culture and Gender in Nineteenth-Century Spain*, ed. Lou Charnon-Deutsch and Jo Labanyi (Oxford: Clarendon Press, 1995), 74–97; Lou Charnon-Deutsch, *Narratives of Desire: Nineteenth-Century Spanish Fiction by Women* (University Park: Pennsylvania State University Press, 1994), 85–112; Wadda Ríos-Font, 'From Romantic Irony to Romantic Grotesque: Mariano José de Larra and Rosalía de Castro's Self-Conscious Novels', *Hispanic Review* 65 (1997), 177–98.

5. Hence Ríos-Font's remarks on the breaking apart of language and experience, of outer and inner, 'From Romantic Irony to Romantic Grotesque', 195.

6. See the comparison made by Kirkpatrick, 'Fantasy, Seduction, and the Woman Reader', 89. Also, on Melchor, Catherine Davies, *Rosalía de Castro no seu tempo* (Vigo: Galaxia, 1987), 295.

7. On the dubious validity of the ending, see, for example, Kirkpatrick, 'Fantasy, Seduction, and the Woman Reader', 81.

8. This analysis suggests a qualification to the openness and ambiguity, the rejection of fixed positions, which many critics discern in the novel (as in the title of Antonio Risco's essay, '*El caballero de las botas azules* de Rosalía, una obra abierta', *Papeles de Son Armadans* 71 (1975), 113–30), because of the apparent interest in certain natural values (hence perhaps also the implicit reference to debates on nature and civilization, with their origins in the Enlightenment, in the Knight's despairing monologue, *CBA* 301). One recalls in this respect the clear social reformist principles discerned by Davies, *Rosalía de Castro no seu tempo*, 284–99.

9. José Manuel Arnáiz, *Eugenio Lucas: Su vida y su obra* (Madrid: M. Montal, 1981), 3–34. The majority of paintings discussed here are reproduced in Arnáiz's

lengthy catalogue. The version of the opening of the waters from Loyoza considered here is reproduced in colour in *Pintura española de la Era Industrial, 1800–1900* (Madrid: Fundación de Arte y Tecnología, 1998); the full range of versions is reproduced in Arnáiz. *El Santero del Escorial* and *Felipe IV, su corte y las meninas* are reproduced in colour in *Eugenio Lucas Velázquez en la Habana* [exhibition cat., Feb.–April 1996] (Madrid: Mapfre Vida, 1996). The most famous Lucas self-portrait appears as the frontispiece to that catalogue.

10. Rafael Santos Torroella, 'Alenza, Lucas, Lameyer', *Goya* 104 (1971), 78–89 at 81; Juan Antonio Gaya Nuño, 'En el centenario de Eugenio Lucas: El glorioso olvidado', *Goya* 98 (1970), 76–85 at 80.

11. E.g. Arnáiz, *Eugenio Lucas*, 86, 93.

12. Ibid., 81.

13. Mariano José de Larra, 'Las antigüedades de Mérida: Primer artículo', idem, *Artículos*, ed. Carlos Seco Serrano (Barcelona: Planeta, 1990), 384–7 at 384.

14. P. A. de Alarcón, 'Bellas Artes' [review of *Exposición de Bellas Artes*, 1858], idem, *Obras completas*, ed. Luis Martínez Kleiser (Madrid: Fax, 1954), 1808–13 at 1809; Manuel Murguía, 'Exposición de Bellas Artes 1858 (I)', *Museo universal* (1858), 153–4 at 153.

15. Arnáiz, *Eugenio Lucas*, 51–2.

16. The points made in this paragraph, and the painting *Felipe IV, su corte y las meninas*, were considered in greater detail and depth in Andrew Ginger, 'Recreating the Golden-Age?', a paper delivered in the University of Edinburgh Nineteenth-Century Iberian and Latin-American seminar series (Nov. 2000).

17. P. A. de Alarcón, 'Agustín Bonnat: Necrología', idem, *Obras completas*, 1785–8 at 1788.

18. Ibid.

19. Arnáiz, *Eugenio Lucas*, 32.

20. Sarah Symmons, *Goya* (London: Phaidon, 1998), 95, 158.

21. Arnáiz, *Eugenio Lucas*, 37.

22. *El Dómine Lucas* (1846), 101.

23. Ana María Freire López, 'La fábula', *Historia de la literatura española*, dir. Víctor García de la Concha, viii: *Siglo XIX (I)*, co-ord. Guillermo Carnero (Madrid: Espasa-Calpe, 1997), 542–8 at 545–6.

24. On Velázquez's *Aesop*, see Jonathan Brown, *Velázquez: Painter and Courtier* (New Haven and London: Yale University Press, 1986), 163.

25. Peter Cherry, 'Murillo's Genre Scenes and Their Context', *Murillo: Scenes of Childhood*, ed. Xanthe Brooke and Peter Cherry (London: Merrell, 2000), 9–41 at 16–20; Brown, *Velázquez*, 163.

26. The source is identified by Francisco Calvo Serraller, 'Eugenio Lucas Velázquez en la colección del Museo Nacional de la Habana', *Eugenio Lucas Velázquez en la Habana*, 25–65 at 62.

27. For images of writing and/or inkpots, see the reproductions in *Sagasta y el liberalismo español* [exhibition cat., 2000] (Madrid: Fundación Argentaria, 2000), 111, 114–15, 205. For an example of *Madre España* and her *hijos*, see José de Espronceda, 'A la patria: Elegía', *Poesías líricas y fragmentos épicos*, ed. Robert Marrast (Madrid: Castalia, 1970), 142–5 at 29–36. The notion is echoed in José Alvarez Junco's recent work on Spanish nationalism, *Mater dolorosa* (Madrid: Taurus, 2001).

28. Cf. Jonathan Brown and Carmen Garrido, *Velázquez: The Technique of Genius* (New Haven and London: Yale University Press, 1998), 125.
29. On fruit, sex and women in Murillo, cf. Cherry, 'Murillo's Genre Scenes', 34–5.

CHAPTER 2

The Rise and Fall of the House of Fontanellas: Narrative, Class and Ideology in Nineteenth-Century Barcelona

Stephen Jacobson

Historians have long been interested in the study of *causes célèbres*. In general, they offer an attractive means by which to penetrate the inner workings of society, often capturing the voices, private lives and concerns of persons traditionally left out of the historical record. Two methodological approaches have characterized their study. First, scholars have often used the *cause célèbre*—like other 'great stories' or 'microhistories'—as a window into viewing the cultural understanding of power, how it is exercised and even undermined outside explicit political and economic structures. Second, *causes célèbres* can also be examined by taking into account their form as well as their content, by understanding how they were told in addition to whom or what they concerned. Providing an interesting intersection between 'real life' and 'fiction', they reveal how narrative constructed political and ideological possibilities. As such, historians have borrowed from the disciplines of cultural anthropology and literary theory in order to inform their analysis; the *cause célèbre* represents a convenient vehicle by which to cross fields.[1]

The *cause célèbre* has existed as long as there were courts, but it emerged as a common feature of the political landscape during the second half of the eighteenth century, most noticeably in France, where it served as a veil for political discussion in a tightly censored environment. The expulsion of the Jesuits in 1764 following the trial of the head of the Order of the West Indies was one of the first high-profile cases on the continent; the most notorious one—the 'Diamond Necklace Affair' (1786)—took aim against the monarchy in the person of Marie Antoinette. These cases and a slew of others revealed that judicial authority could not be used directly against enemies of the state, but that public discussion, rumour, and speculation over forensic matters—multiplied by the power of the written word—could dramatically turn against the state and judicial authority itself. This explosion of *causes célèbres* has been the subject of an insightful study.[2] Sara Maza has noted that *causes célèbres*, not unlike literature and theatre, served to 'desacralize' Old Regime authority by holding it increasingly responsible to 'public opinion'. To Maza, the 'melodramatic imagination' moved from the theatre to the printed page, as the audience expanded out of the aristocratic opera house and into the bourgeois novel- and newspaper-reading public sphere. In the process, political discourse became 'resacralized' to conform to the exigencies of bourgeois morality.

As in much of Europe, *causes célèbres* proliferated with some frequency in Barcelona, the traditional capital of Catalonia. As the accused acquired increased rights during the nineteenth century, trials became increasingly open to public scrutiny, and lawyers were afforded wider latitude in which to frame their defences.[3] Well integrated into the political, economic and aesthetic milieu of Europe, events transpiring in Barcelona were often reflective of those taking place elsewhere. The Old Regime had come to a violent end during the 1830s, and by the mid nineteenth century a bourgeoisie clothed in prototypical European garb—emulating English and French economic, cultural and political practices—had firmly established itself as a powerful governing class. Housing one of Europe's principal textile industries, a remarkable 'Manchesterian' road of industrialization produced sharply-identified social classes perhaps more typical of places east of the Pyrenees than of Iberia.

In the literary sphere, the city initially lagged behind much of Western Europe. Like all of Spain, Catalonia did not develop a prestigious novelistic tradition until the latter decades of the century, as intellectuals were content to compose romantic poetry or drama written in verse. Barcelona produced no equivalent—nor even a cheap imitation—of Paris's Balzac or London's Dickens. Yet it did boast a lively tradition of popular theatre, which featured the typical melodramatic mixture of romance, tragedy and comedy that emulated pan-European plot lines.[4] By the century's end, the city was no longer a literary backwater but in the vanguard. Along with Paris, Munich, Vienna and Prague, Barcelona had become a centre of literary, artistic and architectural modernism.

In short, Barcelona experienced many of the prototypical phenomena associated with the 'great transformation', and, for this reason, provides an interesting setting in which to examine the progression of the *cause célèbre*. The analysis of Sara Maza does not represent the last word, but, as she would undoubtedly agree, it opens the door. After all, it would be poor procedure if not sheer conjecture to conclude that the *cause célèbre* retained the characteristics it exhibited in pre-industrial and pre-revolutionary Europe. What became of the *cause célèbre* following the fall of the Old Regime and the rise of industrial society? What happened once melodrama no longer exerted a 'magical' spell on the listener but became discursively integrated into the popular literary imagination? For it would be a huge leap to assume that the *cause célèbre* functioned as an ahistorical archetype, retaining its destabilizing potential of the late eighteenth century. Nor should we assume that it became immediately stripped of this potential and violently recomposed and brought into line with bourgeois interests. Neither the *cause célèbre* nor literary melodrama moved from their destructive power during the French Revolution to their placid aesthetic quality as expressed in the tabloids and popular novels of the twentieth century. Rather, they had to pass through the nineteenth century, during which time ideological possibilities and class interests became radically rearranged.

At first glance, the Causa Fontanellas, which took place in Barcelona in the 1860s, appears as a typical case of mistaken identity, a derivation of Martin Guerre some three centuries later.[5] It concerned the affairs of the Fontanellas family, owners of one of the most successful financial houses in Barcelona (and all of Spain) during the first half of the nineteenth century.[6] The bank's early history began with Antonio Fontanellas, a man of humble origins who in the late eighteenth century emigrated from a small town outside Barcelona to the Atlantic seaport of Cádiz, then Iberia's most prosperous city, where he made his fortune as a merchant banker, engaged in international commerce with the Americas. He later moved to Madrid, where he celebrated a number of lucrative contracts with the monarchy. With some of his initial profits, he sponsored the education of his younger brothers, who in turn opened branches in Barcelona and Málaga. Around the turn of the century, the three brothers concentrated their wealth in Barcelona, which offered the most promising outlet for their capital and was after all their home. The original entrepreneur Antonio Fontanellas died in the mid 1820s, after the middle brother Francisco had already assumed control of the bank. Francisco further augmented the fortune and eventually acquired the title Marqués de Casa Fontanellas, granted to him by Queen Isabel II.

The spectacular rise of humble town-dwellers into wealthy urban merchant bankers serves as background to the central drama. But the Causa Fontanellas took place during the bank's decline in the 1860s, when the family's fortunes had been going downhill for some time. The first Marquis, Francisco, died in the early 1850s, and his eldest son Lamberto—who possessed neither the ambition nor the acumen of his father and uncles—inherited the title of Marquis and the controlling interest in the bank. The protagonist of the story, however, was a man claiming to be the youngest son, Claudio Fontanellas, who arrived aboard a packet ship in the city's port in May 1861 after having been missing for sixteen years. Summoned in front of a judge, Lamberto initially recognized his 'brother', although he recanted a week later, informing the same judge that he had been harbouring doubts after being informed by friends of the family that he had an imposter living in his home. Relying on this change in testimony as well as the impressions of a number of others, the judge threw the man claiming to be Claudio Fontanellas in jail and commenced summary proceedings. He accused him of being a fraud, another Barcelona citizen named Claudio Feliu y Fontanils, a metalworker who had fled the city in 1857. Even adding more colour to this already vivid portrait, Feliu had also formed part of a popular theatre troupe that had armed the barricades during the failed revolution of 1856. This led to the hypothesis that the entire spectacle was no more than a farce, carefully planned by a group of actors and revolutionaries seeking to capture an inheritance.

The Causa Fontanellas blossomed into a fascinating public scandal owing to the notoriety of the family, multiple irregularities in the judicial proceedings, and the plain fact that the defendant may have been innocent. From the outset, the supposed reappearance of a man claiming to be 'Claudio' immediately raised a few eyebrows, because the original disappearance had been the subject of a small affair in and of itself. Claudio had been a cad ('un calavera') who had frequented the underworld of gambling and prostitution before being kidnapped in September 1845 and never heard from again. Many believed that this kidnapping had also been staged and was strictly a family matter: either a plot by a rebellious son to pay off bad debts and run away, or one by the family to get rid of its black sheep, or some rather unoriginal combination of both.[7]

Furthermore, upon the arrest and imprisonment in 1861, the public's curiosity was further piqued after the alleged imposter fell mortally ill, prompting doctors to diagnose his ailments as poison. This fact cast doubt upon the original accusations, causing many to entertain beliefs that the family had attempted to murder an innocent man—in other words, their blood brother—in order that the case would never have to go to trial. Whatever the truth, the accused survived and a trial did take place. From May 1861 to January 1865, the man with a disputed identity withstood multiple hearings and appeals, as Barcelona society split down the middle as to whether he was Claudio Fontanellas or Claudio Feliu. The case featured more than two hundred witnesses, thousands of pages of proceedings, numerous pamphlets and newspaper articles, and an endless cascade of citywide gossip and speculation. Like most *causes célèbres*, it was chock-full of accusations concerning forged evidence, perjured testimony, the corruption of lawyers and judges and the intimidation, bribery and even murder of witnesses. Whether the accused was innocent or guilty remains a mystery today.

After a summary, a plenary and two appellate hearings, the First Chamber of the Barcelona Audiencia (Court of High Appeals) sentenced the defendant to nine years in prison on 4 January 1865, although he was to die in hospital on 9 May 1871 before completing his sentence. On 11 May 1871, a district court ordered the coroners to perform an autopsy, the results of which are unknown.[8] For their part, the family fared only slightly better. While the case was pending, they declared the bank to be insolvent. With the rise of new, substantially wealthier families during the latter third of the century— the Güell, the López, the Arnús and other members of the so-called 'high Barcelona bourgeoisie'—the Fontanellas dynasty quickly became relegated to the realm of nostalgia and has been surprisingly left out of the history books. After having accumulated one of the most impressive fortunes in the city and having wielded enviable political power, its only meaningful legacy remains this fascinating but now largely forgotten story.[9]

During the four-year duration of the case, Barcelona divided on socio-political lines over the guilt or innocence of the accused. The bourgeoisie sided with the family, while popular classes supported the accused. Gender divisions were also apparent, as the defence relied to a greater extent on the testimony of female witnesses than did the prosecution.[10] Defence lawyers came from the left side of the political spectrum, while a team of advocates representing the city's conservative monarchist elite served as counsel to the family.[11] Taken as a whole, the various oppositions—bourgeois/popular, male/female, monarchist/democratic—present in the Causa Fontanellas reflected the existence of social divisions present in mid-nineteenth-century Barcelona, the tensions that lay therein, and attempts of outsiders or 'others'—such as popular classes, democrats and women—to undermine established hierarchies. This *cause célèbre* simply provided those excluded from political participation an alternative and indeed cathartic mechanism of ideological protest.

In retrospect, the Causa Fontanellas reveals a number of interesting features. Employing a longer view and a broader perspective than those of the interested parties, the case seems to represent a final chapter of a longer story that could be entitled 'The Rise and the Fall of the House of Fontanellas'. This history began in the 1780s, when three brothers, sons of an artisan, earned their fortune by developing triangular trade routes between Spain, Cuba, the United States and Latin America, engaging in the exchange and trafficking of textiles, cotton, sugar and, most likely, slaves. The fall of the bank, although magnified by the hyperbole of courtroom drama, and punctuated by the appearance of an alleged impostor, paralleled a number of similar, less theatrical bankruptcies, given that many financial institutions faced hard times and often insurmountable challenges during this period, when the American Civil War (1861–5) sent cotton prices skyrocketing and the textile business into a tailspin.[12] This worldwide economic crisis signalled the end of this 'virile' epoch of capitalism and accelerated the coming of the era of the joint-stock company, a more 'gentlemanly' way to conduct business.[13] The fall of the House of Fontanellas, then, was an emblematic, if not a spectacular, example of the end of the heady decades of romantic capitalism.

The Causa Fontanellas transpired during what was the romantic era not only of capitalism but also of revolution: Claudio Fontanellas initially disappeared in the aftermath of the failed revolution of 1843; Claudio Feliu originally fled after having participated in another failed revolution, that of 1856; and the entire court case unfolded during the years leading up to the Revolution of 1868. To be sure, politics and economics were not unrelated. In Spain, the economic downturn of the 1860s not only sent many financial institutions into the tank, it seriously destabilized an already decrepit political system, which easily crumbled during the peaceful September or 'Glorious' Revolution of 1868. The Revolution of 1868 in turn ushered in a six-year period known as the 'Democratic Sexennium' (1868–74), a violent time that constituted Spain's first failed attempt at democratic political governance.

In short, the confrontation that took place in the courtroom from 1861 to 1864 between monarchists and republicans and between the bourgeoisie and popular classes revealed social cleavages and tensions that later exploded in 1868. It demonstrated the growing confidence of persons traditionally excluded from political participation, the vulnerability of the Isabeline financial and political elite, and the weakness of governmental and judicial authority. As such, the analysis of this exciting *cause célèbre* produces various snapshots from multiple angles: politics, banking, justice and private life.

Yet the Causa Fontanellas can be interpreted on another level. Not only did the case reveal not-so-latent political divisions and social tensions, but it also can be understood as a story or a narrative, or more precisely, various competing narratives. In other words, the case not only serves as a cultural x-ray of society, but it also provides insight into how literary imagination conditioned political possibilities. To appreciate this latter phenomenon, it will be necessary to analyse the formalistic strategies employed and manipulated in the story's telling.[14] Relevant to this analysis are the theories of Hayden White and Northrop Frye, who have proposed that different modes of emplotment—comic, tragic, romantic and ironic—carry forthright ideological implications.[15]

From the outset, it must be realized that the Causa Fontanellas was not really a case of mistaken identity. Neither the appearances nor the backgrounds of the persons—Claudio Fontanellas and Claudio Feliu—were even remotely comparable. Although they may have been of similar height and weight, they were not of the same age: Feliu would have been twenty-four upon his return in 1861 while Fontanellas would have been thirty-eight; Feliu had light hair while Fontanellas had darker hair; and Feliu, though literate, was born and bred with humble origins, while Fontanellas had received a formal private-school education including French language instruction. Indeed, after carefully examining the Causa Fontanellas, it becomes manifest that one side was simply telling the truth and the other was lying. This meant that—with the exception of a few uninformed, confused or self-deluded witnesses—it is highly possible that one side succeeded in recruiting numerous people to ascend to the witness box, swear to the Spanish constitution and to the infallibility of Jesus Christ, and then tell lies, consciously, studiously and assiduously. The problem is simply that most of Barcelona—like the contemporary historian—had no idea who was telling the truth and who was lying. To be sure, the outcome of the case was not dependent on 'appearance' but on 'representation', or, in other words, which side could tell a more compelling story and stage a more authentic show. This was a high-stakes game bristling with potentially lucrative financial rewards, in which the truth was not so much subjective as it was irrelevant. To convince their audience, various narrators creatively invoked well-known modes of emplotment and genre, easily recognizable, digestible and interpretable to the mid-nineteenth-century listener.

The 'comic' was the first mode that moved to fill the narrative void immediately created upon the arrival of the notorious passenger aboard a ship that had departed Buenos Aires and stopped in Havana and Charlestown before finally docking in Barcelona. The man who claimed to be Claudio Fontanellas cleverly invoked comedy when he answered a summons the day after his arrival. At this point, he had not yet been accused of any crime, and in fact had been favourably identified by the brother Lamberto. During this brief hearing, he narrated to the judge—and hence to the public at large—a truly fascinating story. Playing on rumours that had surfaced years earlier, he wove together a novelistic but nonetheless plausible account. Beginning with his original disappearance in September 1845, he asserted that his father had ordered the original kidnapping by hiring the 'Tarrés Gang', a group of criminals known to have operated in the mid 1840s.[16] He then claimed to have escaped his kidnappers, secured a false passport and set sail for Buenos Aires, where he lived under an assumed name, Santiago O'Donnel. Finding gainful employment both in the navy and army, his story tells of participation in ongoing Argentine civil wars, rising to the post of cavalry officer for the Republic of Buenos Aires and serving in the forces of General Urquiza, one-time president.

In spinning this tale, the man relied upon a well-known Spanish genre, that of the picaresque. The travails of this anti-hero, a string of misfortunes and improvised solutions, read as a saga of perilous yet tragicomic survival. This is not to imply that the narrator was familiar with Spanish Golden-Age literature, or had been leafing through *Lazarillo de Tormes* during the chilly Atlantic crossing. One only has to think of the novels of Charles Dickens to recognize this juxtaposing of picaresque plots with happy endings, typical 'romantic comedies' that no doubt also proliferated in popular theatre in Barcelona and perhaps Buenos Aires as well. For example, Dickens's novel *Martin Chuzzlewit* (1843–4) contains a similar plot, in which an originally selfish and picaresque character returns home from America morally reformed, after which he becomes reintegrated with his family, marries the woman he loves, and inherits the fortune he had been formerly deprived of. With respect to the case at hand, invoking comedy was a skilful manoeuvre, since comic plots tend to culminate in felicitous resolutions, and archetypically feature the triumph of youth. Indeed, at the time when the narrator first recounted his adventures—before there was a Causa Fontanellas—this was precisely what he hoped would occur: the protagonist was literally to return to the bed where he had once slept and thereafter be reconciled with his family. As such, if this story had been believed, it would have ended there: a perfect comic ending. Once it did not take hold, for whatever reason, and the accused found himself in jail, the defence swiftly turned to more radical narrative forms.

The 'tragic' was the second mode of emplotment. This was perhaps the preferred trope of the prosecution and family, who simply strove to demonstrate that ever since the true Claudio had been kidnapped in 1845, the household had been besieged by one con after another, by marginal figures promising to produce information on the whereabouts of their lost brother in exchange for money. According to this theory, his so-called return was no more than the latest of many plots hatched by conspirators—a mixture of former domestic servants, bank competitors, ambitious parvenus and a revolutionary theatre troupe—to capture an inheritance by threatening to air and ultimately by airing much of the family's dirty laundry. To be sure, the defence had at its disposal a well-stocked arsenal of dazzling and stupefying truths and falsehoods, which they presented as evidence, published in newspapers or pamphlets or circulated by word of mouth. In addition to the startling revelation that the first Marquis had possibly contracted organized criminals to kidnap his youngest son, the defence also unearthed the long-forgotten early history of the family by digging deep into court archives. Confirming what many had vaguely recollected, they rehashed and dragged out a previous fraternal conflict in which Francisco Fontanellas initially came into possession of the family bank after defrauding his older brother, Antonio. Other rumours swirled around various dirty financial dealings, an accusation of counterfeiting, the legitimacy of children, the fate of a sister who died in unexplained circumstances in Marseilles and even a strange history of rape and prostitution.

In this tragic melodrama, the family tugged at public sensibilities by portraying themselves as innocent and aggrieved victims of the depravity of the dangerous classes, fronted by out-of-town lawyers and backed by avaricious speculators. Categorically denying the most serious allegations, they none the less acknowledged that even the most proper of families had secrets that deserved to be kept private. Inspired by fiction, the family most likely recycled familiar material. A gentleman unable to escape his past is embodied by the character of Pip in Dickens's *Great Expectations* (1860–1), published just as the Causa Fontanellas was about to unfold and reworked for a Spanish audience by Benito Pérez Galdós decades later in his story *Mendizábal* (1898). Another ambiguous but highly relevant portrayal later appeared in George Eliot's *Middlemarch* (1871–2), where the character of Bulstrode, a rich philanthropist and benefactor of a county hospital, is disgraced by a rogue recently repatriated from the Americas. In this novel, the character known as Raffles blackmails Bulstrode, while revealing a series of unfortunate personal secrets behind the banker's rise from London pawnbroker to Middlemarch banker. Similar but not the same as the Causa Fontanellas, Raffles dies, leading to speculation that the banker poisoned him. The implication is not that the Fontanellas family and the defence borrowed plots from Dickens (although they may have), or that Eliot had caught wind of the Causa Fontanellas (although she may have). Rather, the argument is simply that such plots—though usually less intricate and less stylized—were part and parcel of nineteenth-century narrative, appearing with some frequency in popular theatre, 'true' stories and novels throughout all of Europe and indeed the Atlantic world.

The defence also made use of the tragic mode by relying upon the recognizable tale of the Prodigal Son, a parable prone to metamorphosis. One of the most famous permutations was the sixteenth-century French case of Martin Guerre, in which the 'prodigal son' was in fact a long-lost husband who eventually was discovered to be a fraud. In the nineteenth century, the plot underwent an additional twist. In the Causa Fontanellas: the defence asserted that comedy had become converted into tragedy when an innocent 'prodigal son' became wrongfully accused and thrown in jail as an impostor. Again, this plot-line was by no means original. Balzac's *Colonel Chabert* (1832) also bears much resemblance. In this novella, a hero from the Napoleonic war is unable to prove his true identity, and as a result becomes wrongfully accused as an impostor and robbed of his riches and prestige by his own wife, eager to remarry into the Restoration aristocracy. Interestingly, a similar subplot appears in George Eliot's novel, *Felix Holt* (1866), published just a couple of years after the case closed, although she only deals with it in passing. Irrespective of the origins of this recognizably nineteenth-century story-line, both sides sought to invoke tragedy. Tragedy carried forthright and unmistakable political implications: it dared engage moral and ideological themes that comedy avoided. By appealing to notions of fairness, by portraying and commemorating the plight of persons who wrongfully meet undeserving fates, the tragic mode compels the audience to strive to 'make good' or to 'do justice', even against odds and despite the cruelties and tyrannies endemic to the imperfect and mediocre world in which we live.

Romance, arguably a more radical trope than the 'tragic' or the 'comic', was perhaps the central mode of emplotment.[17] Even before the scandal exploded, the family had long been under the spell of romance, understandably given that their own rags-to-riches saga comprised a storybook tale of success during the heyday of romantic capitalism. Francisco Fontanellas, the first Marquis, initially employed what was most likely his favourite literary genre in his last will and testament, normally a dry, legal document, which he decided to animate by including two rather histrionic provisions. First, he explicitly prevented his son-in-law, a man named Antonio de Lara, from coming into administration or possession of the family wealth. Antonio de Lara had married the Marquis's daughter Joaquina, Claudio's sister, but Joaquina had later become estranged from her husband and returned to the family home. Second, the Marquis left as one of his legacies a sealed envelope to remain unopened until his lost son Claudio had returned. Such a donation would have been unthinkable a century earlier, before the melodrama had been born, or a century later, after it had been dismissed as tacky, pretentious or feminine. But caught in the romantic moment, the Marquis egotistically wove this epic plot into his own death, perversely lending an incentive to the unfolding of this post-mortem drama. Without a doubt, he cast Antonio de Lara as the archetypical villain, Claudio as the 'hero', and his own dead hand as a paternal Merlin, the magical 'donor'.

Defence advocates and sympathizers further adorned and embellished this romantic narrative, a task facilitated by Antonio de Lara's truly novelesque biography. Born in La Mancha and accused though cleared of forgery in 1838, De Lara had married into the family only a few years before Claudio's kidnapping in 1845. After his first wife Joaquina died, he wed another Fontanellas sister, Eulalia. By accumulating inheritances and dowries, and after launching a lawsuit against the new Marquis, the oldest brother Lamberto, he was rumoured to be, and indeed was, in control of the bank. Moreover, since Lamberto was childless, De Lara's son Francisco de Lara y Fontanellas potentially stood to inherit (and probably did inherit) the Marquis's title and the lion's share of the family fortune. According to this theory, then, the appearance of 'Claudio' threatened to undo Antonio de Lara's elaborately conceived plans to take over the family bank, motivating him to concoct a new scheme, in which the innocent 'Claudio' was poisoned and thrown in jail. The defence even contended that the bankruptcy had been fictitious, designed to siphon off and launder the family's wealth in case the defendant prevailed. Irrespective of the merits of these accusations, the elaboration and dissemination of romance offered the widest range of outcomes. It brandished the sharpest sword. Romance is inherently radical: perhaps not as uniformly or predictably inspirational as tragedy, it nonetheless succeeds in achieving what tragedy holds as desirable but also concedes as impossible, the realization of utopia—the triumph of love over hate, of beauty over banality, of liberty over oppression, of justice over tyranny, of good over evil.

The use of comedy, tragedy and romance reveals the presence of a broad phenomenon. Identifying these modes of emplotment is not meant to be an entertaining hermeneutical exercise focusing on an isolated or exceptional event. On the contrary, the agility with which these tropes were marshalled attests to the fact that the citizens of Barcelona frequently and creatively deployed them towards specific and intended goals. This *cause célèbre*, though certainly representing an occurrence out of the ordinary, was indicative of thousands of similar personal stories describing multiple household and workplace conflicts—some verisimilar, others exaggerated and many patently fictive—to be found in everyday street, parlour, tavern and café conversation, within which the critique of political and economic power was omnipresent, ongoing, punishing and, in the long term, destabilizing. Despite recognizable structures and hierarchies, this society was also highly mobile, upwards as well as downwards; it was tightly wound, asphyxiating and claustrophobic. Rags-to-riches stories, such as that of the Fontanellas, were not uncommon; classes were intermixed, and no person could forget their past.

Ultimately, narrative and politics were interdependent, for ambiguous, cross-class and inter-gendered relationships generated emotionally compelling stories that could provide a spark capable of igniting socio-economic tensions. Despite structural differentiation and economic inequality, the exercise of power in the mid nineteenth century was as personal as it was institutional, a fact that must be kept in mind when evaluating the destructive and creative capacities of narrative. As theorized by Hayden White, and as emphasized by Sara Maza, romantic and tragic modes of emplotment—embodied in the melodramatic voice of the nineteenth century—imagined a universe that was cosmically radical or even anarchic. When mixed with politics, romance and tragedy could be explosive, threatening and promising. It was precisely this hegemony of melodrama, in conjunction with social and economic factors, that helps explain why Barcelona and similar European cities were insurrectional tinderboxes in the mid nineteenth century. It also helps explain why the romantic era of both capitalism and revolution eventually proved too aesthetically and materially hazardous for the middle classes to navigate. The experience of the Fontanellas family illustrates the dangers faced by members of the bourgeoisie who dared engage the lower classes in a contest of competing romantic narratives. In the long run, this game would have to be abandoned. The Causa Fontanellas illustrated and exposed the threat to bourgeois stability when both public opinion and capital competed in a market, or perhaps in a labyrinth, that was romantically and tragically constructed.

As an epilogue, it is worth touching on the fall-out or consequences of this interlacing of melodrama with politics and economy. Towards the latter decades of the nineteenth century, high-bourgeois men throughout all of Europe abandoned romance and, to some extent, their air of bravado. The virile entrepreneur and financier—the type represented by Francisco Fontanellas and Antonio de Lara—radically changed his image, financial organization and work-habits. Enlisting new economic mechanisms and discursive techniques, European capitalists recast themselves as ironic, gentlemanly businessmen, holders of shares, persons of limited liability and calculated exposure. Romance and tragedy were deemed frivolous and banal, best suited to women, children and the popular classes. By the turn of the century, privileged and educated men preferred and lent prestige to the satirical mode of emplotment.

In Barcelona, popular narrative eventually gave rise to a prestigious literary tradition, which finally put an end to the city's reputation as a haven for reactionary poets and hack novelists. This new tendency opened with Narcís Oller's *Febre d'or* (1881), a novel whose plot is not unlike the Causa Fontanellas, in which a nouveau-riche family is brought down by the devices of an ambitious but reckless stockbroker's clerk. The novels of Santiago Rusiñol, one of the founders of the first European movement formally known as *modernisme*, continued this tradition, which drew to a close with Josep Maria Sagarra's acrid, entertaining family saga, *Vida privada* (1932). Roughly encompassing the same period as the publication of Marcel Proust's *A la recherche du temps perdu* (1913–26), this new literary movement produced daring, incisive, scandalous and best-selling novels, which exposed the hypocrisy, duplicity and corruption of the wealthy and privileged. However, this high literary tradition represented a significant departure from nineteenth-century narrative; despite the fact that modernist novels constituted seething exposés potentially damaging to those who could be identified with the protagonists, the authors adopted a markedly less threatening style, register and trope. They abandoned melodramatic romantic and tragic modes that had once run so rampant through the streets of the city, when the Causa Fontanellas had shaken the foundations of proper society. Instead, these novels struck a decidedly satirical or ironic note, typical of Barcelona and European modernism. Satire and irony meant clothing critique in the fabric of moral relativism.[18]

This change in high-literary narrative hegemony—the ascendancy of satire and the fading of melodrama—was common throughout Europe and carried clear political implications. The satirical or ironic mode was intrinsically powerful because it embodied philosophical scepticism, and as such discredited and ridiculed the romantic and tragic imagination. More epistemologically adroit than its sibling comedy, irony constructed a conservative matrix for ideas in which ideological possibilities were debunked by means of a steady, systematic discursive deconstruction of truth, beauty, justice, liberty and any and all previously sacrosanct objective realities. As such, the Barcelona bourgeoisie accepted a critique of itself—by literally buying the novels of Oller, Rusiñol and Sagarra—only when narrative became emplotted using ironic as opposed to romantic or tragic forms. This shift was functional, for it allowed the artist to retain his critical, bohemian air without fundamentally threatening the material basis of economy and society. In fact, this latter subject—the 'pact' between the artist and his bourgeois family—constituted the plot of one of the most famous novels of the period, Santiago Rusiñol's *L'auca del Senyor Esteve* (1907).

To conclude, one last theoretical consideration must be addressed. The analytical framework—the identification of the ideological implications of modes of emplotment, and the interpretation of the political consequences of melodrama—has not been universally accepted by all, but has been the subject of an interesting debate. In his seminal *The Political Unconscious*, the Marxist literary theorist Frederic Jameson has criticized the work of Frye and White, and has convincingly argued that romanticism should not be interpreted as a radical narrative trope.[19] Echoing Nietzsche and Lukács, Jameson contends that romanticism, in defining a series of antinomies (good versus evil, beauty versus banality, etc.), constricted and controlled ideological possibilities by embodying, disseminating and ultimately reifying a hegemonic bourgeois moral code. Indeed, although romance may have served as an epic inspiration behind popular mobilization and even revolution, Jameson would attribute this—and all popular beliefs surrounding romance, and any narrative form for that matter—to the presence of 'false consciousness' or, to borrow Lévi-Straussian terminology, the belief in myth. To Jameson, what was really at work was a 'political unconscious' in which textual artefacts and narrative forms constructed a symbolic universe necessary for the smooth operation and progression of capitalism. As such, the advent of modernism did not represent a break with romanticism but the natural evolution of the bourgeois ego from triumphant individualism to depoliticized but nonetheless highly individualized subjectivity.

Jameson's attractive theoretical schema is difficult to evaluate, since the historian has few tools to research the unconscious. What is clear, however, was that in nineteenth-century Europe real, living and breathing people frequently and consciously deployed archetypical narrative structures, trite and vulgar plot-lines and well-known literary genres towards personal and collective ends, which were perhaps more important to them than to the present-day literary critic. Moreover, it is also clear that the bourgeoisie consciously abandoned romance, a form that had perhaps been politically useful when the Old Regime and not the capitalist state was threatened. In Paris, Balzac gave way to Flaubert and then to Proust; in London, Dickens led to Conrad; in Barcelona, romantic poets ceded the path to cynical novelists—in Catalan terms, Verdaguer was replaced by Rusiñol. Although still consumed, melodrama was feminized, relegated to the popular novel, deemed to be the escapist mode of the disillusioned and bored, or the intoxicant of theatrical, populist orators promising false utopias to the uneducated and politically immature. Whether one should believe this change in perception to be a natural unfolding of bourgeois sensibilities and attributes it to the devices of a 'political unconscious', or explain this transformation by means of conscious decisions of persons and classes faced with identifiable political and economic pressures, is difficult to resolve. Suffice it to note that both explanations—though vehemently disagreeing on diagnosis, treatment and remedy—seek to explain a similar historical phenomenon.[20]

Notes to Chapter 2

1. Much of the early path-breaking work of the microhistory or 'great story' genre examined what were essentially early modern versions of *causes célèbres*, many of which were reliant on court, particularly Inquisition, documents. Seminal works included Carlo Ginzburg, *I Benandanti: Stregoneria e culti agrari tra Cinquecento e Seicento* (Milan: Einaudi, 1966), and *Il formaggio e i vermi: Il cosmo di un mugnaio del '500* (Milan: Enaudi, 1976); Emmanuel Le Roy Ladurie, *Montaillou: Village occitan de 1294 à 1324* (Paris: Gallimard, 1975), and *Le Carnival de Romans* (Paris: Gallimard, 1979); and Nathalie Zemon Davis, *The Return of Martin Guerre* (Cambridge, MA: Harvard University Press, 1983).

2. Sarah Maza, *Private Lives and Public Affairs: The Causes Célèbres of Prerevolutionary France* (Berkeley: University of California Press, 1993).

3. Other than the Causa Fontanellas, the most famous *cause célèbre* of the century concerned a lawsuit over compensation for the illegal confiscation of the lands of the Ciutadella by Philip V. These briefs were printed. See Francisco de Paula Vergés, *Alegación en derecho que presenta el Excmo. Sr. Marqués de Ayerbe y de Rubí contra el Excmo. Ayuntamiento de Barcelona* (Barcelona: Jepús, 1886); Mauricio Serrahima, *Alegación en derecho por parte del Excmo. Ayuntamiento de Barcelona en el pleito que, promovido por el Excmo. Sr. Marqués de Ayerbe* (Barcelona: Ramírez, 1886). For an example of a *cause célèbre* taking place at the end of the century, see

Cèlia Cañellas and Rosa Toran, 'Ideologies i actituds professionals, criminologia i positivisme: El·cas Wille', *L'Avenç: Història dels països catalans* 210 (1997): 12–16.

4. For some of the political reasons explaining the lack of a mid-nineteenth-century novelistic tradition in Catalonia, see Josep Maria Fradera, *Cultura nacional en una societat dividida: Patriotisme i cultura a Catalunya (1838–1868)* (Barcelona: Curiel, 1992), 131–211. For popular theatre, see Joan Maluquer i Viladot, *Teatre català: Estudi histórich-crítich* (Barcelona: Renaixença, 1878).

5. The entire case, referred to here as the Causa Fontanellas, has been remarkably safeguarded at the Arxiu de la Corona d'Aragó. The court reporter published the most thorough summary of the facts and testimony. See Esteban de Ferrater, *Resumen del proceso original del estado civil de D. Claudio Fontanellas* (Madrid, Barcelona and Havana: Plus Ultra, 1865). This summary was rebutted point by point by one of the defence lawyers: Fermín Villamil, *Historia justificativa de la defensa en el proceso Fontanellas con las biografías y retratos de las personas interesadas en la causa, de la parte que en ella tomaron, papel que hicieron, y refutación de la obra que sobre lo mismo publica D. Estevan Ferrater, relator de la Audiencia de Barcelona* (Barcelona: Oliveres, 1865).

6. Records reveal that Francisco Fontanellas was either the highest-contributing taxpayer or within a group of highest-paying taxpayers from the 1820s to at least the mid 1840s. See Arxiu Històric Municipal de Barcelona (Casa de l'Ardiaca): Cadastre – serie ix – Indústria i Comerç: ix-8; Cadastre – serie ix – Indústria i Comerç: ix-12; Cadastre – serie ix – Indústria i Comerç: viii–35.

7. For example, on 8 Oct. 1845, the Madrid newspaper *El Heraldo* published a report that Claudio had been kidnapped, but on 14 Oct. 1845, its correspondent stated that he believed the kidnapping to be false, commenting that the disappearance of the son was purely a 'family affair'. In contrast, the *Diario de Barcelona* maintained the version of a kidnapping. These newspaper reports are cited in Villamil, *Historia justificativa*, 20–1.

8. For death and autopsy, see Conrado Roure, *Recuerdos de mi larga vida: Costumbres, anécdotas, acontecimientos y sucesos acaecidos en la ciudad de Barcelona, desde el 1850 hasta el 1900* (Barcelona: El Diluvio, 1925–7), i. 280. In general, Roure presents a concise synopsis of the case, but offers nothing new except for his recollection that an autopsy had been performed.

9. The major histories of the bourgeoisie during this period do not mention the Fontanellas family. See Jaume Vicens i Vives and Montserrat Llorens, *Industrials i polítics: Segle XIX* (Barcelona: Vicens-Vives, 1991; first pubd 1958); Antoni Jutglar, *Historia crítica de la burguesía en Cataluña* (Barcelona: Anthropos, 1984); Gary Wray McDonogh, *Good Families of Barcelona: A Social History of Power in the Industrial Era* (Princeton: Princeton University Press, 1986); and Josep Fontana, *La fi de l'antic règim i la industrialització (1787–1868)* (Barcelona: Edicions 62, 1998).

10. With respect to class, the prosecution relied on about 97 witnesses: 45% could be described as 'bourgeois', 28% as 'white collar', 19% as 'popular' and 8% as unknown; in contrast, the defence relied on approximately 99 witnesses, of whom 11% were 'bourgeois', 10% 'white collar', 75% 'popular' and 4% unknown. With respect to gender, 90% of prosecution witnesses were male and 10% female; in contrast, the defence witnesses were 70% male and 30% female. These figures have been calculated using the information provided by Ferrater, *Resumen del proceso*.

11. For information on the politics of the lawyers, see José Indalecio Caso, *Nueva exposición de hechos para la defensa de D. Claudio Fontanellas y noticia de unos papeles falsos, agenciados en ideas para probar de nuevo que dicho procesado es Claudio Feliu: Opúsculo ameno y edificante* (Madrid: Santa Coloma, 1864), 34, 80.

12. For the effects of the banking crisis of the 1860s in Barcelona, see Francesc Cabana, *Història del Banc de Barcelona (1844–1920)* (Barcelona: Edicions 62, 1978), 37–44.

13. For this argument with respect to England, see Howard Malchow, *Gentlemen Capitalists: The Social and Political World of the Victorian Businessmen* (London: Macmillan, 1991); and Martin J. Wiener, *English Culture and the Decline of the Industrial Spirit, 1850–1980* (Harmondsworth: Penguin, 1992).

14. The prosecution and defence published their briefs in the newspaper during the first hearing. For the accusatory brief of the district court prosecutor, Gabriel Coca, see *Diario de Barcelona* (18 June 1861), 5498–507. For the defence brief of Pelegrín Pomés, see *Diario de Barcelona* (4 July 1861), 5955–78. As the case continued, each of the respective theories was further adorned through publication. The defence was generally more active. See José Indalecio Caso, *Exposición de hechos para la defensa de D. Claudio Fontanellas, hijo del primer Marques de Casa-Fontanellas, en causa pendiente contra el mismo por supuesta usurpación de estado civil* (Madrid: Luis Palacios, 1862); idem, *Nueva Exposición de hechos para la defensa*; idem, *Discursos pronunciados en defensa de D.Claudio Fontanellas suplicando de la Real sentencia de vista de 31 de Diciembre de 1862 por lo que se condenó á dicho procesado á la pena de nueve años de presidio como usurpador de estado civil* (Barcelona: Luis Tasso, 1864–5); and Villamil, *Historia justificativa*. The family's lawyers also published their version: Ricardo Ventosa and Demetrio de Villalaz, *Acusaciones pronunciadas en la causa criminal seguida contra Claudio Feliu y Fontanills sobre usurpación del estado civil de D. Claudio de Fontanellas ante la Excma. Sala Tercera de la Audiencia de Barcelona en grado de Revista seguidas por la sentencia ejecutoria dictada por la misma Real Sala* (Barcelona: Ramírez y Rialp, 1865). If this was not enough, one of the judges also chimed in, although he limited his analysis to rebutting the contention that the case should have been tried not as a criminal but as a civil matter: Vicente Ferrer y Minguet, *La Causa Fontanellas justificada en la esencia de su procedimiento* (Madrid, Barcelona and Havana: Española and Plus Ultra, 1865).

15. See Northrop Frye, *Anatomy of Criticism: Four Essays* (Princeton: Princeton University Press, 1957); Hayden White, *Metahistory: The Historical Imagination in Nineteenth-Century Europe* (Baltimore: Johns Hopkins University Press, 1975). It should be noted that this method of 'genre criticism' has been the subject of critique, most notably in Frederic Jameson, *The Political Unconscious: Narrative as a Socially Symbolic Act* (Ithaca, NY: Cornell University Press, 1981), 103–50.

16. For information on the Ronda de Tarrés, see Roure, *Recuerdos de mi larga vida*, i. 54–6; Josep Benet and Casimir Martí, *Barcelona a mitjan segle XIX: El moviment obrer durant el bienni progressista (1854–1856)*, 2 vols. (Barcelona: Curial, 1976), i. 314–27.

17. This characterization—essentially the contention of Northrop Frye—remained faithful to narrative as it was understood in the nineteenth century. There is, however, an alternative line of criticism. Friedrich Nietzsche, *The Birth of Tragedy*, trans. Douglas Smith (Oxford: Oxford University Press, 2000; first pubd

1872), believed tragedy to be the most radical of all forms, while, in a like manner, Georg Lukács, *The Theory of the Novel: A Historico-philosophical Essay on the Forms of Great Epic Literature*, trans. Anna Bostock (London: Merlin Press, 1978; first pubd 1916), 112–31, contended that romance was a conservative, desultory genre. These latter conceptions have been influential in contemporary criticism as well. Jameson, *The Political Unconscious*, 115–19, for example, asserts that both tragedy and comedy were 'beyond good and evil'.

18. Joan-Lluís Marfany, *Aspectes del modernisme* (Barcelona: Curial, 1990), 13–34, has argued that Catalan *modernisme* represented a politically eclectic tradition, still loosely tied to leftist politics. He contends that it only became associated with conservatism during the first decade of the twentieth century after becoming absorbed into *Noucentisme*, a movement subservient to and sycophantically dependent upon the financial sponsorship of right-wing Catalan nationalists.

19. See n. 15 above.

20. To Jameson, romanticism (which led directly into modernism) is the cancer, and social-scientific critical theory the best of imperfect remedies. To White, the scientific academy—even those members of it claiming to be Marxist such as Jameson—will not likely accomplish or even be able to articulate radical goals, since all voices, including his own, remain ironic. For White's response to Jameson's critique in the *Political Unconscious*, see Hayden White, 'Getting Out of History: Jameson's Redemption of Narrative', *Diacritics* 12 (1982), 2–13, repr. *The Content and the Form* (Baltimore: Johns Hopkins University Press, 1987), 142–68.

CHAPTER 3

Oscar Wilde and Spain: Medicine, Morals, Religion and Aesthetics in the *Fin de Siglo*

Richard A. Cardwell

The discourses employed in the construction of the Symbolist Decadent revolution in Spain were far from literary. In the critical writings of the first founders of the new movement that has come to be labelled *modernismo* we discover an extraordinary interplay of discourses: religious, spiritual, political, social, legal and, especially, medical. Each of these disciplines reacted to and fed upon one another. The discourses of the sciences, evolutionism and medicine belong to the dominant Positivistic mindset of the age. Yet, far from reducing the impact of Idealism, the basis of the new Symbolist experiment, these discourses actually provided a rich source for new literary experimentation. That is, we find a process of cross-culturization, of 'field-crossing'. And nowhere is this more evident than in the elaboration of the identity and character of the modern artist as set out by Enrique Gómez Carrillo and Rubén Darío in their critical assessments of Oscar Wilde.

'No creo que este libro obtenga en Madrid un gran suceso. Fuera de veinte o treinta espíritus cosmopolitas, apenas habrá nadie que lo lea con placer' [I do not believe this book will obtain a great success in Madrid. Apart from a circle of twenty or thirty cosmopolitan souls there is virtually no one who will read it with pleasure], wrote Enrique Gómez Carrillo in the opening chapter of *Esquisses (siluetas de escritores y artistas)* in 1892.[1] Gómez Carrillo, a young Guatemalan diplomat, writer, critic and acute observer of the literary scene in Paris, was thoroughly cognizant of the artistic trends of his age and published an extraordinary range of works incorporating them: novels, literary and art criticism, essays and travel books. He also contributed a regular literary column to newspapers in Paris and Madrid, through which he disseminated the latest fashions from the universally acknowledged centre of European artistic experiment: Paris.

From the late 1880s well into the new century Gómez Carrillo became the 'Francophile propagandist' in Spain.[2] Given the resistance in Spain to outside influence he set himself (virtually single-handed) the task of introducing the 'shock of the new' to the Hispanic world and especially to the young and progressive coteries of Madrid. He had first-hand contact with the artistic and literary scene in *fin-de-siècle* Paris, the cradle of all that was progressive. He was in personal contact with writers like Verlaine, Mallarmé, Morice and Moréas, with critics like Guyau, Paulhan, Bourget and Huret, as well as established figures like Zola. Rather snootily, he tells his readers that they might not know that Naturalism is now dead and that Symbolism, Romanticism and the School of Psychology have superseded it.[3] The stress on a new art for a new age of subjectivity, with its accent on the displaced theologies of Art and the aesthetic, the interest in spiritual and mystical experiences, and the rejection of the scientific and determinist cast of the Naturalist experiment had created, he insisted, a new era, which required new voices and new outlooks (*E* 9). It is not surprising, then, that in *Sensaciones de arte*, published the year before *Esquisses* in 1891, Gómez Carrillo should open his book with an essay on Hokusai, Utamaro and Yosai; his keen nose for all that was new, here Japanese art, never failed him. Nor is it surprising that the second essay should present Oscar Wilde, the modern aesthete *par excellence*, to the Hispanic world.[4]

The homage to Wilde in *Sensaciones* begins with the following autobiographical memoir (*SA* 41): 'Fue en casa de Stuart Merrill, el poeta adorable de *Los fastos*, donde encontré por primera vez, una noche de crudo invierno, al autor ilustre de *Salomé* y del *Retrato de Dorian Gray*.' [It was in the house of Stuart Merrill, the adorable poet of *Les Fastes*, that I first met, one raw winter's night, the famous author of *Salome* and *The Picture of Dorian Gray*.] Gómez Carrillo establishes his literary credentials with the mention of his friendship with Stuart Merrill and his knowledge of his most recent book (1890), and he defers mention of Wilde's name to identify him only by his works. In so doing he conspires with those few (he presumes) who will know of whom he writes. Yet, in spite of this egotism, he is recalling a genuine meeting. We know from Yvanhoe Rambasson, an acquaintance of Wilde's in

Paris in the early 1890s, that, after a lunch with the translator Henry Duvray in the winter of 1891, he and Wilde retired to the Café d'Harcourt, where they were joined by Gómez Carrillo and Verlaine. Wilde, disgusted by the appearance of the latter, addressed his conversation to the Guatemalan and spoke of his life, travels and art. The two became close friends and Gómez Carrillo a confidant.[5] The supper with Stuart Merrill followed that first meeting.

The essay in *Sensaciones* is addressed specifically to Wilde's *Intentions*. Gómez Carrillo is able here to gloss Wilde's theories on Art: his rejection of Nature, the necessary function of Art in improving Nature, the artist in splendid isolation from mundane preoccupations, the artist as a subversive. However, the direct quotations offered, highlighting Wilde's skill as an epigrammatist, are not to be found among the essays of *Intentions*. Possibly inspired by 'The Decay of Lying' (included in *Intentions*) or possibly taken down verbatim from Wilde's own mouth in conversation, these epigrams nevertheless express the principal sentiments of Wilde's revolutionary aestheticism. Gómez Carrillo presents Wilde, in the main, as a profoundly subversive theorist while not overlooking his power as a creative writer.

Most surprising, however, is the initial pen-portrait of Wilde. Gómez Carrillo is struck by his 'manera singular e insinuante de hablar francés' [singular and insinuating manner of speaking French] (*SA* 41). One might compare the same fascination with Wilde's style of speaking in Helen Potter's *Impersonations* of 1891, which offers a detailed account of how Wilde accented and paused for dramatic effect in his American lectures.[6] Second, he describes 'su enorme rostro de adolescente triste y soñador [que] me llenó de interés' [his enormous face, that of a sad and dreamy adolescent, which filled me with interest] (*SA* 41). Again, the adjective *soñador* is soon to become a currency for the modern poet and would be applied to Rubén Darío, the young Juan Ramón Jiménez and other writers whose work was reviewed in the progressive journals of the new century: *Alma Española*, *Helios* and *Renacimiento*. Gómez Carrillo also comments on Wilde's 'envoltura atlética, de cierta distinción especial que atrae las miradas femeninas' [his athletic bulk, of a special distinction that drew the stares of women] (*SA* 41), avoiding any mention of Wilde's homosexuality, of which he was all too aware. He closes this section with a description of Wilde's attire, 'una camiseta descotada de lana roja' [an unbuttoned vest of red wool].

In a visit to Wilde's flat Gómez Carrillo notes 'su robusto torso de luchador [que] me hace pensar en las figuras inmortales de Rubens.

[...] Y cuando trajeado ya con esa cuidadosa *tenue* de los ingleses, le encuentro en cualquier café literario del barrio latino, su talle gigantesco me trae a la memoria un viejo retrato de Tourgénief, que vi hace ya bastante tiempo y ni aun recuerdo donde' [his robust fighter's torso which reminded me of those immortal figures of Rubens. And when, dressed in that studied *tenue* of the English, I met him in one of the literary cafés of the Latin quarter, his giant frame recalled an old portrait of Turgenev, which I saw some time ago and I cannot recall where] (*SA* 41–2). The references to Rubens and Turgenev betray, in their reduction of natural forms to artifice, Gómez Carrillo's obsession with Decadent artifice. Ramón del Valle-Inclán, a contemporary and friend of Gómez Carrillo in the mid-1890s, was soon to adopt the same aesthetic tenets, which both writers derived from Gautier, Baudelaire and Verlaine. Del Valle-Inclán's early prose works, *Epitalamio* (1887) and *Femeninas* (1895) are a token of the acculturation of this type of Decadent writing in Spain, a style soon to be taken up in the early novels of Gómez Carrillo himself.[7]

Gómez Carrillo is reminded of another artistic creation when he describes Wilde's 'ojos largos, húmedos y oblicuos [que] tienen cierta expresión en las pupilas que ni la voz tristeza, ni la voz melancolía alcanzan a denotar; son ojos pálidos, como era pálida la sonrisa de aquella heroina de Catulle Mendès, con la palidez en el dibujo, y no en el color' [huge eyes, watery and slanted, which had a certain expression in their pupils that neither the word sadness nor the word melancholy can properly describe; they are pale eyes, rather like the pale smile of that heroine of Catulle Mendès, with paleness in its outline and not in its colour] (*SA* 42). The reference is probably to Mendès's *Philoméla* of 1863. The terms used—'soñador', 'gigante', 'ojos melancólicos', 'palidez'—are soon to recur in the critical writings and poetic evocations of the young writers and reach a climax in the dedicatory poem of Rubén Darío to Jiménez's *Ninfeas* in 1900. In essence, then, Wilde is evoked as the very model of the aesthete, the refined spirit, the soulful, aloof, feminine and Decadent dreamer, and yet a man of robust and attractive physique. We note again the aestheticism of the evocation where reality (Wilde's body) is transmuted into Art (Rubens, Turgenev, Mendès): the very picture of Dorian Gray and the artist as described by Gautier, Baudelaire and Barbey d'Aurevilly. Even Wilde's 'cabellera blonda, fina y sedeña' [his fair hair, fine and silky], with its arranged central parting covering his 'finas orejas' [fine ears], the aquiline nose and the 'boca sensual'

[sensual mouth] confirm the portrait of the artist as dreamer and aesthete.

Such a description is not an isolated example. Similar portraits of other contemporary artists appear here in *Esquisses* and in later essays. Such pen-portraits, however, are neither unique nor original. If we look at a whole range of essays devoted to arguably the most inspiring and enduring icon of the personal sacrifice to Art and the spiritually troubled life of the artist, we shall perceive the similarities, even though Gómez Carrillo's picture is more detailed in his evocation. The portraits in question are, of course, those of Edgar Allan Poe.

It was French writers, rather than his fellow 'Anglo-Saxons', who rallied to Poe's defence.[8] The artistic and literary vogue for Poe was also fostered by the enthusiastic researches of Poe's most famous and prickly biographer, John Henry Ingram. His first edition of Poe's works in 1874–5 was followed by five further major studies (biographies, opinions on Poe, painterly portraits, etc.) before 1886. Perhaps the most widely read was *Edgar Allan Poe: His Life, Letters and Opinions*, a study of 1880 reprinted in 1891 in the popular Minerva Library of Famous Books. From 1851 with Baudelaire and after 1873 with Mallarmé, followed by many others, the task of translating and paying homage to Poe became a major feature of the French poetic scene until the new century. Both writers penned idealized portraits of their tragic poet-hero who, for Baudelaire in *L'Art Romantique*, was 'l'artiste le plus puissant de l'époque' [the most powerful artist of the age]. In Baudelaire's 'Edgar Allan Poe, sa vie et ses ouvrages' of 1852 and 'Edgar Poe, sa vie et ses œuvres' of 1856, Poe is celebrated as the type of the sensitive artist crushed by an incomprehending public, the visionary poet simultaneously blessed and cursed by his visions and insights. The descriptions of Poe's dress and physiognomy simply confirm the theme.

Mallarmé's portrait in 'Quelques médaillons et portraits en pied', though published in 1894, had been widely discussed in the Mallarmé circle that Gómez Carrillo frequented.[9] The Guatemalan is drawing, then, from an existing literary tradition and working in an established genre. He is depicting Wilde as the true artist, a fitting companion of Edgar Allan Poe. Wilde, as an admirer of Poe, would have recognized the frame of reference, conscious or unconscious. This portrait of the artist was to be further enriched, three years later, in *Les Poètes maudits* of Paul Verlaine, friend and companion of both Wilde and Gómez Carrillo. In the latter's evocation of Verlaine in his hospital bed in

Esquisses, we find once more the formulaic nature of the artist as dreamer and melancholic. We discover, also, the same aestheticizing tendency and the same mixture of the sublime and the subversive and the serious and the ironic, aspects Darío will note later in his own essays on Wilde (*SA* 48):

Y allí le encontré, siempre dispuesto a la burla terrible, en una cama estrecha de su hospital. Su rostro enorme y simpático, cuya palidez extrema me hizo pensar en las figuras pintadas por Ribera, conserva siempre su mueca original. [...] Sus labios gruesos [...] conservan siempre su mueca original, en donde el vicio y la bondad se mezclan para formar la expresión de la sonrisa.

[And there I found him, always disposed to terrible jokes, in a narrow bed in his hospital. His enormous and sympathetic face, whose extreme paleness reminded me of the figures painted by Ribera, still conserved his original grimace. His thick lips still conserved his original grimace, where vice and good nature mingled together to create the expression of a smile.]

What is striking about Gómez Carrillo's pen-portraits of his artist contemporaries is the strong emphasis on physical features: eyes, nose, hair, complexion, physical strength and body contour. In part he reflects the paradigms set down by Ingram and other precursors; in part, however, he is responding to a number of significant departures in art criticism that were to have the most profound effects on the discourses of literary writing.

In 1864, Cesare Lombroso, Professor of Mental Diseases in the University of Pavia, published the first of a series of studies on mental degeneration and the relationship between madness and genius: *Genio e follia*. Eleven years later, in 1875, he published a more substantial and pioneering study on the relationship between mental disease and criminality: *L'uomo delinquente*.[10] His findings were shaped in part by his earlier clinical observations as an army surgeon and Inspector of Prisons before accepting the chair in Pavia. His researches lacked, however, a purely scientific rigour. While influenced by the general intellectual climate of the time and the accumulated body of knowledge inherited from the disciplines of physiology, biology, outdated phrenology and physiognomy and the infant discipline of psychiatry, he allowed personal obsessions and prejudices to intrude upon his conclusions. The work of his predecessors converged in his training and experience to shape his insights regarding the nature and causes of criminal behaviour. While influenced by the earlier work of men like Morel, Maudsley, Lucas and Spencer among others,[11]

Lombroso came to believe that certain individuals were born criminals or were atavistic criminals, biological throwbacks from a primitive stage of evolution. Thus his patients demonstrated unfailingly an inherited disposition to criminal behaviour, evidenced in recognizable physical characteristics. Even though his findings reflect the general theories of heredity and degeneration that ran in parallel with evolutionary theory in mid-century, they also reflect his preoccupation—even obsession—with eliminating from society those elements that might inhibit or hinder the evolutionary development of man to his highest potential.

Lombroso's major contribution to the debates of the time was to link physical characteristics and mental degeneration, generally found, in his view, in the 'criminal type'. Such persons, argued Lombroso, showed specific physical attributes (shape of the head and jaw, posture, alignment of eyes, nose and mouth, etc.) that typified what he termed 'degenerate' types.[12] What was significant in his work, however, was that he introduced a discourse that properly had no place in scientific (medical and pathological) experimentation and research. Lombroso's contribution to science was blemished by his insistence that physically 'degenerate' types were also morally irresponsible or corrupting of 'healthy' society. Thus the binaries healthy/sick or good/evil and moral/immoral entered scientific experimentation, debate and writing.

In *L'uomo delinquente* Lombroso established a framework in which the system of justice and penal control was to operate and reform itself in the late-nineteenth century. Strangely, his work was to have, as a by-product, an enormous impact on literature, notably the Naturalist novel. In Spain his impact was profound.[13] But his greatest influence was to be on discourses of literary criticism, especially after the publication of his *L'uomo di genio* in 1889. The Spanish translation appeared in 1891, the very year of Gómez Carrillo's *Sensaciones de arte* and his essay on Wilde. In this work Lombroso proposed that the artist-genius was not the 'hierophant of the future' and 'seer' that Shelley and Hugo had proposed in the heady days of Romantic heroism and imaginative excess, when the artist, once more, was identified with a special madness. In reality, Lombroso is not concerned with 'genius' as the hallmark of outstanding or mould-breaking intellectual prowess. In the context of the evidence cited it is clear that he applies and restricts the term 'genius' to artists and thinkers. It is also clear that the subject of his analysis is the modern artist, especially the Symbolists and the Parnassians.

Lombroso coins the term *mattoide* [crazoid] to describe his subjects, since they exhibit symptoms of instability, see-sawing between geniality and delirium, altruism and madness. While, in all respects apparently physically healthy, their ideas are absurd and dangerous, unlike the genuine genius. Applying the same flawed model as in *L'uomo delinquente*, he linked moral and physical characteristics with artistic creativity and mental powers to conclude that the modern artist demonstrated 'degenerative psychosis of the epileptic category'. Inspiration was nothing more than a rare form of epilepsy. Thus the modern artist was a spurious 'genius' and, through his eccentric behaviour, presented a danger to society. His moral corruption, his subversive attitudes, his introspection, his alienation from his fellows and other unsocial patterns of behaviour made him a social misfit. As such Lombroso proposed methods for his control and marginalization.

It seems more than coincidental that Gómez Carrillo should emphasize physical characteristics and describe them in such a way as to invert the binary construct of Lombroso's design. The same features that Lombroso perceives as pointers to moral corruption, social peril and subversion, Gómez Carrillo evokes as the necessary and appropriate features and characteristics of the modern artist. Science, tainted with moral, legal and social concerns, ends up serving a literary response of superiority and new ideals. It was also, in the reversion of the binary constructs of healthy/sick, sane/mad, good/evil, a token of subversion and revolt against the controlling centre of the original Lombrosian discourse.

Gómez Carrillo was in touch, as ever, with the latest trends. For him, Wilde is a true artist of the age: only artistic criteria can influence the conception of a work of art and art constitutes the only criterion for its judgment. While he might argue that the artist bears no obligation to established codes, moral or ethical, that he is as noble in his tribulations as he is in his creative work and in his person, the very language he employs betrays his own assertion that Art is distinct from life. His use of the same discourses of the sciences unwittingly vitiates his claim. And the more so when he also employs discourses that belong to another powerful entity in the society of the Spain of the 1890s: religion.

In many ways, as with Rubén Darío's essay on Verlaine in *Los raros* of 1896, we discover in these pen-portraits a type of displaced theology, in which the artist is re-created as a Christ-like figure, a man of vision, a man who preaches a new redemptive religion and a who is martyr to his faith. As such, the portrait was deeply shocking to a conservative and Catholic audience and exhilarating for young Spanish writers eager for any sign that the stranglehold of Restoration civic, religious and moral ideals had begun to weaken. It was this outlook that made Wilde appear subversive and dangerous, and this aspect almost certainly lies in the traces and supplements from medicine, evolutionism, degeneration, the law and criminality and Christian teaching embedded in Gómez Carrillo's evocation of his friend. Indeed, it is, specifically, to the subversive aspects of Wilde that his next Hispanic commentator responds.

Rubén Darío, another of the many Latin-American diplomat-artists resident in Paris and Madrid, also knew Wilde. Through his friend Gómez Carrillo, Darío was drawn into the Wilde circle. In an essay written on 8 December 1900, shortly after Wilde's death on 30 November, Darío depicts his late-lamented friend as a *poète maudit*, a 'poeta maldito', martyr to his artistic ideals. The essay reviews the life and achievements and shows a close acquaintance with *Intentions* and *The Picture of Dorian Gray*. Darío also quotes the letter to Wilde from Mallarmé that Gómez Carrillo had first published in 1892 in *Sensaciones de arte*.[14] He may well have had Gómez Carrillo's essay on his desk. But it is in *Los raros* of 1896 that we discover more clearly the means by which Wilde was acculturated into the progressive artistic scene of Hispanic letters, a process that both confirms and extends the process so far examined, especially since this work is heavily influenced by the pen-portraits of *Sensaciones de arte* and *Esquisses*.

Los raros comprises an introductory essay on the new artistic trends and twenty further essays dedicated to specific artists, mostly French and today mostly forgotten. Several stand out: Poe, Verlaine, Ibsen. But one figure fails to conform to the pattern: Max Nordau, the author of *Entartung* (*Degeneration*). Even more strangely, Darío mentions Wilde in the essay on Nordau.

Now *Entartung* (1893) represented a major contribution to the moral offensive which had begun in the 1870s, with the work of Cesare Lombroso, against the new style of writing we know as the Symbolist Decadence. Nordau was one of the most enthusiastic of Lombroso's supporters and applied Lombroso's theories to specific modern artists including Wilde. In short, both Lombroso and Nordau employ the discourses of the new medical sciences of heredity, degeneration and psychopathology as a literary-critical tool to marginalize and control artistic trends they felt to be deeply subversive, even injurious to society. In a sense, with the added application of ethical and moral criteria and judgements, they sought to 'criminalize' the new writers. The 'man of genius', for Lombroso, was not far from the 'criminal man': both were a threat to society.

Nordau takes up Lombroso's theme enthusiastically and adds evolutionary theory and some half-baked psychological theories of his own to his diatribe to argue that the modern artist was a 'degenerate', an evolutionary failure, an introverted and alienated obsessive and a danger to himself and his fellows. His attack on the poems and the person of Walt Whitman illustrates perfectly the way in which supposedly objective scientific and literary judgements are soon contaminated by personal moral and sexual prejudices:

He was a vagabond, a reprobate, and his poems contain outbursts of erotomania so ardently shameless that their parallel in literature could hardly be found with the author's name attached. For his fame he had to thank just those bestially sensual pieces which first drew him to the attention of all the pruriency of America. He is morally insane and incapable of distinguishing between good and evil, virtue and crime.[15]

In this outburst we see the manner in which the discourses of power of the establishment worked through a system of binaries where the hegemonic centre appropriated to itself the positive aspects of a series of binary forms of specific social and scientific discourses and relegated to the margins the object of judgement in entirely negative terms. Those terms (or variants of the powerful discourses at play) are drawn from disciplines quite inappropriate to the matter at hand, literary criticism, and have no place in an assessment of artistic or aesthetic merit or value. Thus, here, the discourses of the law (vagabond, reprobate, crime), of medicine (erotomania, insane), of sexual morality (bestially sensual, pruriency) and of Christian teaching and religious morals (shameless, morally insane, good and evil, virtue) are brought into play to stigmatize and 'criminalize' and thus to marginalize the modern artist. And it was to this complex interplay of discursive controls, especially in their application to the person and the writings of Oscar Wilde, that the young writers in Spain responded. Their response was to beat Nordau at his own game by the simple process of subverting the discursive pattern, by inverting the binary constructs.

Entartung (the title *Degeneration* says it all) was first published in German in 1893 and in a French translation (*Dégénérescence*) the following year. Darío, as with other Latin-American writers based in Paris and Madrid, was soon to respond. The effect of *Los raros* is to ironize Nordau's position and to offer a riposte in a very special way.[16]

Darío says of the way Wilde is presented by Nordau (*OC* ii. 461): 'al paso de los estetas y decadentes, lleva la insignia de capitán de los primeros' [in passing through the aesthetes and decadents, he bears the badge of the captain of the first rank]. But from direct quotation of Nordau's assessment of Wilde, Darío moves to the offensive in a revision of the discourse employed by Nordau. 'Sí, Dorian Gray es loco rematado, y allá va Dorian Gray a su celda. No puede escribirse con la masa cerebral completamente sana el libro *Intentions*.' [Yes, Dorian Gray is a complete madman, and off goes Dorian Gray to his cell. One cannot write a book like *Intentions* with one's cerebral mass completely sane.] We might note in passing Darío's emphasis on madness, a condition frequently alleged against the modern artist (we have noted the focus on the *mattoide* in Lombroso and the term 'insane' applied by Nordau to Whitman). He then attacks Nordau, rejecting the Austrian's therapies for the degenerate artist who suffers from an 'egoísmo morboso' [morbid egoism], his advice to suppress thoughts concerning 'el misterio de la vida' and 'lo desconocido' [the mystery of life, the unknown], his recommendation that certain works should not be read. He scoffs at Nordau's aetiology of the artist and his 'degeneración como un resultado de la debilidad de los centros de percepción y de los nervios sensitivos' [degeneration as a result of the weakness of the centres of perception and the sensitive nerves] and his suggestion that the modern artist should be quarantined on the margins of society as if the artist were, adds Darío, 'un perro hidrófobo' [a rabid dog] (*OC* ii. 462). We note the discourse of disease and, of course, dis-ease. This adoption of the discourse of medicine, especially the science of psychopathology, colours the way in which both Nordau and Darío depict Wilde.

Increasingly from the late 1870s onwards, we find the appropriation of the discourse of medicine in debates concerning the nature and role of the artist and especially in literary criticism. Such a process is not a question of vogues or fashions where one area of culture or learning adopts the language and lexicon of another, even if the second is, as medicine was, a powerful one. The process is neither innocent nor accidental. Michel Foucault has shown how a dominant culture maintains its status by a process of division whereby one pole of a given binary contrast is condemned to silence and marginalization.

The binary healthy/sick was one such; sane/mad was another. The powerful institution forces expression into straitjackets of permissibility. Both groups contend, in their employment of the powerful discourse, to privilege and legitimize their position and, thereby, marginalize and confine their opponents.[17]

Thus, when Nordau stigmatizes Wilde for his 'queer costumes' (especially apt in the present meaning of the word, which he cannot have foreseen), 'his hysterical craving to be noticed', his 'anti-social megalomania', his 'pathological aberration' and his 'perversion', he employs a medical discourse.[18] But he also, principally, employs moral categories to condemn and marginalize. The two forms of control, in these *fin-de siècle* literary debates and confrontations, are often inseparable. Wilde's apparent deviation from the norm of 'normal' behaviour demands that he be controlled not only through the powerful discourse of establishment morality but also through the authority of medicine, especially that branch of the discipline (note again the coercive aspect of the discourses of the professions) that is concerned with mental health and disease. Thus, for Nordau, Wilde is a 'fool', a 'buffoon' who acts from 'a malevolent mania for contradiction'.[19] We note, however, that the criterion for acceptance is physical, social and moral 'health'. Since Nordau finds Wilde wanting, he is quarantined and incarcerated as a 'madman'. This is the idiom that Darío employs in his presentation of Wilde. This becomes very clear in Darío's reply to the accusation of Wilde as a subversive. In Wilde's obituary a chastened Darío, with no little irony amidst the seriousness of his comment, wrote the following (*OC* iii. 471):

Este mártir de su propia excentricidad y de la honorable Inglaterra aprendió duramente en el *hard labour* que la vida es seria, que la *pose* es peligrosa; que la literatura, por más que se suene, no puede separarse de la vida; que los tiempos cambian, que Grecia antigua no es la Gran Bretaña moderna, que las psicopatías se tratan en las clínicas, que las deformidades, que las cosas monstruosas deben huir de la luz, deben tener el pudor del sol, y que a la sociedad, mientras la destruya o que la dé vuelta como un guante, hay que tenerle, ya que no respeto, siquiera temor, porque si la sociedad sacude, pone la mano al cuello, aprieta, ahoga, aplasta. El burgués a quien queréis *épater* tiene rudezas espantosas y refinamientos crueles de venganza. Desdeñando el consejo de la cábala, ese triste Wilde *jugó al fantasma y llegó a serlo*; y el cigarrillo perfumado que tenía en sus labios las noches de conferencia era ya el precursor de la estricnina que llegara a su boca en la postrera desesperación, cuando murió, el *arbiter elegantiarium*, como un perro.

[This martyr to his own eccentricity and to honourable England learned harshly in hard labour that life is serious, that the *pose* is dangerous; that literature, whatever is said, cannot be separated from life; that times change, that ancient Greece is not the same as modern Great Britain, that psychiatric disease is treated in clinics, that deformities, that monstrous things should flee from the light, should be ashamed of the sun, and that society, while it destroys or can turn itself inside out like a glove, must be held, if not in respect, then in fear, because if society shakes itself, puts its hand on one's neck, it squeezes, chokes, crushes. The bourgeois you desire to shock has a horrifying coarseness and a refined cruelty in its vengeance. Distaining the advice of the cabal, this sad Wilde played at being an outsider and became one; and the perfumed cigar that he held in his lips during the nights of literary discussion was already the precursor of the strychnine that would be in his mouth in his last agony, when he died, the arbiter of elegance, like a dog.]

And, as Darío knew full well (*OC* iii. 469–70):

Pero no se puede jugar con las palabras, y menos con los actos. Los arranques, las paradojas son como puñales de juglar. Muy brillantes, muy asombrosos en manos del que los maneja, pero tienen punta y filos que pueden herir y dar la muerte. El desventurado Wilde cayó desde muy alto por haber querido abusar de la sonrisa. La proclamación y alabanza de cosas tenidas por infames; el brummelismo exagerado; el querer a toda costa *épater les bourgeois* —¡y qué *bourgeois* los de la incomparable Albión!—, el tomar las ideas primordiales como asunto comediable; el salirse del mundo en que se vive rozando ásperamente a ese mismo mundo, que no perdonará ni la ofensa ni la burla; el confundir la nobleza del arte con la parada caprichosa, a pesar de un inmenso talento, a pesar de un temperamento exquisito, a pesar de todas las ventajas de su buena suerte, le hizo bajar hasta la vergüenza, hasta la cárcel, hasta la miseria, hasta la muerte. Y él no comprendió sino muy tarde que los dones sagrados de lo invisible son depósitos que hay que saber guardar, fortunas que hay que saber emplear, altas misiones que hay que saber cumplir.

[One cannot play with words, and even less with actions. Emotional outbursts, paradoxes are like the daggerstroke of a minstrel entertainer. Brilliant, astonishing in the hands of those who know how to accomplish it, but it also has a point and an edge that can wound and kill. Luckless Wilde fell from on high because he decided to abuse the smile. The public announcement and lauding of things held to be odious; the exaggerated behaviour of a Brummell; the desire at all costs to *épater les bourgeois*—and what *bourgeois* are the citizens of incomparable Albion!—the taking of basic and central ideas as a matter for comedy; sauntering out of the world in which one lives roughly rubbing up the wrong way that very world, which will not pardon the offence or the joke; the confusing of the nobility of art with a capricious parade of wit, in spite of an exquisite temperament, in spite of all the advantages of good fortune, he was led to sink even into shame, to the prison cell, to misery, to death. And he only realized too late that the sacred gifts of the invisible are treasures one must hoard, fortunes one must know how to use aright, high missions one must know how to accomplish.]

Wilde's (and the modern artist's) ludic attitude to Art and the game of upsetting a bourgeois public by eccentric gestures and outrageous proclamations is, insists Darío, a two-edged sword. Like the discourses employed and their binary versions and reversions, the artistic *pose* can, all too quickly, rebound on itself. By 1900 Darío was all too aware, also, that the ironic pose and the mocking laughter that concealed would be misconstrued, as it had been for Byron and others,[20] in a Positivist and mercantile age that took levity as a sign of anti-social behaviour. Art was not a game but a sacred mission, even though the artist had come to defend himself, through the ironic pose and the mocking laugh (noted also by Gómez Carrillo in Verlaine), from the terrible insight that the desire for an artistic ideal was ever menaced by an inherently self-destructive urge and the belief that the true artist was fated by the gods to endure madness and rejection.[21] Thus Darío's descriptions of Wilde (like those of Gómez Carrillo before him) are a defence of the tragic condition of the artist's life and genius as much as an attempt to reverse the binary construction of Nordau's claim that Wilde was a degenerate.

In the context of Darío's decision to include Nordau in his gallery of *raros*, his friendship with Gómez Carrillo, as much as his reading of *Entartung*, is arguably an important feature. Gómez Carrillo had met Nordau in 1893 or 1894, at the time of the French translation of *Entartung*, and had discussed Decadent literature with him in 1891, and thus one might reasonably suppose he had learned something of the Austrian's attitude to modern art and culture.[22] Thus both Latin-American writers respond with a positive portrait of Wilde. As Foucault has noted, any discourse, however powerful, is incapable of resisting revisions and reversals where fissures open up and the margins are able to reclaim the centre. So, too, with the portraits of Wilde by Gómez Carrillo and Darío. Against the degenerate figure of Wilde depicted by Nordau and against the attacks of Lombroso on the artist-genius, the two Latin-American writers evoke a picture of a man who is physically strong, for all the distracted gaze of the poet-dreamer.

For Darío the Wilde of 1899 had the mien of an abbot with an air of perfect distinction. In conversation he found Wilde's dexterity in framing phrases to be singular. Wilde also spoke of matters of high moment, of pure ideas and questions of beauty. His vocabulary was picturesque, fine and subtle (*OC* iii. 473). Darío's account of *The Picture of Dorian Gray* and *Intentions* is similarly positive, a view underlined by the reproduction of the letter from Mallarmé, which he must have culled from earlier articles of Gómez Carrillo or directly from the Guatemalan himself. In his *Autobiografía* of 1912 Darío recalls the same meeting described in the 1900 article and repeats, with minor differences of detail, the same picture of Wilde. But he adds: 'Rara vez he encontrado una distinción mayor, una cultura más elegante y una urbanidad más gentil' [Rarely have I encountered a greater distinction, a more elegant culture and a more charming urbanity] (*OC* i. 149).

The artistic establishment consciously and unconsciously responded to the contending discourses of power rooted in the debates concerning the nature of the artist-genius first raised by Lombroso and subsequently given notoriety in Nordau's *Degeneration*. As such Wilde became a rallying point and an icon for the young Hispanic disciples of aestheticism. Yet it was the paradoxical state of art within the existing social order that brought another reaction to Wilde. The modern artist seemed to stand apart from the concerns of the age, and yet was profoundly concerned with the mysteries of life and with the more degenerate aspects of society. Wilde's *The Soul of Man under Socialism*, published in the *Fortnightly Review* in February 1891, was well known to the Spanish critical and artistic establishment, especially among its radical coteries. But, for all Wilde's attempt to incorporate the spell of art into an age made ugly by the pursuit of materialism and the inroads of industrialism, the late years of the 1890s reacted negatively to Wilde. It was not until after 1900 that the 'literary war' with the conservative establishment in Spain really began. In part it was Nordau's attack on Wilde's immorality, his want of decorum and his anti-social poses that conditioned opinion, especially after the publication of the Spanish version of *Degeneration* in 1902. Gómez Carrillo and Darío were lone voices. But it was also the reaction against the idea of Decadence (in the sense of evolutionary paralysis or the reversal of progress) and the attempt to arrest what was considered to be a rapid national decline and a failure of the national will (fed now by the writings of Nietzsche and the Disaster of 1898), that prevented any widespread admiration for the views put forward by Wilde. Aestheticism seemed to have no positive role to play in the process of national regeneration along the lines suggested in the works of Lucas Mallada, Rafael Altamira, Pompeyo Gener, Macías Picavea and Joaquín Costa. The journal *Vida Nueva*, arguably the most progressive and militant review of the time, was fervently anti-establishment in its Republican politics and its commitment to a more open society. It had little time for aestheticism and gave its support to Zola (especially after his essay *J'accuse*) and Tolstoy's essays on the role of art in a modern society. In October 1898, only months following Spain's national humiliation after the twin naval defeats at the hands of the fleets of the United States and the loss of the last of its overseas colonies, an article under the title 'Los estetas' appeared in *Vida Nueva*. The editor wrote:[23]

Este nombre [estetismo], que en un principio sirvió para designar una escuela artística, ha caído hoy no en el arroyo sino en la cloaca. Si hoy aparece en las columnas de *Vida nueva*, es para nombrar lo que nuestra desventurada política ha puesto en vergonzosa evidencia. Al copiar lo que acerca de los estetas han descrito autores tan ilustres como Max Nordau y Zola, aspiramos a contribuir a que se borre de nuestra sociedad esa lepra cuyo nombre sólo mancha el papel en que se estampa.

[This word (aestheticism), which at the outset served to define an artistic school, has today fallen not into the stream but into the sewer. If it appears today in the columns of *Vida Nueva*, it is to make public what our unfortunate editorial policy has placed in shameful evidence. In copying what has been written of the aesthetes by such famous men as Max Nordau and Zola, we hope to contribute to the cleansing of this leprosy whose name only sullies the paper on which it is printed.]

Underneath the editor reproduced Nordau's section on 'Aestheticism', including the section on Wilde. In addition, the editor appended Zola's description of Wilde as a moral and physical degenerate. Once more the binaries are reversed, and we note the process of the crossing of fields of discursive practice. Aestheticism is, once more, a sewer to be disinfected and a disease to be eradicated. *Vida Nueva* must act as a reluctant but necessary sanitary inspector to cleanse society of a highly infectious disease rather than as an arbiter of aesthetic taste and judgement. The article is not about literary and aesthetic issues; it is about public health. It does not employ the lexicon of literary criticism but the discourses of medicine and of hygiene.

It was not until the end of the first decade of the new century, long after the victory of aestheticism over conservative aesthetics, long after the scandal of Wilde's impeachment and imprisonment, that Wilde's fame finally began to grow in Spain. In 1908 Methuen Press ventured to re-publish Wilde's collected works in England, and within months a review appeared in the quality literary journal *Prometeo*, soon to be followed by the first of a series of translations. From then on Wilde was not only influential and popular, especially for his plays, but bankable. He became fashionable and popular with the theatre-going public. His works soon became a part of the currency of the early avant-garde and form a chapter that as yet has fully to be studied, but a chapter that will reveal the continued process of cultural transfer and the crossing of fields.[24]

Notes to Chapter 3

1. Enrique Gómez Carrillo, *Esquisses (siluetas de escritores y artistas): Oscar Wilde, Armand Silvestre, Charles Maurras, Paul Verlaine, etc.* (Madrid: Viuda de Hernández, 1892) [abbreviated *E* in text], 7.

2. See J. W. Kronik, 'Enrique Gómez Carrillo, Francophile Propagandist', *Symposium* 21 (1967), 50–60; see also L. Alberto Sánchez, 'Enrique Gómez Carrillo y el modernismo', *Atenea* [Chile] 117/299 (1950), 185–205.

3. 'Para ellos [the young writers in France] ya no es un misterio, como lo es en Espana, la muerte del Naturalismo. Para ellos ya no es un tema de discusión los paralelos entre la escuela de Zola y la escuela de Hugo. [...] Las escuelas que hoy se discuten entre esos jóvenes [...] son: el Simbolismo de Maurice, el Romanismo de Moréas y el Psicologismo de Bourget.' [For them (the young writers in France) the death of Naturalism is no mystery, as it is in Spain. For them the parallels between the school of Zola and that of Hugo is no longer a topic for discussion. The schools discussed today among these young men are Maurice's Symbolism, Moréas' Romanism and Bourget's Psychologism.] Gómez Carrillo, *Esquisses,* 8.

4. Enrique Gómez Carrillo, *Sensaciones de arte* (Paris: G. Richard, 1891) [abbreviated *SA* in text], 41–52.

5. Richard Ellmann, *Oscar Wilde* (London: Hamish Hamilton, 1987), 324.

6. Helen Potter, *Impersonations* (New York: Edgar S. Werner, 1891).

7. See Richard A. Cardwell, 'The War of the Wor(l)ds: Symbolist Decadent Literature and the Discourses of Power in Finisecular Spain', *Symbolism, Decadence and the Fin de Siècle: French and European Perspectives*, ed. Patrick McGuiness (Exeter: University of Exeter Press, 2000), 225–43.

8. See Patrick F. Quinn, *The French Face of Edgar Poe* (Carbondale: Southern Illinois University Press, 1957).

9. See 'Notes et variantes', Stéphane Mallarmé, *Œuvres complètes*, ed. H. Mondor and G. Jean Aubry (Paris: Pléiade and Gallimard, 1945).

10. Cesare Lombroso, *Genio e follia: Prelezione al corso di clinica-psychiatrica* (Milan: Chiusi, 1864); idem, *L'uomo delinquente* (Milan: Hoepli, 1876). The French translation, *L'Homme criminel*, appeared in 1887 (Paris: Alcan) with a second

edition in 1888. It was probably this translation with which Gómez Carrillo was acquainted.

11. See M. E. Wolfgang, 'Cesare Lombroso', *Pioneers in Criminology*, ed. Hermann Mannheim (London: Stevens, 1960), 168–277.

12. See for example this entry in a report: 'At the sight of that skull, I seemed to see all of a sudden, [...] the problem of the nature of the criminal—an atavistic being who reproduces in his person the ferocious instincts of primitive humanity and the inferior animals. Thus were explained anatomically the enormous jaws, the high cheek-bones, prominent superciliary arches, solitary lines in the palms, extreme size of the orbits, handle-shaped or sessile ears found in criminals, savages and apes, insensible to pain, extremely acute sight, tatooing, excessive idleness, love of orgies, and the irresistible craving for evil for its own sake, the desire not only to extinguish life in the victim, but to mutilate the corpse, tear its flesh, and drink its blood.' Quoted in the Introduction to Gina Lombroso-Ferrero, *Criminal Man according to the Classification of Cesare Lombroso* (New York: G. Putnam's Sons, 1911), pp. xiv–xvi. In this statement we see how Lombroso rode roughshod over the scientific method to include moral and social categories for judgement. We also discover the sensationalist aspect of his portrayal of the 'criminal type', which reflects the sensationalist reporting of crime at the time, yet another example of the way in which 'fields' cross.

13. See Pura Fernández, *Eduardo López Bago y el Naturalismo radical: La novela y el mercado literario en el siglo XIX* (Amsterdam: Rodopi, 1995); *Historia de la literatura española*, dir. Víctor García de la Concha, ix: *Siglo XIX (II)*, co-ord. Leonardo Romero Tobar (Madrid: Espasa-Calpe, 1998), § 7.2: 'El Naturalismo radical', 753–4; Remigio Vega Armentero, *¿Loco o delincuente? Novela social contemporánea (1890)*, ed. Pura Fernández (Madrid: Celeste, 2001). The title of this novel defines exactly the debate concerning madness and criminality. See also Luis Maristany's seminal study of the impact of Lombroso on the intellectuals of *fin-de-siècle* Spain: *El gabinete del doctor Lombroso (Delincuencia y fin de siglo en España)* (Barcelona: Anagrama, 1973).

14. Rubén Darío, 'Purificaciones de la piedad', idem, *Obras completas*, 5 vols. (Madrid: Afrodisio Aguado, 1950) [abbreviated *OC* in text], iii. 468–74.

15. Max Nordau, *Degeneration*, trans. G. L. Mosse (New York: Howard Fertig, 1968), 265.

16. See Richard Cardwell, '*Los raros* de Rubén Darío y los médicos chiflados finiseculares', *Rubén Darío y el arte de la prosa: Ensayo, retratos y alegorías*, ed. Cristóbal Cuevas, Actas del XI Congreso de literatura española contemporánea, 10–14 de noviembre de 1997 (Málaga: Publicaciones del Congreso de literatura española contemporánea, 1998), 55–77.

17. See Michel Foucault, *Les Mots et les choses: une archéologie des sciences humaines* (Paris: Gallimard, 1961).

18. Nordau, *Degeneration*, 316–18.

19. Ibid., 319.

20. See e.g. Byron's comment in *Don Juan*, Canto IV, 3–4: 'And the sad truth which hovers o'er my desk / Turns what was once romantic to burlesque. // And if I laugh at any mortal thing, /'Tis that I may not weep; and if I weep,/ 'Tis that our nature cannot always bring / Itself to apathy, for we must steep/Our hearts first in the depths of Lethe's spring / Ere what we least wish to behold will sleep.'

21. See Richard Cardwell, 'Darío and *El arte puro*: The Enigma of Life and the Beguilement of Art', *Bulletin of Hispanic Studies* 48 (1970): 37–51.
22. Enrique Gómez Carrillo, 'Notas sobre las enfermedades de la sensación, desde el punto de vista de la literatura' (1894), idem, *Obras completas*, 20 vols. (Madrid: Mundo Latino, n.d. [1920?]), xi. 83–145.
23. 'Los estetas', *Vida Nueva* 21 (1898), n.p.
24. This essay is indebted to the pioneering essay by Lisa E. Davis, 'Oscar Wilde in Spain', *Comparative Literature* 35 (1973), 136–52.

CHAPTER 4

Norah Borges Illustrates
Two Spanish Women Poets

Roberta Quance

The illustrations the Argentine artist Norah Borges (1901–1998) provided for two books of poetry by Spanish women associated with the Generation of 1927 are interesting as an example of how this artist's aesthetics could accommodate two quite different poetic stances on the part of women writers who were negotiating their way through the avant-garde. The books in question are *Canciones de mar y tierra*, published in Buenos Aires in 1930 by Concha Méndez (1898–1986), already well-known in Madrid as one of the few women moving in avant-garde circles, and *Júbilos*, published in Murcia in 1934 by Carmen Conde (1907–1996), a younger writer from Cartagena who had made her first publishing contacts through Juan Ramón Jiménez.

Norah Borges was Jorge Luis Borges's younger sister. Both were introduced into *ultraísta* circles in Spain shortly after their arrival in Seville in 1919, where they soon became major figures in the Spanish branch of the movement.[1] Unlike her brother, however, Norah, who married the young Spanish critic and poet Guillermo de Torre in 1928, maintained strong ties with Spain. Although it was said that she had made her husband promise that they would live in Argentina, the young couple returned to Spain in 1932.[2] And there they remained— both devoting their time to literary and artistic pursuits—until civil war broke out. By 1938, after a brief stay in Paris, they were back in Buenos Aires.

Concha Méndez did not know Norah Borges in Spain but rather met her on a trip she made to Argentina in 1929, when she looked up Guillermo de Torre, whom she had met once in San Sebastián.[3] Carmen Conde, on the other hand, made Norah's acquaintance in Madrid when

Norah and Guillermo returned to Spain to live, in the heady days following the proclamation of the Second Republic.[4] The link between the three women may very well have been Guillermo, and that is not strange, really, when one considers that he had acted as the *secretario de redacción* [deputy editor] for *La Gaceta Literaria* (1927–32), to which both Concha Méndez and Carmen Conde had contributed poems, and that he had made a name for himself as a literary critic with the publication of his *Literaturas europeas de vanguardia* in 1925.

By 1929, in any case, Norah Borges was a much-sought-after illustrator of literary journals. In Spain her work had appeared in several little magazines associated with *ultraísmo* (such as *Grecia* and *Ultra*), and when that movement waned her woodcuts, linoleum prints and drawings were featured in *Alfar*. Her early friendship with Guillermo de Torre and her close relationship with her brother had led her to produce a woodcut for Guillermo's first book of poems, *Hélices* (1923), and another that same year for the cover of her brother's *Fervor de Buenos Aires*. By the end of the decade Norah had also made her mark as a painter. In 1925 she participated in the Exposición de Artistas Ibéricos in Madrid, and the following year she had a one-woman show (comprising 75 works) at the Amigos del Arte in Buenos Aires.

Although *ultraísta* critics were struck originally by the way Norah's graphic work had assimilated the formal lessons of Expressionism and Cubism,[5] as her work evolved and became more representational in the general postwar *retorno al orden* [return to order], her themes and what was seen as her poetic vision commanded more attention. According to Augusto Mario Delfino, who reviewed Norah's show at the Amigos del Arte, 'De los setenta y cinco trabajos que expone, son sus ángeles la nota destacada.' [Of the seventy-five works that she is exhibiting, her angels are the most striking note.] In almost the same breath he observed that even more of her figures could be considered angels: 'no sólo las figuras que ella clasifica de tales, sino también esos niños que andan "buscando ángeles"' [not only the figures she classifies as such but also those children who are 'looking for angels'].[6] Manuel Rojas Silveyra was even more emphatic: 'En su pintura no hay sino niños y ángeles' [there is nothing but angels and children in her painting].[7]

This critical line extended to Spain where Benjamín Jarnés, writing in *La Gaceta Literaria* in 1927, echoed the Argentines: 'Los dibujos de Norah Borges representan preferentemente ángeles y niños' [Norah

Borges's drawings show a preference for angels and children]. He saw a quality of innocence and lack of *gravitas* in the work, which suggested to him that the world Norah's art projected was a prelapsarian one with a humankind still full of grace. Jarnés believed that these themes and the treatment of them were signs of the painter's femininity: 'Pocos casos de tan exquisita feminidad como el de Norah Borges. Por eso prefiere luchar con la materia más leve, más dócil' [There are few cases of such exquisite femininity as that of Norah Borges. That is why she prefers to grapple with the lightest, most docile of materials].[8] Although Norah's graphic work and painting were more varied than these judgements suggest, later critics tended to enlarge upon the qualities these men had defined. The Argentine Córdova Iturburu, for example, some three years later, described the artist's world view thus:

Los personajes de Norah Borges [...] están separados del mundo por una defensa de pudor. [...] Por eso dan esa sensación de meditación recogida, de dulce defenderse, de tímida afirmación de una personalidad definida y frágil, en cuyos ojos brilla la llama de una intimidad que se defiende extendiendo las manos, como un niño, para que nadie se aproxime. Extranjeros serían entre los hombres, tan extranjeros como los ángeles del Beato Angélico, nostálgicos de la patria celeste. [...] ¿No es éste el destino del espíritu? ¿Y no es así, justamente, la personalidad de Norah Borges, delicada y feliz con la felicidad triste de los frágiles?

[Norah Borges's characters are separated from the world by a barrier of modesty. That is why they give the impression of meditative withdrawal from the world, of sweet defensiveness, of timidly affirming a definite and fragile personality, in whose eyes shines the flame of a private world that defends itself by putting up its hands like a child so that no one will come near. They would be foreigners among men, as foreign as the angels of Fra Angelico, homesick for their celestial birthplace. Is this not the destiny of the spirit? And is this not precisely what Norah Borges's personality is like, delicate and happy with the sad happiness of the fragile?][9]

Although the critical strategy here might seem arbitrary inasmuch as it identifies the object(s) represented with the artist's own subjectivity, Norah herself seemed to encourage this approach. In 1928 she published a text entitled 'Nueve dibujos y una confesión: Lista de las obras de arte que prefiero' [Nine drawings and a confession: A list of my favorite works of art], which could be taken as a poetics, for in it she enumerated many of the objects that filled her paintings and drawings.[10] This suggested that in her work she was building up an ideal, personal world, a world that was better and perhaps happier than the one she knew. As for her person, some of the photographs taken of Norah at the time showed her to be ill at ease with publicity, as if she preferred to work from the sidelines.[11]

Norah Borges's children and angels would prove to be ambiguous signs. To begin with, as Jarnés pointed out, one could not be sure that the angels were not really children or the children angels (angels are children with wings, and children are angels without wings, he said). On closer inspection, one might be tempted to think that her adults also were both child-like and angelic. So a basically Romantic hierarchy suggests itself: adults, children, angels, in ascending order. To the extent that the figure one step below participates in the qualities of the figure immediately above, that figure is promoted— one step closer to perfection. But sex and gender, too, must be factors in this discussion. Norah Borges's figures all have something androgynous about them (to resurrect this word in the sense in which it has been analyzed by feminists, as that which is male or masculine overlaid with the female or the feminine). Her angels and men may be boys, yet they are boys who bear a delicate expression that makes them seem like twins of the girls that she portrays. Consider, for example, the portraits of lovers: *Pablo y Virginia* (1927), *Urbano y Simona* (woodcut 1924; oil painting, 1930), or her own oil portrait with Guillermo, *El herbario* (1928). As her figures rise on the spiritual ladder, transcending the human, they become ever more androgynous. By the time they are angels, sporting wings, they are entitled to wear a skirt and long hair, as we see from the illustrations for Jarnés's article on her work.[12]

This sort of androgyny—however suspect it might seem to us now—was at the time a retreat from the ideology of the avant-garde Ortega had analyzed in *La deshumanización del arte* (1925). In that essay (and elsewhere) Ortega declared that the modern movement was stamped with a masculine character. And that it had specifically repudiated the values of a *feminine* past, by which he seemed to mean anything smacking of nineteenth-century Romanticism.[13] Ortega certainly had no women in mind when he wrote.

Nonetheless, Norah Borges's androgynous angels, angelic children and child-like adults, because they keep a toehold in the world of youth and play, do not altogether elude Ortega's account of avant-garde values. And it is only on a *spiritual* plane that femininity reasserts itself.[14] Perhaps we can consider Norah's child-like, celestial androgyny a way of resolving the contradictory values women artists associated with the avant-garde were presented with, caught as they were between the *juvenil* [youthful] and the *deportivo* [sporty]—to follow Ortega—and the wish to build on the values of their own upbringing as girls.

Norah's work as an illustrator could and did look both ways in this respect. It was at once tactful and suggestive. Very early on, as May Lorenzo has noted, out of deference to the text she was illustrating, the artist developed a style that featured clear, simple lines against a white background.[15] Thus she could address the work of a poet who represented the avant-garde ideals of which Ortega had spoken (Concha Méndez) and then turn to the work of another poet who sought her models in a more traditionally feminine world (Carmen Conde).

Concha Méndez's *Canciones de mar y tierra* (1930) has been analysed as an effort on the part of a woman poet to embody the ludic and sporting ideals of an avant-garde aesthetic forged by men. But what is most striking in this collection of neopopular verse is the speaker's heartfelt desire for emancipation, for which the sea and sailing serve as metaphors. We see this in the very first poem, 'Navegar' (*CMT* 23–4):[16]

> Que me pongan en la frente
> una condecoración.
> Y me nombren capitana
> de una nave sin timón.
>
> Por las mares quiero ir
> corriendo entre Sur y Norte
> que quiero vivir, vivir,
> sin leyes ni pasaporte.
>
> Perdida por los azules
> navegar y navegar.
> Si he nacido tierra adentro
> me muero por ver el mar.
>
> [Let them place a decoration
> upon my brow.
> And name me the captain
> Of a vessel without helm.
>
> Over the seas I would go
> Running North and South,
> For my only wish is to live
> Without passport or law.

Lost amidst the blue,
Sailing and sailing along.
Though I was inland born,
I'm dying to catch sight of the sea.]

There is no fixed destination here—and hence no need for a rudder or helm (as we also read in 'Barca de luna', *CMT* 76). The point is that the speaker—whom Norah imagines to be a girl still—wishes to live freely, like a female version of a Romantic hero, on the margins of society ('sin leyes ni pasaporte' [without laws or passport]). As Alfonso Sánchez Rodríguez has pointed out, this is not just (Romantic) literature but an exact expression of the motives which in real life led Concha Méndez to set sail for London or Buenos Aires against her family's wishes and in violation of the standards of decorum for a young woman from the upper class.[17] In one simple poem where the poet makes the case for the importance of travel for the sense of self, she asserts that to go—to sail—is to be (*CMT* 75):

Mi vida en el mar. Yo voy
saltando de puerto a puerto.
Y en mi aventura yo soy
como un corazón despierto.

[My life on the sea. I go
Skipping from port to port.
And in my adventures I am
Like a heart now woken.]

The rhymes in lines 1 and 3, 'voy' and 'soy', which because of the enjambment are actually more visual than aural in character, encourage us to 'see' an almost philosophical affirmation in the celebration of sailing. According to Catherine Bellver, the poet is flouting the age-old association of women with passivity and immanence, qualities which find symbolic expression in fixity and horizontality. Thus she argues that poems such as 'Escalas' stake out a masculine symbolic space.[18] Women writers of the twenties and thirties, she asserts, adopted the theories and values men were promoting. Certainly the 'verticality' in some of the poems suggests that Méndez had internalized the symbolism that was prevalent in two important *ultraísta* texts from 1920, one by Guillermo de Torre, 'Manifiesto Vertical', which appeared as a supplement of *Grecia* (1 Nov. 1920) and a reply by Jorge Luis Borges, 'Vertical', which appeared in the first and only issue of *Reflector* (Dec. 1920).[19]

There is nothing in Norah Borges' illustrations of the book to buttress such 'faloforia' [phallophoria], as her brother called it. But to the extent that they evoke the sea and seashore and a solitary young female protagonist, her drawings do lend support to the ideal of female emancipation. They do this by bringing out the less obvious strains in the book, having to do with female sexuality and a dream of unobserved and unfettered being, which the sea induces in the would-be sailor. Norah envisages the female voyager as a young girl in her sailor shirt, catching the echo of the sea in her ear as if it were a seashell (Méndez's metaphor),[20] or leaning in a reverie against the ship's rail. Thus her drawings place the accent on interiority—a dimension that comes only gradually into view in the book—and shifts attention away from the many senses in which the protagonist of the verse, in seeking adventure on the seas, could be said to emulate masculine ideals or models. The decontextualization of the drawings—their lack of reference to a specific time and place, their assertion of a lyric present, and their isolation on a sea of white paper—encourages us to read the protagonist's actions and aspirations as a fantasy that will ultimately unfold on an island or happen to an island-self (*CMT* 184):

Recuerdo; era nadadora en el Cantábrico. El Cantábrico tenía —tiene— una isla pequeñita; mi primer puerto de broma. Y todos los días yendo a mi puerto por los caminos del mar, soñaba yo con las velas que a la isla debieran nacerle para irse —irnos— a navegar por el mundo.

[I remember; I was a swimmer in the Cantabrian Sea. The Cantabrian had—has—a tiny little island: my first toy port. And every day on the way to my port over the sea-roads, I dreamt of the sails that the island would have to grow in order for it—for us—to sail about the world.]

Through metonymy, the island destination becomes a metaphor for the female self who in turn becomes again, metonymically, a boat that has set sail.

Norah's drawings also imply a celebration of physicality. Consider her sunbather, for example, or her bare-breasted young woman. The heroine she imagined for the book is a sturdy athlete (the strong swimmer that we know the author in fact was) but at the same time one who embraces the sensuous pull of the sea and the lack of restraint in a seaside existence. Wishing, perhaps, to feel what a mermaid might feel in the ocean depths, such a character could give voice to the poem entitled 'Verdes', a poem which John Wilcox has said calls for the inner voyage of rebirth (*CMT* 66):[21]

¡Ay, jardines submarinos,
quién pudiera pasear
por vuestros verdes caminos

hondos de líquenes y olas,
radiantes, y estremecidos
de peces y caracolas.

Y volver a la ribera:
verdes ojos, verde el alma
y verde la cabellera!

[Oh gardens beneath the sea
if only I could tour
your deep green roads

of lichens and waves,
radiant and quivering
with conch-shells and fish.

And return to the shore:
green eyes, green soul
and green mane of hair!]

Méndez's poems exalt liberty and a proud unconcern for love, as is clear from 'Mi soledad' (*CMT* 141), which frankly equates 'soledad' [solitude] and 'alegría' [delight] or 'A todas las albas' (*CMT* 29–30), which suggests that to take a lover implies a landbound existence. Yet Norah chose to give the speaker a male counterpart: an athletic young bather with a dreamy expression, who is seemingly content to live off the fruits of the sea and ruminate verse. In her defence, she could surely have pointed out that, even though the heroine declares herself 'novia del mar, o su amante' [sweetheart of the sea, or his lover] ('Canal de Bristol', *CMT* 49) or 'barca sin dueño' [boat without an owner] ('Nocturno', *CMT* 143), some of her poems do allude to a possible male accomplice.[22]

Making only the slightest concession to contemporary details (that is, the heroine's stylish bathing suit), Norah understands this girl-woman to be so far ahead of her time that one would have to look backward to classical sources to trace her physical type. This sort of futuristic nostalgia, as we know, permeated other artists' work from this period as well, such as Picasso's bathers from the early twenties, which may have inspired Norah's.

The illustrations Norah did for Carmen Conde's *Júbilos* (1934) all centre on children, even though this collection of prose-poems, written in the first person and autobiographical in nature, is not exclusively about children, as its subtitle indicates: *Poemas de niños, rosas, animales, máquinas y vientos* [Poems about children, roses, animals, machines and winds]. In her prologue, however, Gabriela Mistral offered unstinting praise for the texts about childhood, noting that while the author did not use a child's language ('El libro es mejor *sobre* niños que *para* niños') [The book is better *on the subject* of children than it is *for* children], she had indeed captured a child's perspective. Conde had tapped most convincingly memories of her own childhood in Melilla and Murcia. As she welcomed Carmen Conde into the poetic fold, Mistral voiced the opinion that this was particularly a woman's gift:[23]

Nosotras, Carmen, estaríamos destinadas —y subraye fuerte el *destinadas* porque sería un destino pleno— a conservar, a celar y a doblar la infancia de los hombres, las corrientes de frescura y de ingenuidad que arrancan de la infancia en ellos, y que después, muy pronto, se encenagan, se paran, o se secan en su entraña.

[We women, Carmen, may very well be destined—and underline *destined* because it is no doubt a full destiny—to preserve, watch over and duplicate the childhood of men, those streams of freshness and ingenuity which well up in them from their childhood and which later, very soon, grow muddy, stop flowing, or dry up in their insides.]

One might very well ask why this should be the case. Although Mistral does not go into reasons, her own work evidenced the belief that women had privileged access to the world of childhood because they were mothers.[24] Thus, in seeking support from Gabriela Mistral, who was famous for her poems inspired in motherhood, Carmen Conde was beginning to formulate a poetics of sexual difference that departed from what some saw as a norm of masculinity imposed by the avant-garde.

Of the six illustrations Norah did for this book, five refer to specific poems, incorporating a phrase or sentence from each as a caption beneath the drawing, as if she were illustrating a primer for children. They do not, however, sit strictly beside the texts. Thus, 'Escuela' (*J* 21) is illustrated on p. 29 with a drawing of ABCs. The text 'Freja' (*J* 31) from a sequence entitled 'Niñas moras' is illustrated on p. 77, with a drawing of little girls with their hair in tight plaits resembling cornrows, hair that had been treated according to a traditional

Moroccan recipe of egg yolk and honey. Another of the texts from the same series, 'Pies desnudos' (*J* 33), in which the young Carmen learns to go barefoot like the Moroccans, has a corresponding illustration on p. 47. 'Masanto' (*J* 38), a text about a little Jewish girl ('una hebreílla'), is illustrated on p. 89 with a drawing of the cookies one got in her house; and 'El niño limpio' (*J* 54) finds illustration on p. 125 in a drawing of an exercise book. Only one drawing (p. 129) of two little peasant girls at play, one somewhat older than the other and so the leader in the game, is not geared to a specific text. It seems, in fact, to be a simplified version of a painting Norah had done in 1933 entitled *Tres niñas españolas*.[25] In both the painting and the drawing the girls are rendered in the simple geometrical shapes and with the wide eyes and timid expression that had become Norah's personal style.

Since three of the drawings refer to the author's North African playmates, it is fair to say that these are the texts that Norah Borges found most suggestive. She went unerringly to a phrase or passage in each that appealed not only to the sense of sight but to the other senses as well—taste, smell, touch—which had been stirred by the young girl's exposure to an exotic household. She also focused on texts that recorded Conde's experience in the schoolroom teaching youngsters their ABCs. She does not adopt the adult perspective of the writer, however: it is a little girl's hand, for example, (not the teacher's) which is seen tracing the letters of the alphabet. The enlarged size and child-like simplicity of the drawings suggest that quite possibly, like Gabriela Mistral, the illustrator had envisaged children as potential readers of at least some of these texts and that she sought to engage them through reference to their own action of reading and, in the case of the little boy filling his exercise-book, writing, too.

When Concha Méndez published her book of poetry, as her memoirs reveal, she hardly knew who Norah Borges was.[26] Carmen Conde, on the other hand, had no doubt read Méndez's book, and in view of the several articles that had appeared on Norah's work in the Spanish press, as we have seen, it seems likely that she was well aware of the artist's reputation. An unsigned review of Concha Méndez's book, which appeared in the journal *Sudeste*, edited by Conde's husband and mentor Antonio Oliver Belmás, had mixed praise for the poetry but unqualified admiration for the artwork:[27]

Todo el ímpetu viajero de Concha Méndez Cuesta, no ha bastado a apartarla de las fuentes líricas donde primeramente bebió. Sin embargo, sería interesante verla romper esas últimas amarras y acercarse más a sí misma, como ya consigue en muchos poemas. Norah Borges de Torre, ha prestado a este libro la belleza de unos finos dibujos, poemas ellos también alusivos al mar.

[Not all of Concha Méndez's passion for travel has been enough to lure her away from the sources where she first drank of poetry. Nonetheless, it would be interesting to see her cut loose from those last moorings and move closer to herself, as she already does in many of her poems. Norah Borges de Torre has added a touch of beauty to the book with her fine drawings, which are themselves poems about the sea.]

Perhaps it was upon seeing Méndez's book (which included a poem dedicated to her) that Conde conceived a desire to see her own work illustrated by this artist. After all that had been written about Norah Borges's angels and children and her femininity, she may very well have thought that here was an artist who would feel a special sympathy for her writing. (There could have been an element of rivalry with Concha, too.)

Be that as it may, Norah Borges's art came to illustrate two very different images of the woman poet. In Concha Méndez it served as a counterpoint to the image of a freewheeling spirit who had arrogated to herself the male prerogative of travel and autonomy. In Carmen Conde it reinforced the bonds with a traditional woman's world that some women thought could and should be exploited literarily.

Notes to Chapter 4

1. For details, see Sergio Baur, 'Norah Borges, musa de las vanguardias', *Cuadernos hispanoamericanos* 610 (April 2001), 87–96; also *El ultraísmo y las artes plásticas,* ed. Juan Manuel Bonet (Valencia: IVA and Centre Julio González, 1996). For a rough chronology of Norah's life and work see *Norah Borges, casi un siglo de pintura* [exhibition cat., July–Aug. 1996] (Buenos Aires: Centro Cultural Borges, 1996).
2. Reported by Ernesto Giménez Caballero, 'Itinerarios jóvenes de España: Guillermo de Torre', *La Gaceta Literaria* 44 (15 Oct. 1928), 7.
3. See James Valender, 'Concha Méndez en el Río de la Plata (1929–1930)', *Una mujer moderna: Concha Méndez en su mundo (1898–1936),* ed. James Valender (Madrid: Publicaciones de la Residencia de Estudiantes, 2001), 149–63. For her own account, see Paloma Ulacia Altolaguirre, *Concha Méndez: Memorias habladas, memorias armadas,* foreword by María Zambrano (Madrid: Mondadori, 1990), 72–82.
4. As Norah maintained in an interview with Juan Manuel Bonet, 'Hora y media con Norah Borges', *Renacimiento* [Seville] 8 (1992): 5–6 at 5.
5. See, for example, Guillermo de Torre, 'El renacimiento xilográfico: Tres grabadores ultraístas', *Nosotros* [Buenos Aires] 161 (1924), 274–6. Norah's

excellent training in Switzerland earned her the respect of other young *ultraístas* as well. According to Eugenio Carmona, 'Bores ultraísta, clásico, nuevo, 1921–1925', *Francisco Bores: El ultraísmo y el ambiente literario madrileño* [exhibition cat., Sept.–Nov. 1999] (Madrid: Publicaciones de la Residencia de Estudiantes, 1999), 13–51 at 23, it was she who probably taught Francisco Bores the Expressionist technique in woodcuts.

6. Augusto Mario Delfino, 'La exposición de Norah Borges en "Los Amigos del Arte"', *El Diario* [Buenos Aires] (23 Oct. 1926); repr. Patricia Artundo, *La obra gráfica de Norah Borges, 1920–1930* (Buenos Aires: n.p., 1993), 164.

7. Manuel Rojas Silveyra, 'La exposición de Norah Borges', *La Prensa* [Buenos Aires] (n.d.); repr. Artundo, *Norah Borges*, 162–4 at 162. See also Alberto Prebisch, 'Los dibujos de Norah Borges', *Martín Fierro* 36 (1926), 1; repr. Artundo, *Norah Borges*, 165: 'Angeles, niños, adolescentes de ojos lánguidos, todos ellos impregnados de una gracia y una ternura que no son el menor atractivo de este arte tan delicadamente femenino.'

8. Benjamín Jarnés, 'Los ángeles de Norah Borges', *La Gaceta Literaria* 7 (1 Apr. 1927), 2.

9. Córdova Iturburu, 'Definición de Norah Borges de Torre', *La Gaceta Literaria* 73 (1 Jan. 1930), 5–6 at 5.

10. Norah Borges, 'Nueve dibujos y una confesión: Lista de las obras de arte que prefiero', *La Nación* [Buenos Aires] (12 Aug. 1928), repr. Artundo, *Norah Borges,* 157; also repr. Ramón Gómez de la Serna, *Norah Borges* (Buenos Aires: Losada, 1945), 25–6.

11. See *Norah Borges, casi un siglo de pintura*; Roberta Quance, 'Un espejo vacío: Sobre una ilustración de Norah Borges para el ultraísmo', *La Revista de Occidente* 239 (2001), 134–47.

12. Henry Mayr-Harting, *Perceptions of Angels in History* (Oxford: Clarendon Press, 1997), 17–18, speculates that with the 'celesticization of angels' in the twelfth and thirteenth centuries, there came a 'sex change', and the angels formerly thought of as male became androgynous. As a well-travelled young woman with a strong preparation in the fine arts, Norah would certainly have absorbed this idea and made it her own. In Ramón Pérez de Ayala's *Los trabajos de Urbano y Simona* (1924), a novel which Norah admired, according to Artundo, and which inspired a woodcut and at least one oil painting, we read: 'Tengo leído en Santo Tomás de Aquino, si no me equivoco, que los ángeles no se casan porque son andróginos, como las azucenas.' Idem, *Obras completas*, ed. José Garcia Mercadal (Madrid, Aguilar, 1963), iv. 387.

13. See José Ortega y Gasset, *La deshumanización del arte* (Madrid: Revista de Occidente en Alianza Editorial, 1998; first pubd 1925), 51–2. For more on this, see Quance, 'Un espejo vacío'.

14. Interestingly, Guillermo Díaz-Plaja, 'Tres discos románticos', *La Gaceta Literaria* 96 (15 Dec. 1930), 7, who saw signs around 1930 (the centenary of Victor Hugo's *Hernani*) of a return to a Romantic sensibility in literature and fashion, bantered that one would not achieve 'una vitalización total de esta conmemoración romántica hasta que el ángel de luz [for example, Espronceda's Teresa] vuelva a ser la mujer'.

15. By implication the drawings 'no debían apropiarse de la página; por respeto al

autor, dejaban blancos para que la imaginación los llenara con el texto'. See May Lorenzo Alcalá, 'Norah Borges, ilustradora', *Noticias: Voz e imagen de Oaxaca* [digital edn.] (11 March 2001), (accessed 21 Feb. 2002, no longer accessible); first publ. in *La Nación* [Buenos Aires], Cultura (18 Feb. 2001), 1, 8.

16. Concha Méndez Cuesta, *Canciones de mar y tierra,* foreword by Consuelo Berges (Buenos Aires, n. p., 1930), 23–4. All quotations refer to this edition, abbreviated *CMT* in the text.

17. Alfonso Sánchez Rodríguez, 'Concha Méndez y la vanguardia: Apuntes para un retrato de mujer moderna', *Una mujer moderna,* ed. Valender, 115–33 at 130.

18. Catherine Bellver, *Absence and Presence: Spanish Women Poets of the Twenties and Thirties* (Lewisburg, PA: Bucknell University Press, 2001), 63–6.

19. Both repr. *El ultraísmo y las artes plásticas* [exhibition cat., 27 June – 8 Sept. 1996] (Valencia: IVAM, 1996), 140–1 (Torre); 150 (Borges): 'posee ante la democracia borrosa del medio ambiente todo el prestigio audaz de una desorbitada faloforia en un pueblo jesuítico'.

20. As the poet herself recalls (*CMT* 184): 'Todo tiene sabor de músicas lejanas,— que yo llevo en el caracol de mis oídos y en los oídos de mi alma.' [Everything has the savour of distant music—which I carry in the conch-shell of my ears and in the ears of my soul.]

21. John C. Wilcox, *Women Poets of Spain, 1860–1990* (Urbana and Chicago: University of Illinois Press, 1997), 104.

22. See the poems 'A la isla' (*CMT* 99) and 'Coplilla' (*CMT* 105). In 'A todas las albas' (*CMT* 30), however, a lover is associated with a landlocked existence which the lyrical subject vows to leave behind: 'Y no me quedaré en tierra, / no me quedaré, no, amante' [And I will not stay on land, / no , I will not, no, my lover.]

23. Gabriela Mistral, Foreword to Carmen Conde, *Júbilos: Poemas de niños, rosas, animales, máquinas y vientos,* drawings by Norah Borges de Torre (Murcia: Sudeste, 1934), 13. All quotations refer to this edition, abbreviated *J* in the text.

24. See Mistral's early works *Desolación* (1921) and *Ternura* (1923). María Teresa León, 'La narradora', *La Gaceta Literaria* 85 (1 July 1930), 8, whose first collection of stories was for children, laments the fact that women of her day, in order to 'hombrearse', or place themselves on a par with men, lose touch with childhood.

25. This painting is reproduced in black and white in Gómez de la Serna, *Norah Borges,* plate 20.

26. 'Tenía la dirección de Guillermo de Torre, a quien años antes había conocido en San Sebastián. Norah Borges, su mujer, era muy graciosa. Recuerdo su voz de niña una de las veces que comí con ellos. "Mira, Guillermo, Concha tiene carita de Goya; sus ojos son enteramente de personaje goyesco". Norah hacía unos dibujos ingenuos, preciosos y, además, sabía muchísimo de pintura. Otra tarde recibí de sus manos un ramo pequeñito de violetas, envuelto en un papel de china: "Toma".' See Ulacia Altolaguirre, *Concha Méndez,* 73.

27. Anon. review of Méndez, *Canciones de mar y tierra, Sudeste* 4 (1931), 4. For discussion of influence, see Sánchez Rodríguez, 'Concha Méndez y la vanguardia'.

CHAPTER 5

❖

Gifts from the Poet to the Art Critic

Jacqueline Cockburn

Lorca met Sebastiá Gasch, the most documented and influential critic of modern art in Catalunya, at the house of the Uruguayan painter Rafael Pérez Barradas in 1927. Barradas was a stage designer, and Gasch knew Josep Dalmau who owned a gallery in Barcelona. Lorca was staying with Dalí in Figueras and working on 'Mariana Pineda', which was to take place at the Teatro Goya towards the end of May 1927. The three men met at the Café Oro del Rhin in Barcelona. Gasch had never heard of Lorca, but Lorca knew who Gasch was. Gasch recounted the meeting: 'Tan pronto como cambié cuatro palabras con el misterioso personaje, fui víctima del flechazo. De un modo fulminante, repentino, me sentí atraído, hacia aquel apasionado muchacho como por un imán.' [As soon as I had exchanged four words with this mysterious character, I was the victim of love at first sight. In an explosive, unexpected way, I felt attracted like a magnet to that passionate boy.][1] In Lorca's first letter to Gasch he mentioned his drawings and promised to bring some to their first meeting.[2] In the second half of May 1927 Lorca first started to show Gasch his drawings either personally or in letters. In fact he was ultimately to gift Gasch with 22 of his drawings.

It is important to note that by January 1927 Lorca was already expressing dissatisfaction with his written work, and a feeling that his intentions were misunderstood and that the public as yet had not realized the seriousness of his creative personality. An article in 'Verso y prosa' of that month described him as up and coming but only mentioned his 'Impresiones y paisajes', which had been published nine years earlier. It also described him as a gypsy, responding perhaps to *Romancero gitano* (1924–7); this enraged him further: 'me va molestando mi mito de gitanería. Confunden mi vida y mi carácter.'

[the myth of my being a gypsy is bothering me. They are confusing my life and my character.][3] He had spent an idyllic and much-documented time with Salvador Dalí before meeting Gasch, and he had begun to draw.[4] Dalí's own 1925 exhibition at the same gallery contained seven paintings with Lorca as their main theme. Dalí helped to arrange the first of the two exhibitions of his drawings during his lifetime. This took place at the Dalmau Gallery in Barcelona from 25 June until 2 July 1927 and gave Gasch the chance to write about him. From their meeting in May to the opening in June, Lorca and Gasch began their discussions about art. Lorca's exhibition at the Dalmau gallery lasted just one week, and although it did not attract much critical attention, Gasch published an article in *L'Amic de les arts* in the July issue, which later appeared in *La Gaceta Literaria* in March 1928.

In fact the press seemed confused by the drawings. The *Revista de Catalunya* referred to the drawings as 'Art Surrealista' and the *Ciutat* called them products of 'poscubismo'.[5] Gasch commented on the fact that the 'bureaucrats of art' would lack understanding of the work. In fact he went further and advised the timid and the sedentary to stay away from them. He also used the opportunity to attack the transcendentalists, the pretentious and what he called responsible people, those who feared ridicule and unknown adventures and those who were weighed down with worry.[6] In a sense he damned with faint praise, suggesting that the drawings were aimed at the pure and the simple and those who could feel without understanding; he called the drawings puerile, anti-artistic, anti-transcendental objects:[7]

Federico García Lorca, el poeta, el poeta auténtico, el poeta altísimo, siente a menudo la necesidad, como Jean Cocteau, como Max Jacob, de plasmar sus sueños plásticamente [...] y nacen automáticamente sus dibujos [...] dibujos presentidos, dibujos adivinados, dibujos vistos en un momento de inspiración, y que pasan directamente de lo más profundo del ser del poeta a su mano [...] Pensamos también en los dibujos de Miró, que vive atento a las visiones de su mundo interior, y que las fija rápidamente sobre el papel al presentarse de la misma manera que el poeta anota en su carnet la metáfora que acaba de crear.

[Federico García Lorca, the poet, the authentic poet, the well-regarded poet, often needs, like Jean Cocteau, like Max Jacob to transform his dreams plastically. and his drawings are born automatically. Drawings that foresee, drawings that guess, drawings seen in a moment of inspiration, they come from the depths of the poet's being to his hand. We are reminded of Miró's drawings, which are indications of his inner world that he fixes quickly on paper, presenting them in the same way as the poet, who notes down in his exercise book, the metaphor he has just created.]

Lorca was, however, delighted to be praised, and he replied to this article on 31 July 1927: 'Su artículo [...] me gusta y le doy mis gracias efusivas. Usted ya sabe el extraordinario regocijo que me causa el verme tratado de pintor.' [I like your article and send you my heartfelt thanks. You understand the pleasure I get when I'm treated like a painter].[8] By showing his drawings publicly, Lorca was able to enter the current artistic debate between Cubism and Surrealism. He chose carefully which works to display, showing those that clarified his own line of argument.[9]

Lorca entered the artistic debate for three reasons. First, to rid himself of the reputation of 'gypsy'. Secondly, to resolve the difficulties he was experiencing in writing poetry. It is significant that he almost stops writing poetry at this point, yet the process he begins he refers to as 'escribir y [...] dibujar poesías' [writing and drawing poems].[10] Thirdly, to enter the raging debate about creativity. If he turned to the same artistic medium, it brought him closer to Gasch and Dalí. He needed to be functioning in the same currency before he could operate on the same level. The 'currency' is the primary level of exchange, in that he could seek approval and intellectual nurture more easily. His drawings are consequently part of an intellectual exchange or field-crossing, as they engendered a debate between himself and the art critic and kept that debate alive between them. So the summer of 1927 was a critical moment in both the poetic work and the graphic work and the fusion between them.

1927 was an important year for other reasons too. Henri Bergson had been a frequent visitor at the Residencia de Estudiantes, where Lorca had been a student, for ten years between 1918 and 1928. Bergson also won the prestigious Nobel Prize for literature in 1927 and enjoyed the status of a cult figure whose lectures attracted large crowds. His lecture given in 1916 was in fact published in the magazine of the Residencia in 1926.[11] Einstein, H. G. Wells and a number of other key scientists and philosophers had also spoken at the Residencia. Debates about instinct and intellect provide much of the background to the debate between Lorca and Gasch. Bergson juxtaposed instinct with analysis and posited that intuition was the key to the real world. Debates about non-Euclidian geometry and the fourth dimension excited much speculation at the time, suggesting that reality was merely an appearance, behind which lay some order or energy or essence of a different kind. Bergson stressed the importance of human freedom and creativity in the face of causal accounts and human consciousness. His brilliant use of metaphor and analogy made his work accessible at that time to a large following. To what extent Lorca understood Bergson is not the issue here. What is clear is that his name was a buzzword at the time. Bergson was topical, trendy perhaps.

Let us look at, for example, the debate about *Totalismo* in the light of Bergson's writing. The references to this concept in *L'Amic* and *La Gaceta Literaria* between the beginning of 1927 and the end of 1928 are constant. Lorca, in his drawings was clearly responding to Gasch's call for *Totalismo,* which he had been writing about in both journals at the time. *Totalismo,* as understood by Gasch and interpreted by Lorca, was a hybrid expression that many artists were experimenting with at the time: that is, the fusion between the arts and the interdependence and possible personal development that could come out of experimentation. Gasch applauded what he called poetry and plasticity at the same time and found it mostly in Picasso. Gasch had set the challenge in *La Gaceta Literaria:*[12]

Esperamos ávidamente la obra genial que aproveche las conquistas técnicas del cubismo, que las enriquezca con la poesía del superrealismo, que fusione, finalmente la abstracción y la realidad, que una finalmente la inteligencia y la sensibilidad. Esperamos ávidamente el nuevo Picasso que canalice las aguas desordenadas del río inquieto de la pintura de ahora, que conduzca finalmente a buen puerto el buque pictórico que flota a la deriva sobre el mar agitado de la plástica actual.

[Avidly we await the ingenious work that takes advantage of the technical conquests of Cubism, that enriches these with the poetry of Surrealism, that fuses, finally, abstraction and reality, that unites, finally, intelligence and sensitivity. Avidly we await the new Picasso who channels the disordered waters of the river of the paintings of our time, who pilots finally, the pictorial vessel that floats adrift over the agitated sea of current plasticity, into safe harbour.]

It is clear that he was advocating intelligence and sensitivity in line with Bergson's arguments about analysis and intuition. Lorca responded to Gasch's challenge by putting forward a number of 'Cubist' images for the Dalmau exhibition; he put forward 24 drawings in total. Perhaps he was grateful for the mention of his ode, which he had written to Dalí in response to Dalí's 1925 exhibition, or perhaps he saw himself as the new Picasso. The works, as we shall see, contain echoes of Bergsonian concepts and Picasso and Braque's project, but they also look back to the conventions of earlier still lifes. They are a direct response to Gasch's requirements and are meant to convince Gasch that he is serious.

Lorca drew in order to work out problems, as the title of his drawing *Teorema de la copa y la mandolina* (1927) suggests. He also drew to communicate his feelings or emotions. Gasch was scathing about early Cubist practices and also criticized Dalí, but was very much in favour of Miró, who he felt was independent of imitation.[13] It is clear that in *Teorema de la copa y la mandolina* the drawing process is laboured or intellectual and opens the debates in terms of the validity of Cubism over Surrealism or what Gasch calls 'intelligence and sensitivity' and their possible fusion.[14] *Teorema de la copa y la mandolina* announces itself as theoretical. The format inside the rectangular paper is reminiscent of eighteenth-century formats later used by Braque and Picasso.[15] This stresses the notion that we are looking at a work of art and not at a view through a window.

At first glance the language is clearly that of Cubist practices. The image is centred as Analytical Cubist works emphasized, yet the insistence on surface nods in the direction of Synthetic practices. If we look at Picasso's *Naturaleza muerta con mandolina* (1924), we see that Lorca is repeating certain shapes and colours.[16] Lorca is working with shapes and picture planes in true Cubist tradition as he saw it. He is schematizing the act of looking and analysing objects in relation to one another and to the space around them. The subject matter engages with Cubist practice, but it also echoes the Spanish still-life tradition. On Lorca's part this is also a reaction to Gasch's call for *Totalismo*. The musical instrument is in the image not just as a reminder of the abstract quality of music but also to highlight its importance within the artistic debates at the time. The earlier still lifes were filled with allegorical meanings, often alluding to Christian themes such as the transience of life. The Cubist vocabulary stresses the moment and the notion that any symbolism is fluid and constantly changing. We are reminded once again of the Bergsonian debate about time understood at the level of human consciousness or by the intellect.

The playing card in *Teorema de la copa y la mandolina*, which Lorca also echoed in one of his drawings of Dalí, *Slavador Adil* (1925), suggests randomness and the chance encounter. Lorca added the notion or equivalent of the Venn diagram in order to explore use of space and mixings of primary colours. He also used numbers in his poetry to create tension. Picasso said that he painted forms as he thought them, not as he saw them. Here the general effect is of flatness as if objects have been splayed and yet they are fragmentary and abstract. The numbers also suggest a notion of the kind of abstract quality found in mathematics and physics, which obviously fascinated Lorca.[17] On the drawing he calls a 'Teorema' he puts the equation 'A = A', from Niels Bohr's theory of complementarity. Lorca was clearly interested in the binary notion of reality/absence. On the one hand, it suggests a working out or positioning process, but the equation seems also to stress the notion of exchange and equality so vital to Lorca's intentions.

In *Merienda* (1927),which he also prepared for viewing at the Gallery, he reworked the same principles in a slightly more sophisticated way. Once again the format is oval, but the composition is structured by means of a rising triangle that is based on an invisible horizontal line about a quarter of the way up from the bottom of the paper. The signs are less visible in this drawing, and the suggestive shapes stress tonally tilted planes and a shallow use of space. Lorca invites the viewer to seek for clues in an ambiguous visible world. He insists on surface patterning and texture, as Picasso did in *Guitarra* (1913).[18] He also explores the idea of the description of three-dimensionality in a two-dimensional way; which he did not attempt, or consciously avoided, in his line drawings. The overlapping stresses the possibility of a fourth dimension and a realignment of time.

Gasch made a clear connection between Cubism, seen as cerebral and plastic, and Surrealism, seen as instinctive and poetic. The ideal work is a fusion of the two senses and two art forms. But Gasch seemed less convinced about Surrealism, which he referred to as the orphan of plastic values and somehow shipwrecked from pure literature. The tensions between the forces of reason and the imagination, between intellectual control and intuition, are explicit in many of Lorca's own comments about the act of drawing. What Gasch approvingly called Lorca's 'tendencia plástica/poética' would seem to be the fusion not only between the literary and artistic arts but also between Cubism and Surrealism: 'Los dibujos de Lorca no imitan al natural. Una cosa es la naturaleza y otra cosa es el arte [...] Lo esencial para el artista son las resonancias de su mundo interior al chocar con el mundo exterior.' [Lorca's drawings do not imitate the natural world. One thing is the natural world and the other is art.

What are fundamental for the artist are the harmonies of his interior world when they collide with his exterior world.][19] Suggesting that what Cubism and Surrealism had in common was a construction of the world, that was not based on mimesis, Gasch ends this particular article by acknowledging:[20]

Poesía, mucha poesía, en los dibujos de Lorca. Plástica, también, mucha plástica. Los dibujos de Lorca, no son, como casi la totalidad de dibujos de literato, simples pasatiempos de la fantasía sin un andamiaje plástico que los sostenga. Plástica, mucha plástica en los dibujos de Lorca. Equilibrio de líneas, dimensión, relación de tonos. No armonía querida, sin embargo, si la voluntad se mezclara en este juego, el juego perdería toda su importancia. Armonía instintiva, simplemente. Sentido plástico instintivo que se opone decisivamente a la caída en la divagación literaria.

[Poetry, lots of poetry in Lorca's drawings. Plasticity too, lots of plasticity. Lorca's drawings are not like nearly all the drawings of literary people, simple doodles without any plastic scaffolding to hold them up. Balance of lines, dimension and tonal variations. No beloved harmony, though, for if desire becomes enmeshed in the game, the game itself loses all its importance. Simply instinctive harmony, instinctive plasticity, which opposes outright any fall into literary rambling.]

   Lorca knew that Gasch had criticized Dalí for allowing his intelligence to prevent the free expression of his instinct. But he praised Lorca for his lyricism, which was 'la traducción de un estado de alma por medio de ritmos de líneas y colores' [a translation from the state of the soul by means of the rhythms of lines and colours].[21] Once again the debate between Cubism and Surrealism is opened. The 'estado de alma' is important but must be depicted with rhythms. Lorca's Surrealist works sparked fiery discussions between the men. Yet many of Lorca's words in his correspondence with Gasch seem to echo Surrealist practices. Drawings such as *La vista y el tacto* (1929–30) show clearly the idea of a drawing that could be synonymous with a map, and the reader could be guided on a journey. The mind could wander like the pen. The poet would go to the hunt, clean, serene and, as Lorca expressed it, 'almost disguised'.[22] The map became a record of an inner reality: 'la imaginación está limitada por la realidad: *no se puede imaginar lo que no existe,* la imaginación tiene horizontes, quiere dibujar y concretar todo lo que abarca'. [Imagination is limited by reality: it is not possible to imagine what does not exist, the imagination has horizons, it wants to draw and make concrete everything within its grasp.][23]

Lorca wrote that he felt uplifted by the act of drawing: 'Desde luego me encuentro en estos momentos con una sensibilidad ya casi física que me lleva a planos donde es difícil tenerse de pie y casi se vuela sobre *el abismo*.' [So, in those moments, I find myself in a state of almost physical sensitivity, which takes me to levels where it is difficult to stand and I nearly fly over the abyss.][24] One feels that Lorca is struggling with Surrealist notions of abandonment, possibly in homage to Dalí but at the same time wanting to please Gasch, who had been openly critical of Lorca in a review of *Poema del cante jondo*. Gasch disliked all things Surrealist and denounced Lorca as a pseudo-Surrealist. Referring to Lorca's text at times as 'intense' and at others 'pungent', he felt that Dalí had been a bad influence on him.[25]

If Lorca's drawings are a direct diagram of thought as in the kind of Surrealist practices mentioned above, it is problematic to seek to find the thought. They are perhaps diagrams of thought-processes. The issue of 'spontaneity' is also problematic in that it suggests a possible tapping of an unconscious mind, which was of course popular in the 1920s. It is possible that in many of the drawings sent to the Dalmau we are dealing with deliberate thought-out acts of artistic production. They are more a product of the aforementioned reflection and debate, and arguably they give very few clues to any 'sense' of person. This explains the importance of the drawing *Manos cortadas* (1935). The hand, which is normally a controlling factor in creation, has lost that control, or is attempting to hang on through the veins. Automatic writing was of course a crucial Surrealist activity. Gasch expressed concern about Lorca's Surrealist side, and Lorca appeased him somewhat by laying no claim to knowledge, assuring him that 'Yo estoy y me siento con pies de plomo en arte.' [I am and feel very unsure when it comes to art.][26]

Lorca had intimated to Gasch that he saw drawing as very personal and intimate and was apparently initially against their reproduction: 'Mis dibujos gustan a un grupo de gente muy sensible, pero es que se conocen poco. Yo no me he preocupado de reproducirlos y son en mí una cosa privada.' [A group of very sensitive people like my drawings but they are not well known. I haven't bothered to reproduce them for they are very private.][27] Yet he mentions their editing and reproduction a number of times in this particular correspondence and states that if it was not for 'los catalanes' he would not have continued drawing. This reiterates notions of emotional need and sharing on Lorca's part. Mario Hernández, the critic who collated the drawings, saw this as a critical moment in terms of his artistic development: 'his rich correspondence with the art critic Sebastiá Gasch denotes the blending of his surrender to drawing and his parallel aesthetic reflection on his creations and the principles, which uphold them'.[28] It is interesting to note that Gasch also commented on Lorca's use of the hand, as if severed from the body:[29]

dibujos vistos en un momento de inspiración, y que pasan directamente de lo más profundo del ser del poeta a su mano. Una mano que se abandona, que no opone resistencia, que no sabe ni quiere saber dónde se la conduce, y que para sin esfuerzo, sin tortura, con optimismo, con alegría, con la misma alegría del niño que llena de garabatos una pared, esas maravillosas realizaciones que alían la más pura fantasía, el más exacto equilibrio de líneas y colores.

[drawings seen in a moment of inspiration, they come from the depths of the poet's being to his hand. A hand that lets itself go freely, that does not resist, that does not know, nor want to know where it is going and that stops effortlessly, free from torture, with optimism, with happiness, with that happiness of a child who fills a wall with scribbles, these wonderful perform-ances which align the purest fantasy with a perfect balance of line and colour.]

Lorca was perhaps more insistent in his desire to gift Gasch than others. He dedicated 22 drawings to him, but did not give them all to him. He desired approbation, and the public dedications were statements to people in general. His clear insistence that lines only have emotion suggests that he saw drawing as a much more personal act than poetry.

Lorca's letters to Gasch in the summer of 1927 point to the need to draw as part of the creative process, not necessarily divorced from poetry but to enhance or enliven creativity. Lorca's admiration for Gasch led him to struggle to adhere to the critic's call for *Totalismo*. Gasch also insisted on the resonance of the artist's interior world and its collision with his exterior world. The exchanges between Lorca and Gasch are clearly fundamental to Lorca's process of creation. Lorca wrote in January 1928, 'Tú sabes perfectamente que coincidimos y que nuestras conversaciones nos provechan a los dos de igual manera. Yo siempre digo que tú eres el único crítico y la única persona sagaz que he conocido y que no hay en Madrid un jóven de tu categoría y tu ciencia artística, ni tampoco de tu sensibilidad.' [You know perfectly well that we agree and that we both get an equal amount from our conversations. I always say that you are the only critic and the only wise person that I have ever known and that there is no other

young person in Madrid in your league and with your artistic
knowledge, much less your sensitivity.][30] Lorca's oleaginous approach
continued as he assured Gasch that he must not let their friendship
influence his writings. Gasch had clearly been a little concerned about
his Castilian, but Lorca assured him that it is not the language that
matters but the ideas.

It is clear that Lorca described and could find simultaneity in the
creative process:[31]

Estos dibujos son poesía pura o plástica pura a la vez. Me siento limpio,
confortado, alegre, *niño*, cuando los hago. Y me da horror *la palabra* que
tengo que usar para llamarlos. Y me da horror la pintura que llaman *directa*
que no es sino una angustiosa lucha con las formas en las que el pintor sale
siempre vencido y con la obra *muerta* [...] Tienes razón mi queridísimo
Gasch, hay que unir la abstracción. Es más, yo titularía estos dibujos que
recibirás (te los mando certificados), *Dibujos humanísimos*. Porque casi todos
van a dar con su flechita en el corazón.

[These drawings are pure poetry or pure plasticity at the same time. I feel
clean, comforted, happy, child-like, when I do them. And I hate the word
that I have to use to name them. And I hate what they call direct art, which
is merely a battle of forms from which the artist emerges beaten and the work
of art is dead. You are right, my dear Gasch, you have to unite abstraction.
Moreover, I would call these drawings which you will receive (I send them
registered) very human drawings, because nearly every one strikes a little
arrow in the heart.]

In a letter to Gasch of the same year containing the drawing *San
Sebastián* (1927) he excitedly describes the process of drawing:[32]

Estos últimos dibujos que he hecho me han costado un trabajo de
elaboración grande. Abandonaba la mano a la tierra virgen y la mano junto
con mi corazón me traía los elementos milagrosos. Yo los descubría y los
anotaba. Volvía a lanzar mi mano, y así con muchos elementos, escogía las
características del asunto o los más bellos e inexplicables, y componía mi
dibujo [...] Unos dibujos salen así como las metáforas mas bellas, y otros
buscándolos en el sitio *donde se sabe de seguro* que están. Es una pesca. Unas
veces entra el pez solo en el cestillo y otras se busca la mejor agua y se lanza
al mejor anzuelo a propósito para conseguir. El anzuelo se llama *realidad* [...]
He procurado escoger los rasgos esenciales de emoción y de forma, o de
super-realidad y super-forma, para hacer de ellos un *signo* que como llave
mágica, nos lleva a *comprender mejor* la realidad que tiene en el mundo.

[The most recent drawings that I have done were me a lot of work as they
were extremely elaborate. I would abandon my hand to virgin territory, and

my hand, in conjunction with my heart, would bring miraculous elements to me. I would discover them and note them down. I would throw my hand again, then with many elements, I would choose the characteristics of the subject or the most beautiful and inexplicable ones, then I would compose my drawing. Some drawings just come out like that, like the most beautiful metaphors, and others have to be found, in the place where you know for sure they are. You fish for them. Sometimes the fish enters the net alone, other times you look for better waters and cast a better hook in order to succeed. The hook is called reality. I have tried to choose the essential lines of emotion and form or superreality or superform, to make from them a sign that, like a magic key, will help us to understand better what reality is in this world.]

Once again the words seem to echo a limited understanding of Bergson and a continuing debate with Gasch. Lorca was, as has been discussed, certainly aware of the Surrealist practice of automatic writing and drawing. This is also why Lorca's drawings cannot simply be seen as doodles. They are consciously constructed, created as part of the creative process, helping him as a kind of therapy to tap his own emotions and feelings. They serve as a stream of consciousness. In the drawings *San Sebastián* and *Amor intelectualis* (1927) line cuts through the page with no hatching or shading, no attempt at three-dimensionality. These drawings are direct diagrams of thought, done with assured lines and a clear structure and rhythm. They are linked in that both Dalí and Lorca identified themselves and their relationship with Saint Sebastian and in *Amor intelectualis*, which is a portrait of Dalí.

Lorca seems to be challenging the argument of reason versus the senses. In *San Sebastián* the body of the saint is represented by one eye on the left of the drawing, and by a circle or mouth which encloses a point or a bull's eye. This circle with a point in it falls in the centre of the drawing and functions as both a symbol and a metonym. As a symbol it could be the ancient symbol of the sun. As a metonym it could of course be that unwounded anus mentioned by Lorca and Dalí in their letters.[33] The arrows fall near it but do not penetrate it. To suggest the whole body with the eye and the anus allows 'a kind of privacy' to language. Lorca's drawings contain codes and references, which can only be understood by those who have the key. The face is suggested by heavy circles (the pen point is bled into the paper) and all the arrows terminate to form a sort of half circle. Thus the eye and the mouth or anus serve to perform the act of suffering.

The direction of the arrows leads the viewer towards the central drama but also up and beyond. It is possible to see different elements which are charged with more concrete meaning and are easily identifiable. Yet there are also 'magic keys' which evoke the reality of martyrdom in the viewer and carry him into the centre of the tragedy. The arrows are also reminiscent of Bergson's use of the famous paradoxes of the ancient Greek philosopher, Zeno which reveal the inadequacy of the intellect's understanding of time. He argued that an arrow shot by Achilles must pass through an infinite number of points en route to its target, but he questions how it ever reaches its target if it must traverse infinity.

In one letter to Dalí in August 1927, Lorca is clearer than ever about how he views Saint Sebastian and how they differ in their interpretations of him: 'Las flechas de San Sebastián son de acero, pero la diferencia que yo tengo contigo es que tú las ves clavadas, fijas y robustas, flechas cortas *que no descompongan*, y yo las veo *largas...* en el *momento* de la herida. Tu San Sebastián de mármol se opone al mío de carne que muere en todos momentos, y así tiene que ser.' [Saint Sebastian's arrows are made of steel, but the difference between us is that you see them nailed, fixed and strong, short arrows which do not decompose, I see them long... in the moment of the wound. Your Saint Sebastian is marble, which is the opposite of mine, which is flesh which dies at every turn, it has to be that way.][34] The arrow is an important metaphor for the men, but it forms part of an on-going discussion between them, which goes beyond the image itself and borders on notions of time. In *Amor intelectualis* Lorca has fused Cubist notions of intellect and geometry and instinct and feeling. One is aware of the non-Euclidian curve in the centre of the drawing.

Lorca dedicated one particular drawing, *Leyenda de Jerez* (1927), to Gasch. Done with India ink and crayons on paper, its dedication seems more important than its title, which is in parenthesis. It contains the word TABERNA, and Mario Hernández states that the word ALMA is written below the reflected crosses.[35] This is clearly a response to the comment about the importance of expressing the 'estado del alma'. Many of the doubling effects of this image are fascinating. Here the figure appears in the foreground in clown costume with another figure behind it. There is a correlation between the doubling of the figure and the doubling of the medium (verbal and visual). This image announces itself as a study in doubling. The crosses are echoed in what might be water, but there are so many different planes or grounds (Lorca identified six) that the image is once again migratory and shimmering, defying any one reading. The title suggests a narrative structure, although Lorca subtitled it 'Poema Surrealista'. Lorca called 1926 the year of Surrealism, and the closed eyes of the one figure suggest a dream reference. Yet he had written to Gasch, 'abomino el arte de los sueños' [I hate dream art].[36]

The drawings provided an excuse or vehicle to exchange thoughts with Gasch and to support and maintain a mutual admiration between the two men. They provided food for a debate that interested both men, who had worked with different mediums, and gave them a continuing reason to debate current theories about perception. The field-crossing is clear. Philosophical debates gave rise to artistic ones. Writers, poets and art critics joined forces with painters, sculptors, musicians and others to depict and make sense of an ever-changing world.

Notes to Chapter 5

1. Sebastià Gasch, Foreword 'Mi Federico García Lorca', Federico García Lorca, *Cartas a sus amigos*, ed. Sebastià Gasch (Barcelona: Cobalto, 1950), 7–14 at 9.
2. Federico García Lorca, *Obras completas*, ed. Arturo del Hoyo, 22nd edn. (Madrid: Aguilar, 1986), iii. 951.
3. Letter from Lorca to Jorge Guillén, Jan. 1927, ibid., iii. 902.
4. Ian Gibson, *Federico García Lorca: A Life* (London: Faber & Faber, 1989), 171–204, esp. 175.
5. See Antonina Rodrigo, *Lorca–Dalí: Una amistad traicionada* (Barcelona: Planeta, 1981), 142.
6. Sebastià Gasch, 'Lorca dibujante', *La Gaceta Literaria* 30 (15 Mar. 1928), 4.
7. Ibid.
8. Lorca, *Obras completas*, iii. 953.
9. For the most up-to-date catalogue of the drawings see Mario Hernández, *Libro de los dibujos de Federico García Lorca* (Madrid: Fundación Federico García Lorca, 1990).
10. Letter from Lorca to Gasch, 31 July 1927, Lorca, *Obras completas*, iii. 953.
11. Henri Bergson, 'Bergson en la Residencia', *Residencia* 2 (1926), 174–6.
12. Sebastià Gasch, 'Del Cubismo al Superrealismo', *La Gaceta Literaria* 20 (15 Oct. 1927), 121, cited in Juan Manuel Rozas, *La Generación del 27 desde dentro* (Madrid: Istmo, 1986), 144–53 at 153.
13. Miró's poetry in the 1920s inspired him to structure his paintings as if they were a kind of free verse. Sometimes he would also attribute poetic titles to his paintings and stencil words onto the canvas. Miró's later letters to Gasch, written in April 1932, suggest that he too cared about the critic's opinion. Gasch was to review Miró's *Jeux d'enfants*, which came to Barcelona in May 1933.
14. Cited in Rozas, *La Generación del 27*, 153.

15. See Simon Shaw-Miller, *Visible Deeds of Music* (New Haven and London: Yale University Press, 2002), chap. 3, 'Instruments of Desire, Musical Morphology in Picasso's Cubism', where he analyses the ambiguity of coexisting oppositions in the work of Picasso.

16. See Jacqueline Cockburn, 'Learning from the Master: Lorca's Homage to Picasso', *Fire, Blood and the Alphabet: One Hundred Years of Lorca*, ed. Sebastian Doggart and Michael Thompson (Durham: University of Durham, 1999), 123–42.

17. For an interesting chapter on scientific debates at the turn of the century, see Adriano Bergero, 'Science, Modern Art and Surrealism: The Representation of Imaginary Matter', *The Surrealist Adventure in Spain*, ed. C. Brian Morris (Ottawa Hispanic Studies 6; Ottawa: Dovehouse, 1991), 19–39.

18. See Robert Rosenblum, 'The Spanishness of Picasso's Still Lifes', *Picasso and the Spanish Tradition*, ed. Jonathan Brown (New Haven and London: Yale University Press, 1996), 61–93 at 80.

19. Gasch, 'Lorca dibujante', 4.

20. Ibid.

21. Ibid.

22. Federico García Lorca, 'La imagen poética de don Luis de Góngora', *Obras completas*, iii. 236.

23. Federico García Lorca, 'Imaginación, inspiración, evasión', *Obras completas*, iii. 259.

24. Fragment of letter from Lorca to Gasch, Lorca, *Obras completas*, iii. 968.

25. Gibson, *Federico García Lorca*, 171–204, esp. 181.

26. Lorca, *Obras completas*, iii. 967.

27. Ibid., iii. 964.

28. Mario Hernández, 'El arte del dibujo en la creación de García Lorca', *Federico García Lorca: Saggi critici nel cinquantenario della morte*, ed. Gabriele Morelli (Rome: Schena, 1988), 119–34 at 121, cited in Cecilia J. Cavanaugh, *Lorca's Drawings and Poems: Forming the Eye of the Reader* (London: Associated University Presses, 1995), 184.

29. Gasch, 'Lorca dibujante', 4.

30. Lorca, *Obras completas*, iii. 957.

31. Ibid., iii. 970.

32. Ibid., iii. 969.

33. Rafael Santos Torroella, *Salvador Dalí escribe a Federico García Lorca (1925–1936)* (Madrid: Ministerio de Cultura, 1987), 46.

34. Federico García Lorca, *Epistolario completo*, ed. Christopher Maurer and Andrew A. Anderson (Madrid: Cátedra, 1997), 511.

35. Hernández, *Libro de los dibujos*, 191.

36. Lorca, *Obras completas*, iii. 970.

CHAPTER 6

Ignacio Sánchez Mejías Blues

Xon de Ros

'When a woman gets the blues she hangs her head and cries, / When a woman gets the blues she hangs her head and cries, / But when a man gets the blues, he grabs a train and rides.' These lines come from a classic blues ('Freight Train Blues') popularized by Trixie Smith in a Paramount recording made in 1924 in New York. The lyrics reflect what Juliana Schiesari has called the cultural gendering of melancholia, in which women's experience of grief is insidiously represented as debilitating and men's as enabling.[1] The early 1920s was the golden era of the black female blues singer. In fact the term 'classic blues' is applied to the music of urban women singers of the stature of Ma Rainey, Bessie Smith, Roberta Hunter and Ida Cox, who came to dominate the vaudeville circuit of Chicago and New York as well as the recording market. During his visit to New York in 1929, Federico García Lorca had the opportunity to experience at first hand the 'Harlem Renaissance' phenomenon with its vibrant musical scene. His sympathy with idioms derived from popular music, combined with the receptivity of his poetic language to music, made it possible for him to incorporate the spirit of black music into his collection *Poeta en Nueva York,* where its influence is most evident.

This essay explores the presence of this type of music in his later poem *Llanto por Ignacio Sánchez Mejías,* suggesting that Lorca's invocation of the blues clashes with the poetic tradition to which the poem is tributary. Despite their common elegiac mood, the different ideologies of the poetic elegy and the blues, particularly in relation to questions of gender politics, made the reconciliation enacted in Lorca's poem a problematic enterprise whose tensions are articulated in the conflict the poem expresses.

Although it seems Lorca never referred specifically to the blues, its presence is inescapable in his poem 'Norma y paraíso de los negros' from *Poeta en Nueva York*, with its insistence on the word 'azul' [blue]. In the title we can read an allusion to one of the earliest jazz clubs in Harlem—Smalls' Paradise—frequented by Lorca, which was the home in the twenties and thirties of Charlie Johnson's Paradise orchestra, and which unlike other similar establishments was popular with white and black patrons alike.[2] The nocturnal, hallucinatory tone and elegiac mood that this poem shares with the *Llanto*, together with their common water imagery, calls for an exploration of 'blueness' also in the elegy for Sánchez Mejías.

Because of its subject, *Llanto por Ignacio Sánchez Mejías* has often been interpreted in connection with Lorca's lecture 'Juego y teoría del duende' (1933), where Lorca had made bullfighting one of the repositories of his *duende*. But Lorca himself never singled out Sánchez Mejías for this elusive aesthetic category. However unflinching in the face of death ('No se cerraron sus ojos / cuando vio los cuernos cerca' [His eyes did not close / when he saw the horns near]), the bull-fighter's attributes highlighted in the poem are closer to those pro-vided by the angel and the muse, which Lorca made a point of distinguishing from *duende*.

According to the *Diccionario de la Real Academia Española*, to possess *duende* is 'traer en la imaginación cosa que le inquieta'; that is, to be inspired with disquiet. And Lorca had seen in this disquiet an intimation of death that can manifest itself in most of the arts but is more prevalent in music and dance—particularly in the flamenco tradition—and last but not least, in spoken poetry. It has been noted that *duende* only enters Lorca's vocabulary after his visit to America in 1929, where he expressed an interest in and fascination with the folklore of the black community. In one of his letters home he establishes a parallel between Negro religious songs and *cante jondo*. The comparison is hardly surprising: he had referred elsewhere to *cante jondo* as fundamentally an expression of grief—*pena*—and black spirituals were frequently termed 'sorrow songs'.

Predictably, Lorca's emphasis on the performative quality of *duende* and on the strong rapport that it establishes with its audience has been compared with the notion of 'soul' in music.[3] Both terms evoke the emotional and spiritual depth of oral, non-literate cultures persecuted by unrelenting oppression—African-American and Gypsy Andalusian, respectively—which, having been marginalized by the dominant society from its political, economic, social and cultural institutions, found in music a powerful vehicle for expression. However, by the time Lorca was in New York, the term 'soul', as used to define the cathartic and liberating experience of African-American music, had still to gain currency and the term 'blues' served to describe this effect. The grief of the blues lacks both the consolatory promise of spirituals and the tempering exuberance of jazz. As a musical and oral genre it certainly has the potential to inspire with disquiet, and as a poetic form of lament it shows an affinity with the modern elegy, which has been characterized as unredemptive and anti-consolatory.[4]

The interpretation of a literary form that incorporates in its discourse and structure the work of mourning can be easily accommodated within a psychoanalytic critical framework.[5] However, the elegy not only re-enacts the psychological processes associated with secular mourning, but also, and perhaps more urgently, it reveals the difficulties and tensions of the act of writing about it. Recent criticism focusing on the metapoetic dimension of elegiac literature highlights the contradictions of its ideology. To begin with, from the perspective of gender politics, elegy is a problematic form. Since classical antiquity, mourning—the outward manifestation of grief for a mortal loss—has been associated with women, with excess and hysteria that renders them incoherent and speechless.[6] Nevertheless, the elegiac tradition is an essentially masculine one, one of its foundation myths being that of the poet-mourner Orpheus.[7]

Unsurprisingly, anxieties of sexuality and gender are articulated and dramatized in the narrative of Orpheus and Eurydice, in which the female characters occupy a space of negativity: from the dark underworld of Persephone, where the silent, disembodied Eurydice is confined, to the murderous, undifferentiated Maenads who dismember Orpheus. Moreover, the mourning Orpheus is an ambiguous figure. Even if his preaching of homosexual love is seen as a displaced desire after the loss of Euridyce, his gentle disposition, communing with nature, makes him an unlikely male hero. But even though the genre, linked to the pastoral, may cast the poet in a feminine role, the consolation traditionally provided by the elegy represented a suppression or internalization of grief that is associated with masculine melancholia.

However, in the secular world of twentieth-century elegy there is little room for consolation, as Lorca's reference to the medieval *planctus* in the title of *Llanto por Ignacio Sánchez Mejías* suggests. In the rhetorical form of the *planctus*, the display of grief, which lacks the renewal of hope of the traditional elegy, was intended to move the audience to compassion for the grieving speaker. Lorca's poem alludes to and reformulates some of the conventions of consolation and celebration within the elegy tradition, such as the encomium or the imagery related to fertility rites and Christian redemption, but, as critics such as Jones and Scanlon and more recently Anderson have demonstrated, these conventions have a desolate character or are exposed as meaningless.[8] This simultaneous acknowledgement and distancing is characteristic of the elegiac genre, concerned as it is with issues of identification and separation, which, as Melissa F. Zeiger argues in her study of the literary and cultural politics of the genre in the twentieth century, not only involve the living and the dead but also a wide range of contingent alignments and disconnections.[9]

Lorca's poem is informed by the myth of Orpheus and in particular by the sequence of Eurydice's death,[10] which is considered to be 'the germinal episode for elegiac rewriting' of the myth.[11] Eurydice has died as the result of a snake-bite, and Orpheus with the magic power of his music gains entry into the underworld to retrieve his wife, but in their return journey he turns to give a fateful backward glance to Eurydice, contravening the gods' interdiction not to look upon or communicate with her during their ascent. As a result, she returns to the underworld, leaving Orpheus to mourn. His song then becomes a lamentation. The antinomy between sound and vision is at the centre of the narrative: Orpheus's song being an enabling power to transcend boundaries, his gaze restoring those boundaries.

The dichotomy between sound and sight, voice and visibility, is also central to Lorca's poem, and its articulation foregrounds the symbolic workings of gender in the elegy. The encoded masculinity of the elegy form, together with the notion of the bullfighter as a male hero, underscore Lorca's complex relation to ideals of masculinity as well as his own outsider relation to the masculine conventions. Already the dedication of the poem to Encarnación López Júlvez, 'La Argentinita', highlights the absence of female figures in the poem, or more precisely their presence outside the text. A dedication, in Gérard Genette's view, 'implicates the addressee as a kind of ideal inspirer'.[12] La Argentinita, Sánchez Mejías's lover, was a popular vaudeville singer and dancer with whom in 1931 Lorca had recorded some traditional Spanish songs compiled and scored by the poet and accompanied by himself on the piano.

If La Argentinita's paratextual position suggests that the feminine is located outside the process of cultural production, her presence in Lorca's legacy as a disembodied voice only reinforces her association with Eurydice. The symbolic exclusion of women is consistent with the ideology of a literary tradition that concerns itself with the rescuing of fertility from biological death.[13] Conceived as re-generative, death is identified with birth and by extension with women, whose power is appropriated by the elegist. As we shall see, it is with some resistance that the poet submits to the gender-dynamics of the form, and even though the structure of *Llanto por Ignacio Sánchez Mejías* reflects the elegy's usual split between initial despair and subsequent affirmation, the poem's expression is ambivalent in relation to the achievement of the elegiac project.[14]

In the first section, 'La cogida y la muerte' [*Cogida* and Death], the alternate lines give the effect of the live poet moving between the dead man's consciousness and his own. The insistence on images of vulnerability and invasion suggest the poet's entrance in the masculine interchange of the elegy. And yet the suspension of time represented in the refrain '*a las cinco de la tarde*' [*at five in the afternoon*] indicates a resistance to the coercive linearity of tradition, a resistance whose expression recalls what in the jargon of the blues is called 'riffing', with the rocking back and forth of swing.

The musical connection is not too far-fetched if we look at the antiphonal effect created by the section's typeface pattern. Whereas the call-and-response form is related to the origins of the ceremonial elegy, it is also one of the oldest and strongest structural features of black music. Characteristically, black spirituals start with a chorus preceding the first verse, and then alternate lines are sung by the whole congregation. The way their imagery features vivid phrasal juxtapositions, broken only by some vocal interjections, offers another parallel with Lorca's poem, especially the last two stanzas' final lines and the exclamation '¡Ay qué terribles cinco de la tarde!' [Ah, that fatal five in the afternoon!].

Likewise, the numb atmosphere conjured up in this section is reminiscent of the alleged trance-like state induced by the singing and rhythms of spirituals among members of the congregation. The dividing line between the blues and some kinds of spirituals cannot be sharply drawn. Both convey to listeners the same blues feeling. The difficulty in distinguishing the two kinds of songs is exemplified in the category of the blues-spirituals, which subsumes them in the same experience. This experience, in the context of New York in the late 1920s, was perceived as fundamentally feminine, related to the genre of 'classic blues' mentioned above. This is a significant fact because by incorporating the blues idiom, the poem appropriates a mode of grieving associated with women, implictly reinserting the feminine into the text.

The emphasis on sound carries on to the next section, 'La sangre derramada' [The spilled blood], where the implied call-and-response pattern of the syncopated opening line, '¡Que no quiero verla!' [I don't want to see it!*], together with the emotional and performative general tone, finds a correspondence in the singing style of the blues. In this context, the semi-vowel in the repeated word 'quiero' may bring to mind the notion of a 'blue note'.[15] The insistence on repetition, from alliteration to anaphora, the short interjections, the exhortative and apostrophizing mode, which reaches its climax in the final double exclamation, endow the section with a strong aural quality, which, combined with the individual, subjective and assertive tone, can again be associated with the blues idiom, with its mixture of pathos and self-assertion.

It is also in this section that the Orphean subtext emerges. And it does so with a significant twist: instead of being forbidden to look, Lorca's Orpheus seems to be pressed to do it against his will. We can identify the musical language that permeates the section with the figure of a Dionysian Orpheus, whose music is an extension of his own emotional life. However, here we find not only one but two different voices at play. The Apollonian Orpheus—the civilizing hero-inventor of poetry—is also invoked in the conventions of elegiac poetry that the section incorporates. The amalgamation of the two voices creates, as in the original myth, 'an oscillation between the power of form to master intense emotion and the power of intense emotion to engulf form'.[16]

The image of the river, of which the section becomes a figure, articulates the tension between these two forces. The river, a traditional symbol of life and fertility and one of the stock elegiac images, is transformed into a deadly stream of blood and is described as 'una larga, oscura, triste lengua' [a long, dark, sad tongue]. The figurative meaning of the word 'tongue' as language is brought out earlier, when the same phrase 'triste lengua' appears related to the enigmatic 'vaca del viejo mundo' [cow of the ancient world]. This image, together with the stony 'toros de Guisando' [bulls of Guisando] suggest the hieratic ceremonies and rhetoric of the genre, which the section re-enacts. The bullfighter begins a climb towards heroic status surrounded by the structures and codes of the traditional elegy: the encomium, the religious imagery, his mythical translation into a constellation; but his disorientation suggests a distance between the subject and its textual representation. The weariness of the Guisando bulls, the sombre final note of the panegyric, the indistinctness of the voices, the general gloom and bleakness, ending up with the stagnant image of Ignacio's blood, more of a black hole than a constellation, indicate a retreat from the conventions. Moreover, the river of blood also articulates female-encoded anxieties of excess and disembodiment.

If the elegy is a way of reaffirming patriarchal inheritance, then the reluctance or incapacity to adopt the comforting voice and formal rhetoric of tradition has disquieting implications for the male poet. With its rejection, the appropriate distance between mourner and mourned is destabilized, and so is the gendered economy of the elegy. The singing blood in the poem recalls images of the aftermath of Orpheus's decapitation, when his head, still singing, floats down the river Hebrus. His body has been torn apart by the raging Ciconian matrons/Maenads in vindication of the laws of nature they represent and to which he has refused obedience. 'Madres terribles' [terrible mothers] indeed, whose admonitory heads are raised in Lorca's poem. The concluding line's frenetic emphasis on the negative '¡¡Yo no quiero verla!!' [No, I will not see it!*] may express the poet's resistance to the need to conform to traditional poetic imperatives, but the pleonastic 'yo' already anticipates the self-positioning that the next section 'Cuerpo presente' [The laid-out body], with the emphasis on presence and embodiment that its title suggests, will effect.

In the radical discontinuity between the two sections, the poem reasserts the absolute rupture that divides life from death, which traditional elegy reintegrates in a regenerative continuum. The inertness of the dominant image in 'Cuerpo presente', the stone, surrounded by an enforced silence, registers a change of mood from mourning to melancholia.[17] The masculinity of the form is reasserted with the banishing of the feminine and the emotional, starting with images ('agua curva' [curving waters] and 'lluvias' [showers]) that had first appeared in the poem 'Norma y paraíso de los negros' associated with the blues. Even though the scenario has changed from the feminized world of the dead to one of masculine detachment ruled by a dispassionate stare, the voice in the poem is still one of longing.

The plea for guidance to the summoned 'hombres de voz dura' [men of hard voice], who stand for the traditional invocation of a male deity, underlines the masculine gender affiliation. However, in its unrelenting focus on bodily disintegration there is an implicit questioning of acts of commemorative rescue as well as an awareness of the transactions of the form, which assimilates the dead person into the fabric of the poem. The final apostrophe to Mejías represents Orpheus's turning round and brief contact, followed by the estrangement and the definite separation from Eurydice. In the concluding section, and just as a worldly loss is a figure for other losses, the lament for the irrevocable loss of the individual person leads the poet to reflect on the impermanence of his own work, and along with the assertion of the poet's voice there is an implicit acceptance of its transience in the use of the adverb 'luego' [later].

The last two lines, 'Yo canto su elegancia con palabras que gimen / y recuerdo una brisa triste por los olivos' [I sing of his elegance with words that groan / and I remember a sad breeze through the olive trees], contain what can be read as a disclaimer of the elegy's compensatory economy of poetic gain from human loss. The nostalgic memory of the form's favourite trope, the pathetic fallacy, suggests that the literary achievement might have been at the cost of dehumanizing nature. Also the association of the wind with Orpheus and music re-evokes the figure of Eurydice, who as a source of poetic inspiration enables the poet but whose presence has been relegated to invisibility. It is in the light of this final image that the section's title, 'Alma ausente' [Absent soul], seems to acquire a musical, albeit anachronistic, undertone.

While recasting the elegy for a secular age, revisiting its conventions and questioning their significance—sceptical in particular with regard to its traditional consolations—Lorca's poem is nevertheless complicit with the androcentric ideology of traditional elegies, 'poems that summon woman, occlude her, and move towards an identification with mirroring images of masculine power'.[18] The prestige inherent in a form that legitimates a masculine poetic identity confers cultural respectability on the poet himself. This self-consecration in turn is defined against a culturally demarcated feminine space occupied by popular art forms. *Llanto por Ignacio Sánchez Mejías* begins with an attempt to reconcile its high-art status as an elegy with the popular-art form of the blues, but the fracture that occurs in the middle acknowledges a failure to do so.

However, to interpret Lorca's final assertion of his writerly masculinity as an act of bad faith would be to fall into a reductive mechanistic view, which feminist criticism may run the risk of adopting. The engagement that the poem undertakes with the tradition does not take place in the confined space of its poetics but is embedded in political and social discourses from which the poet cannot be separated. Likewise, as Bourdieu reminds us, we need to take into account the 'space of the possibilities bequeathed by previous (literary) struggles'.[19] In this case, the nonutilitarian emphasis in the modern idea of literature, which once had been a sign of resistance to the dehumanizing power of capitalist values, had also been, despite its significance, a contributing factor in divesting poetry of social relevance. If the adoption of a masculine sexual identity as a writer indicates a critical desire to engage and shape society, the concluding wistful tone of Lorca's poem implies an acknowledgement of poetry's alienation from social power. The cultural powerlessness of poetry in a society that feminizes the literary is identified, through the poem's musical allusiveness, with those whose access to the public sphere has been historically denied.

In *Llanto por Ignacio Sánchez Mejías*, the lament for the death of his bullfighter friend becomes also a lament for the loss of poetry's civilizing power and cultural agency, more pressing in the context of Spain's socio-political turmoil in the summer of 1934 and of Lorca's own increasing Republican commitment. Going back to his lecture on *duende*, there is certainly scope for *duende* in the confrontation with death that the poem dramatizes, but the disquiet it inspires may have come from different sources.

Notes to Chapter 6

1. Juliana Schiesari, *The Gendering of Melancholia: Feminism, Psychoanalysis and the Symbolics of Loss in Renaissance Literature* (Ithaca, NY, and London: Cornell University Press, 1992), 15 and *passim*. Following Schiesari, this essay refers to melancholia rather than melancholy to distinguish the cultural category associated with men from the pathological condition theorized by Freud in his 1917 essay 'Mourning and Melancholy'.

2. The reference is made by Derek Harris in his edition of Federico García Lorca, *Romancero gitano; Poeta en Nueva York; El público* (Madrid: Taurus, 1993), 141. For *Llanto por Ignacio Sánchez Mejías*, see Miguel Ángel García Posada's edition, *Primer romancero gitano; Llanto por Ignacio Sánchez Mejías; Romance de la corrida de toros en Ronda; y otros textos taurinos* (Madrid: Castalia, 1988). Except for two instances, marked with an asterisk (*), where the translations are my own, the following

English translations have been used: *Lament for Ignacio Sánchez Mejías*, trans. Stephen Spender and J. L. Gili, *The Selected Poems of Federico García Lorca*, ed. Francisco García Lorca and Donald M.Allen (New York: New Directions, 1961); *Poet in New York*, trans. Greg Simon and Steven F. White, ed. and introd. Christopher Maurer (Harmondsworth: Viking Penguin, 1989); 'Play and Theory of the Duende', in *Deep Song and Other Prose*, ed. and trans. Christopher Maurer (London and New York: Marion Boyars, 1982).

3. Carlos A. Rabassó and Fco. Javier Rabassó, *Federico García Lorca entre el flamenco, el jazz y el afrocubanismo* (Madrid: Libertarias, 1998), 371.

4. Jahan Ramazani, *Poetry of Mourning: The Modern Elegy from Hardy to Heaney* (London and Chicago: University of Chicago Press, 1994), 142.

5. A seminal text for this critical approach is Peter M. Sacks, *The English Elegy from Spenser to Yeats* (Baltimore and London: Johns Hopkins University Press, 1985).

6. Melissa F. Zeiger, *Beyond Consolation: Death, Sexuality and the Changing Shapes of Elegy* (Ithaca, NY, and London: Cornell University Press, 1997), 26.

7. The most influential texts concerning Orpheus are Ovid's *Metamorphoses*, 10, 1–85 and 11, 1–66 and Virgil's *Georgics*, 4, 453–527. For an informative study of the variations between the two versions of the myth, see Charles Segal, *Orpheus: The Myth of the Poet* (Baltimore and London: Johns Hopkins University Press, 1993).

8. R. O. Jones and Geraldine M. Scanlon, 'Ignacio Sánchez Mejías: The "Mythic" Hero', *Studies in Modern Spanish Literature and Art, presented to Helen F. Grant*, ed. Nigel Glendinning (London: Tamesis, 1972), 97–108; Andrew A. Anderson, *Lorca's Late Poetry* (Leeds: Cairns, 1990). See also Calvin Cannon, 'Lorca's *Llanto por Ignacio Sánchez Mejías* and the Elegiac Tradition', *Hispanic Review* 31 (1963), 229–38. For general studies on the Spanish elegiac tradition, see Eduardo Camacho Guizado, *La elegía funeral en la poesía española* (Madrid: Gredos, 1969); Bruce W. Wardropper, *Poesía elegíaca española* (Salamanca: Anaya, 1967); María Paz Díez Taboada, *La elegía romántica española: Estudio y antología* (Madrid: Instituto Miguel de Cervantes and CSIC, 1977).

9. Zeiger, *Beyond Consolation*, 168 and *passim*.

10. See Xon de Ros, 'Science and Myth in *Llanto por Ignacio Sánchez Mejías*', *The Modern Language Review* 95 (2000), 114–26.

11. Zeiger, *Beyond Consolation*, 3.

12. Gérard Genette, *Paratexts: Thresholds of Interpretation*, trans. Jane E. Lewin (Cambridge and London: Cambridge University Press, 1997), 136.

13. See Louise O. Fradenburg, '"Voice Memorial": Loss and Reparation in Chaucer's Poetry', *Exemplaria* 2 (1990), 169–202 at 185.

14. A similar predicament is identified by Zeiger in Swinburne's elegy for Baudelaire, in her illuminating essay 'Unwriting Orpheus: Swinburne's "Ave atque Vale" and the "New" Elegy', *Beyond Consolation*, 26–42.

15. According to the *Oxford Companion to Music* (2002), s.v., 'blue notes' are notes of unstable pitch somewhere between the minor and major forms of the 3rd and 7th degrees of the otherwise major scale.

16. Segal, *Orpheus*, 8. As Segal points out, Orpheus's duality is more explicit in Virgil's rendering of the myth than in Ovid's.

17. 'Mourning' here refers to the cultural practice associated with women rather than merely the affect of grief. See the works cited in nn. 1, 6 above.

18. Ramazani, *Poetry of Mourning*, 61.

19. Pierre Bourdieu, *The Rules of Art: Genesis and Structure of the Literary Field*, trans. Susan Emanuel (Cambridge: Polity Press, 1996), 206.

CHAPTER 7

Parallel Trajectories in the Careers of Falla and Lorca

D. Gareth Walters

In an autobiographical note written during his stay in New York in 1929–30, Lorca relates his decision to become a poet to thwarted musical ambitions: 'Como sus padres no permitieron que se trasladase a París para continuar con sus estudios iniciales, y su maestro de música murió, García Lorca dirigió su (dramático) patético afán creativo a la poesía' [Since his parents did not allow him to go to Paris to continue with his initial studies, and his music teacher died, García Lorca turned his (dramatic) pathetic creative urges towards poetry].[1] This statement, like so many of the writer's, needs qualification. Several commentators have observed that the sentence is in the third person, but not that it is only at this point in the autobiographical jotting that the more usual first-person presentation was abandoned. Perhaps this change of perspective indicates a conscious effort on Lorca's part to supply an interpretation of his life, as opposed to mere detail, and thus invest the events of more than a decade earlier—the parental opposition, the death of his music teacher Antonio Segura— with a more clearly causal impact than they really possessed. What Lorca does not mention in this note is that two weeks after the death of Segura he set out for Baeza on his first study trip with Domínguez Berrueta, professor of history of art at the University of Granada. The rest is history—or, more correctly, literature.

But would it have been different if Manuel de Falla, the leading Spanish composer of his day, had settled in Granada in 1916, rather than in 1920 as he was to do? Lorca was at an impressionable age, and his talents as performer and, seemingly, as a composer were ripe for development. But the nature of the relationship between the two was such that we could not confidently say that Falla's arrival in Granada would have been a decisive influence on Lorca's future career. From the evidence of the letters, their friendship was warm but never close, even though it lasted until the very end of Lorca's life, when Falla pleaded in vain with the military authorities on his behalf. It was not so much the generation gap—Falla was twenty-two years older than Lorca—as differences of character that may have accounted for the note of reserve and respect in Lorca's letters to the composer. Falla was an austere man, endowed with what Stravinsky described as the most unpityingly religious nature he had ever encountered. It would not be surprising then if the gregarious and hedonistic Lorca should have been a little wary of someone so timid and fastidious.

What is striking too is the lack of artistic collaboration. One might well have expected initiatives of this kind, not only because of Lorca's musical interests and abilities but also because of Falla's fondness for literature as a stimulus for composition, as testified by his settings of Mallarmé and Góngora and, notably, his most ambitious project, the unfinished cantata setting parts of Verdaguer's *L'Atlàntida*. Indeed the fate of their one and only joint venture, a projected opera entitled *Lola, la comedianta* for which Lorca wrote the libretto, is illuminating. Although Falla started work on his part of the project to the extent of providing marginal indications about the music required on a synopsis that Lorca had supplied, he did not follow it through. Ian Gibson speculates that he may have had doubts about the morality of the work and the depiction of the eponymous heroine even though it was a comic opera.[2] Such an interpretation of why the piece never came to fruition is plausible if we bear in mind the composer's misgivings about the morality of some of his own works, especially the ballet *El amor brujo* with its elements of sorcery and superstition.

We are thus left with no more than traces of influence between the two. We could point to a scene towards the end of Act I of Lorca's *La zapatera prodigiosa*, where the Vecinas crowd the stage in a dance-like fashion when they come in to gloat over the Zapatera's misfortune. This scene is reminiscent of the Neighbours' Dance in Falla's *El sombrero de tres picos*, the plot of which, based on a short novel by Pedro de Alarcón, has affinities with Lorca's play. As an instance of influence in the other direction, it is also likely that Falla's puppet opera *El retablo de Maese Pedro*, based on a scene from *Don Quixote*, emerged from the composer's rediscovered interest in the puppet theatre. As a child, Falla like Lorca had made up and performed puppet plays for

his own amusement, and around the time that *El retablo* was begun
they had devised a Twelfth-Night entertainment consisting of *Los
habladores* of Cervantes, a mystery play about the Three Kings, and a
piece by Lorca now lost.[3]

The most significant collaboration, however, was administrative,
not creative. Not long after moving to Granada in 1920, Falla,
together with Lorca and the local businessman Miguel Cerón Rubio,
set about organizing a *cante jondo* festival in the form of competitions
for various categories. Falla felt strongly that primitive Andalusian
song was in decline as a result of its debasement through com-
mercialization in the *café cantante*. The 'concurso' was conceived as a
corrective measure: to restore purity and dignity to the form. But,
contrary to general belief, the festival was not a success. Aside from
the embarrassing dispute about what was to be done with the the
profits—something that especially shocked Falla—the organizers
failed to acknowledge the contribution that professional performers
could have made to the event. In their zeal to promote *cante jondo* as
an art of the people and by a kind of inverted snobbery, they
overlooked several leading singers whose art did not in any case make
any concessions to commercialism. As a consequence many of the
amateurs who took part in the competitions were mediocre, with the
result that prizes in some categories had to be witheld.

The organization of the festival produced artistic spin-offs for
Lorca. In the February preceding the festival he delivered a lecture on
cante jondo to the Arts Club in Granada, both consulting and citing
Falla.[4] More significant, though, was the set of poems written in the
previous November and published ten years later. The *Poema del cante
jondo* dates from the period when Lorca was working on his *Suites*,
and in form and style it has much in common with them, notably the
grouping together of short poems in small cohesive sub-groupings.

But if the festival coincided with Lorca's active involvement with
Andalusian art it was not so with Falla, whose Andalusian phase, to
use Ronald Crichton's term, had already been and gone. It was
roughly the second decade of the twentieth century that saw Falla's
composition of works inspired by Andalusia, a period that was by far
his most productive. The evolution of the composer's art in this
period is, moreover, intriguingly similar to that of what might be
termed Lorca's own Andalusian phase—a period of similar duration,
roughly from the earliest unpublished poems of 1917 through to the
completion of *Romancero gitano* in 1927.

The starting-points for this developing response are Falla's *Noches en los jardines de España*, subtitled 'Symphonic Impressions for Piano and Orchestra', and Lorca's earliest poetry on the subject of his native region. In this initial stage of development, both artists betray an acceptance of the standard aesthetic view of Andalusia as a romantic location, a vision that largely derives from nineteenth-century literature and painting, much of it the work of foreigners. Accordingly the realization is lush, overblown and clichéd in the case of Lorca, and imbued by a desire for beauty. Falla's *Noches* is the most sensuous composition of this ascetic man. Ann Livermore recounts how, when she attended a rehearsal of the work under the composer's direction in Barcelona before the Civil War, Falla told the orchestra at one point to play slower, because, as he concisely observed, 'son nocturnos'.[5] Livermore was sitting next to Falla's sister Doña María del Carmen, who added to what Falla had said the words 'del poeta americano'. Livermore subsequently discovered that the 'poeta americano' was Rubén Darío, and that the three movements of the *Noches* were inspired, in part at least, by three poems from the Nicaraguan poet's *Cantos de vida y esperanza*, two of which were entitled 'Nocturnos'.

The first and third movements have titles that clearly designate an Andalusian inpiration: 'En el Generalife' and 'En los jardines de la Sierra de Córdoba'. The former has an exotic, oriental tinge, as with the piano's first entry after the mysterious hushed opening. It is, of course, difficult on the basis of impression alone to be precise about parallels between music and words, but in the light of Livermore's discovery there is no mistaking how such evocative and melancholy music could appear as appropriate for lines like these from one of Darío's 'Nocturnos', not least because of the poet's characteristic recourse to a musical analogy:[6]

> Lejano clavicordio que en silencio y olvido
> no diste nunca al sueño la sublime sonata,
> huérfano esquife, árbol insigne, oscuro nido
> que suavizó la noche de dulzura de plata ...
>
> Esperanza olorosa a hierbas frescas, trino
> del ruiseñor primaveral y matinal,
> azucena tronchada por un fatal destino,
> rebusca de la dicha, persecución del mal ...
>
> [Distant clavichord that in silence and oblivion
> never gave that sublime sonata to sleep,

an orphan skiff, an illustrious tree, a dark nest
that softened night with the sweetness of silver ...

A hope fragrant with fresh herbs, the trill
of the spring and morning nightingale,
a lily cut down by a fatal destiny,
the search for happiness, the pursuit of evil ...]

Gardens figured too in Lorca's first published work, *Impresiones y paisajes* (1918). The core of the book comprises recollections of the poet's travels in Castile and Galicia in the preceding year, but it is supplemented by a miscellaneous section that includes sketches of Granada and meditations on gardens. In his earliest poetry, too, Lorca, very much under the influence of the *modernistas*, communicated the same exotic and vaguely oriental conception of Andalusia that was evident in Falla's Darío-inspired sound picture of the Generalife. The very first of the unpublished poems, dated in Lorca's notebook 29 June 1917, is in the same vein, albeit more erotic in content than Darío's 'Nocturno':[7]

Fue una noche plena de lujuria.
Noche de oro en Oriente ancestral,
noche de besos, de luz y caricias,
noche encarnada de tul pasional.

Sobre tu cuerpo había penas y rosas,
tus ojos eran la muerte y el mar.
¡Tu boca! Tus labios, tu nuca, tu cuello ...
Y yo como la sombra de un antiguo Omar ...

[It was a night full of lust.
A night of gold in the Orient of old,
a night of kisses, light and caresses,
a red night of passionate tulle.

On your body there were sorrows and roses,
your eyes were death and the sea.
Your mouth! Your lips, your nape, your neck ...
And I, like the shadow of an ancient Omar ...]

Where Lorca differs from Falla at this point in their respective Andalusian phases is in the quality of their productions—understandable, naturally, if we realize that the poet was a novice while Falla was by now a highly experienced composer. More than evocation, what Lorca commonly supplies is description, where simple enumeration replaces development or meditation, though, in fairness, in this he is guilty of nothing more than an inability to transcend his models. If his long poem 'Jueves Santo', written in March 1918, is a cliché-ridden picture of Andalusia in Holy Week, it is in truth no worse than what we read in Manuel Machado's *Cante hondo* (1912). It suffices to compare these lines from Lorca's poem:[8]

> ¡Ah Jueves Santo de Andalucía!
> Vino, guitarra, llanto y saetas.
> Cópulas hondas entre miradas.
> Quedan las almas enmarañadas
> en las mantillas vagas e inquietas.

> [Ah, Holy Thursday of Andalusia!
> Wine, guitar, weeping and *saetas*.
> Deep copulas among glances.
> The souls remain tangled
> in the vague and unquiet shawls.]

with ones from the older poet's work:[9]

> Vino, sentimiento, guitarra y poesía
> hacen los cantares de la patria mía.
> Cantares ...
> Quien dice cantares dice Andalucía.

> A la sombra fresca de la vieja parra,
> un mozo moreno rasguea la guitarra ...
> Cantares ...
> Algo que acaricia y algo que desgarra.

> [Wine, feeling, guitar and poetry
> are what the songs of my homeland make.
> Songs ...
> Whoever says songs says Andalusia.

> In the fresh shade of the old vine,
> a dark youth strums the guitar ...
> Songs ...
> Something that caresses and something that tears.]

The second stage of the Andalusian phases of Falla and Lorca involves a learning process, almost as though to correct the overconventional vision we have just witnessed. It is a stage that could be described as one of investigation. Falla's folk-song settings, *Siete canciones populares españolas*, date from 1914. These were composed when *Noches en los jardines de España* was near completion. The two songs of Andalusian origin, the 'Nana' and the 'Polo', are perhaps in their differing ways the most striking of the set. The oriental inflections of the lullaby and the unmistakable *cante jondo* traits of the latter—the strongly-accented guitar figures for the piano, the melismas, and the vocal interjections of anguish—have the ring of authenticity. In the opinion of Crichton, Falla 'selected (and sometimes retouched) the tunes and worked the accompaniments with fastidious and penetrating insight'.[10]

Lorca's investigative phase is manifested in two activities. In 1920 Ramón Menéndez Pidal, engaged as he had been for years in research into popular ballads surviving in the oral tradition, came to Granada. Lorca accompanied him in his visits to the Gypsies of the Albaicín and Sacromonte. Menéndez Pidal was later to write of how interested Lorca was in the subject; indeed, the philologist transcribed several ballads from a servant of the García Lorca family. Gibson suggests that Menéndez Pidal's visit, together with Falla's move to Granada in 1920, would have strengthened Lorca's interest 'both in folk music in general and that of the local Gypsies in particular'.[11] Then in the following year Lorca took flamenco guitar lessons from two Gypsies from his native Fuente Vaqueros and quickly learnt to accompany a range of songs, as he admitted in a letter to Adolfo Salazar in August 1920. In the same letter he speaks of his enthusiasm for this art, which he could now perform and which was to have such an impact on his poetry in the early to mid 1920s: 'me parece que lo flamenco es una de las creaciones más gigantescas del pueblo español' [It seems to me that flamenco is one of the most gigantic creations of the Spanish people].[12]

Hard on the heels of *Siete canciones* came Falla's ballet *El amor brujo*. The work arose as a response to a request from the gypsy singer Pastora Imperio; indeed, at the first performance at the Teatro Lara in Madrid in April 1915, she not only danced the role of Candelas but also performed the songs accompanying the ballet. This is a tale of love, jealousy and the supernatural, which Falla derived from legends recounted to him by Pastora's mother. Its *cante jondo* hallmarks are especially pronounced in the vocal sections, as the initial 'Canción del amor dolido' with its decorative chromatic runs and the exclamations of lament. But, while there is no mistaking the gypsy pedigree of this music, Falla claimed that he did not use a single folk-tune—a sign of how surely he had absorbed the manner and spirit of Andalusian gypsy music.

A similar claim for authenticity could be made for the parallel work by Lorca. Like Falla (and other folk-song 'collectors') he was disposed to assimilate rather than replicate when it came to creating his own *Poema del cante jondo* in November 1921. So, despite his high regard for the poetry of *cante jondo*, Lorca never incorporates it verbatim in his book. Only occasionally does he adopt its lexical mannerisms or turns of phrase, as with the similes of the poem entitled 'Puñal' [Knife]: 'entra en el corazón / como la reja del arado / en el yermo'; 'como un rayo de sol, / incendia las terribles hondonadas' [goes into the heart / like the ploughshare / into the barren land; like a ray of sun, / it sets the terrible ravines on fire].[13] Moreover, the poet has advanced from the picturesque banality of a poem like 'Jueves Santo' to a genuinely evocative mode, where restraint and sobriety of diction and metaphor, as opposed to the florid rhetoric of the *modernista* phase, are effective in conveying the timeless and telluric essence of the *cante jondo* experience. For what Lorca interpreted in his essay on the *duende* as 'un canto sin paisaje' [a song without landscape] a spareness of articulation was appropriate. Unlike Manuel Machado's strenuous reaching out for a lexicon of expressiveness there is in Lorca at this time a marvellous fastidiousness. The poetry resonates with the echo or, more suggestively, the memory of song, so that such similes as we find in 'La guitarra'—one of the emblematic poems of the book—are less about precision and detail than indicative of an opposite process—a moving away, a withdrawal:[14]

> Es inútil
> callarla.
> Es imposible
> callarla.
> Llora monótona
> como llora el agua,
> como llora el viento
> sobre la nevada.
>
> [It is futile
> to silence it.
> It is impossible
> to silence it.
> It weeps monotonously
> as the waters weep,
> as the wind weeps
> on the snowfield.]

Such similes shadow a fading sound and register the immensity of impact, such is their sheer sense of size and space.

By the time Lorca wrote this work in a surge of inspiration, when the plans for the *Cante jondo* festival were well advanced, Falla's Andalusian phase was over. Its concluding composition was a virtuoso piano piece, the *Fantasía baetica*, written in response to a commission from Arthur Rubinstein in 1919. In structure this is Falla's most strictly classical work, combining in its single movement sonata form with a slow intermezzo in lieu of a development section. Its ABA form is thus an amalgam of the first movement and all three movements (fast–slow–fast) of a classical sonata. But within this rigorous structure Falla unleashes some of his harshest and most dissonant effects. He does this especially in the part of the fast section (A) of the piece that corresponds to the second subject of the sonata-form design. It occurs with the repetition of a dramatic *cante jondo* recitative. In its first presentation it might well have strayed out of a composition by Albéniz, but when it appears a second time it has the discordant intervals of the seventh and the ninth rather than the expected octave doubling such as we find in a piece like Albéniz's *Sevillanas*. It may be stretching the point to consider such a realization of *cante jondo* as a parody, though there is an angry, biting quality about this music. But what we can say is that it constituted a musical cul-de-sac: after the *Fantasía baetica* Falla moved definitively away from 'lo andaluz'.

There is likewise something of an extreme and end-of-the-line quality about the work that concludes Lorca's Andalusian phase: the *Romancero gitano*. Here the gypsy experience is transformed into a mythical and eclectic dream-world. There is a parallel to the dissonance of the *Fantasía baetica* in the sheen and brilliance of the word-pictures and metaphors. If Falla's composition has the percussive and steely qualities we should expect from a heady stylistic mixture of Scarlatti and Bartók, then the *Romancero gitano* resounds to a similar clang of metal and galloping hooves. The sounds of the anvil or of horses in motion are evoked or echoed in poem after poem, from the opening ballad, 'Romance de la luna, luna':[15]

> Cuando vengan los gitanos,
> te encontrarán sobre el yunque
> con los ojillos cerrados.
> Huye luna, luna, luna,
> que ya siento sus caballos.
> Niño, déjame, no pises
> mi blancor almidonado.

El jinete se acercaba
tocando el tambor del llano.
Dentro de la fragua el niño
tiene sus ojos cerrados.

[When the gypsies come,
they will find you on the anvil
with your little eyes closed.
Run away, moon, moon, moon,
for now I hear their horses.
Child, leave me alone, don't tread
on my starched whiteness.

The horseman was approaching,
playing the drum of the plain.
Inside the forge the child
has his eyes closed.]

to the conclusion of the whole series, the ending of 'Thamar y Amnón':[16]

Violador enfurecido,
Amnón huye con su jaca.
Negros le dirigen flechas
en los muros y atalayas.
Y cuando los cuatro cascos
eran cuatro resonancias,
David con unas tijeras
cortó las cuerdas del arpa.

[Enraged violator,
Amnon flees on his pony.
Blacks fire arrows at him
from the walls and watchtowers.
And when the four hooves
were four echoes,
David with some scissors
cut the strings of the harp.]

The reasons why *Romancero gitano* should constitute the end of a process in Lorca are more complex than in the case of Falla. The unfavourable response to the collection by Dalí and Buñuel and Lorca's own unease about his 'mito de gitanería' [myth of the gypsy world] complicate the issue. But the parallel experience of Falla enables us to acknowledge how his evolution had an aesthetic rationale as well. Lorca was too good and too restless a creative artist to repeat or even to vary himself. So just as Falla, increasingly less productive in the last two decades of his life, moved from Andalusia to the Spain of Cervantes for the *Retablo de Maese Pedro* and to the pan-Hispanic vision of Verdaguer for *L'Atlàntida*, so Lorca was to leave Andalusia both physically and spiritually for the poetry inspired by New York and Galicia and, up to a point, for the theatre of the women of the villages of Spain. The flame of specifically Andalusian inspiration for these artists from Cadiz and Granada was never extinguished, but it is evident that it burnt intensely for only one period of their careers, and, then, in strikingly similar ways.

Notes to Chapter 7

1. Federico García Lorca, *Obras completas*, ed. Arturo del Hoyo, 5th edn. (Madrid: Aguilar, 1967), 1698.

2. Ian Gibson, *Federico García Lorca: A Life* (London: Faber & Faber, 1989), 125.

3. See Ronald Crichton, *Manuel de Falla: Descriptive Catalogue of his Works* (London: J. & W. Chester and Wilhelm Hansen, 1976), 36–7.

4. His more famous lecture on *cante jondo*, 'Teoría y juego del duende', dates from much later (1933). There was no mention of *duende* in the lecture delivered in Granada in 1922.

5. Ann Livermore, *A Short History of Spanish Music* (London: Duckworth, 1972), 193.

6. Rubén Darío, *Cantos de vida y esperanza*, 12th edn. (Madrid: Espasa-Calpe, 1971), 86.

7. Federico García Lorca, *Poesía inédita de juventud*, ed. Christian de Paepe (Madrid: Cátedra, 1994), 25.

8. Ibid., 189.

9. Manuel Machado, *Antología*, 6th edn. (Madrid: Espasa-Calpe, 1959), 11.

10. Crichton, *Falla: Descriptive Catalogue*, 22.

11. Gibson, *Federico García Lorca*, 107.

12. Federico García Lorca, *Epistolario*, 2 vols., ed. Christopher Maurer (Madrid: Alianza, 1983), i. 38.

13. Federico García Lorca, *Poema del cante jondo; Romancero gitano*, ed. Allen Josephs and Juan Caballero, 8th edn. (Madrid: Cátedra, 1985), 156.

14. Ibid., 146.

15. Ibid., 225.

16. Ibid., 300.

❖

Angels, Art and Analysis: Rafael Alberti's *Sobre los ángeles*

Helen Laurenson-Shakibi

The publication in 1929 of Rafael Alberti's poetic collection, *Sobre los ángeles*, marked a watershed in both the style and content of the Andalusian poet's work. With its rejection of traditional poetic models and motifs, this seminal poetry of crisis appears to mark a schism between Alberti's initial neopopular phase and a more mature poetic expression. Critics concur about the apocalyptic character of the vision presented and recognize the primacy of the poet's individual experience. For example, C. Brian Morris comments that 'Alberti is his own theme',[1] while Judith Nantell examines what she terms 'the battleground of the self'.[2] Both contemporaneous and more recent critical analysis converge in their use of specifically Catholic terminology to describe the collection, articulating Alberti's personal crisis almost exclusively in terms of religious referents. C. M. Bowra, whose study of *Sobre los ángeles* has been described by Alberti himself as 'muy importante y extenso' [very significant and thorough][3] considers the poems collectively to be 'a *confession* of a tremendous crisis in his [the poet's] life. A struggle and an agony.'[4] Pedro Salinas, whose close knowledge of the text in draft form led to his suggestion of the title to Alberti, describes *Sobre los ángeles* as 'una visión del mundo, angustiosa y siniestra, con un temblor medieval' [an embittered and radical world vision, with a medieval tremor].[5]

Biographical investigation can benefit the analysis of a complex and hermetic text such as *Sobre los ángeles*. This essay seeks to examine Alberti's work in light of poetic and psychoanalytical discourses, and open out the poetic text to a non-literary framework, namely that of art, which discloses the author-function, exposing the poet as a 'site of struggle'. But why the recourse to psychoanalysis, and what benefits does a theory of mind bring to an analysis of poetry? Psycho-analysis explores the connection between the latent and the manifest, between the subjective and the formal. The communication of subconscious or psychic material across the aesthetic boundaries of poetry emphasizes the active role played by the genre in the provision of a balanced mental space, a literary matrix through which the poet delineates an experience through the act of composition. The psychological implications of this poetic process are succinctly described by Dylan Thomas: 'I hold a beast, an angel, and a madman in me, and my enquiry is as to their working, and my problem is their subjugation and victory, downthrow and upheaval, and my effort is their self-expression.'[6]

In 1927, at the age of 25, the Spanish poet Rafael Alberti (1902–1999) suffered a nervous breakdown. Several primary texts reveal that the reasons for this are diverse and that the presentation of psychotic symptoms is curious, exhibiting a distorted engagement with reality.[7] A series of events propelled the young man towards a personal and spiritual crisis: the death in 1921 of his father, academic failure, his own diagnosis with tuberculosis and an unsuccessful love-affair. The most closely contemporaneous statement by the poet is dated 1 January 1929 and gives detailed information regarding his state of mind: 'Cubrí mi cabeza con ceniza. Me estoy quemando vivo. Atufadme de braseros y rodeadme de infiernillos azules, porque estoy de muy mal humor.' [My head I covered with hot ash. I am burning alive. Fan me with braziers and surround me with blue flame for I have a sick disposition.][8] Later, and with the benefit of hindsight, the poet expands upon the context of his personal malaise: 'Me encontraba de pronto como sin nada, sin azules detrás, quebrantada de nuevo la salud, estropeado en mis centros más íntimos.' [I suddenly found myself as if with nothing, no blue backdrop, my health shattered and my most intimate spirit in crisis.][9]

Sobre los ángeles, published in 1929, is the product of this personal crisis and functions as a lyrical displacement of neuroses. The poems present a gallery of divine incarnations described by Alberti as 'Los ángeles, no como los cristianos, corpóreos, de los bellos cuadros o estampas, sino como irresistibles fuerzas del espíritu, moldeables a los estados más turbios y secretos de mi naturaleza' [angels, not as the Christian figures of artistic tradition, but rather as unstoppable spiritual forces reflective of my most chaotic and secret moods] (*AP*

I/II, 264). What makes the composition of *Sobre los ángeles* even more interesting is an evident overlap between the poet's visions and the emergence of a rich and dense poetic text, whose very intention is to impose structure and logic on a paranoiac state. In his recent book, Robert Havard refutes comments made by Luis Monguió and Geoffrey Connell that the discernible form and discipline of the poems of *Sobre los ángeles* effectively preclude any type of irrationality from the work, with no possibility of Surrealism. Havard comments:

In short, the notion that the unconscious consists of and generates totally random impulses is a mistake. Paranoia, in particular, is characterized by this structuring orientation. One point to be drawn from these observations, I suggest, is that evidence of linguistic structure or systematization in a text, far from precluding paranoiac input, will tend rather to confirm it and, more generally, the presence of the unconscious at work.[10]

Alberti's visions had begun several years earlier in the course of the winter of 1919, during interminable walks through Madrid. He admitted (*AP I/II*, 126): 'El andar fuera de casa me obsesionaba. Las visiones, los insomnios cruzados de pesadillas me hacían llegar al alba con los párpados rotos y los ojos casi ensangrentados. Sufría de miedos, de terrores incontenibles.' [Walking outdoors obsessed me. Dawn saw me with painful and blood-stained eyes owing to my constant visions, insomnia and nightmares. I suffered blinding panic-attacks.] In his memoirs, Alberti recalls precise visions, including 'unos frailes extáticos encapuchados de un blanco amarillento' [several friars in ecstasy and hooded in parchment white]; during the composition of *Sobre los ángeles*, he specifies 'un inmenso pulpo negro que estuvo debajo de mi cama' [an enormous black octopus underneath my bed]. There can be no doubt that the balance of the young poet's mind was disturbed during this period, and that this imbalance presented itself in an acutely visual way. As late as 1987 Alberti elaborated upon his capacity for visions, saying 'nunca están marcados los límites de estas imágenes o apariciones. Me surgen de improviso, al mirar de soslayo, cuando menos los espero y pensando en nada o en cualquier algo incoherente' [there are never any clear boundaries to these images or visions. They appear suddenly, if I glance one way or the other, when I least expect them and at my most abstracted] (*AP III/ IV*, 355–6). What makes Alberti's psychological disorder interesting is that his confabulation is initially visual then transposed on a verbal level through the poems of *Sobre los ángeles*.

The Argentinian writer Ernesto Sábato, who also suffered from 'tremendas pesadillas, alucinaciones, sonambulismo y un caos general' [incredible nightmares, visions, sleepwalking and a general inner chaos], comments on the relationship between words and images:[11]

El inconsciente se manifiesta con imágenes, es como el cine mudo. Uno transmite por imágenes directamente el objeto poético que es el inconsciente, al escribir se le mete en el entresueño, en la duermevela. El pintor tiene la ventaja de transmitir la imagen directamente a la imagen, en cambio el escritor tiene que hacer palabras que son abstracciones. Tiene que ir reconstruyendo esa imagen del inconsciente y ahí se logra la poesía, que es siempre misteriosa, polivalente, que se presta a diferentes lecturas.

[The unconscious is made up of images, just as in silent film. The poetic motif too is communicated through image just as with the unconscious, when it is written it enters a sort of limbo, a semi-conscious realm. A painter has the distinct advantage of transposing the image directly with an image, whereas the writer uses abstract words. The image derived from the unconscious is thus recreated and from here we approach poetry, which equally is always mysterious and with multiple meanings and readings.]

For Alberti, such visions emerged from 1919 onwards, a period during which he was establishing himself as a painter and spending long hours both in the Museo del Prado and in El Casón del Buen Retiro, exhibiting in El Ateneo de Madrid in 1920. Alberti describes the Prado Museum as 'la casa más fantástica que he tenido y que yo me sabía de memoria' [the most fantastic house I have ever had and which I knew back to front].[12] Interestingly, the boundaries of artistic expression began to merge for him in 1921, and a liminal space was created between art and poetry: 'Aún veía en líneas y colores, pero esfumados entre una multitud de sensaciones ya imposibles de fijar con los pinceles' [Whilst I still saw in lines and colours, everything was blurred amidst a multiplicity of feeling that could no longer be defined with a paintbrush] (*AP I/II*, 144). Vicente Aleixandre, recalling 'estos lienzos flameantes [que] se colgaban en las paredes del Ateneo de Madrid' [these fluttering canvases hanging on the walls of the Madrid *Ateneo*], also recognized the innate pictorial qualities of Alberti's poetry, stating, 'pero miradle qué bien dibuja, todavía, en el verso, el verso [...] pero ¿y la pintura, la otra, la real, la del pintor qué había sido? La pintura dormía, la bella durmiente, ay, no en el bosque' [but look how well he still paints, in poetry, in verse—but what of the real painter that he had been? Painting was slumbering, sleeping beauty, aye, but not in the forest].[13] This blurring of categories is reiterated by Vittorio Bodini, critic and personal friend of Alberti, who comments that 'Il suo passaggio dalla pittura alla poesia è abbastanza coerente: il suo programma poetico è quello di dipinger la poesia. Ma forse soprattutto disegnarla.' [His journey from painting to poetry is quite straightforward: his poetic plan is to paint poetry. But perhaps above all to draw it.][14] It may be observed that the poetic texts of *Sobre los ángeles* emerge at the confluence of several sources: a psychological disintegration on the part of the poet, manifest through acute visions; the expression of these visual and psychical motifs through the structured framework of poetry; and the influence of Spanish art in their transposition from visual to written entity.

Bowra's 1949 *The Creative Experiment*, one of the earliest comprehensive studies of *Sobre los ángeles*, emphatically stresses the implicit and important notion of subjectivity in the poetic text, terming the poet 'a complex, self-analytical character [whose] catastrophe is private and personal'. Bowra continues: 'Alberti found his subjects more and more in himself, in his own struggles and contradictions and problems. This is an extremely intimate, self-examining, self-revealing poetry. Alberti turns the full strength of his intellectual passion to understanding his state.'[15] Bowra's comments herald later studies on the cathartic role of poetry, in which definitions of subjectivity are generally based on the linguistic implications of the first-person pronoun, and on an analysis of what spaces this *I* or *yo poético* demarcates. In *Sobre los ángeles* it is Alberti's intention to understand his state by rendering the internal external, making objective the subjective, and above all by drawing an impression through poetry of the dark situation of his spirit. This aspect of intimate revelation and confession through written text renders poetry and psychoanalysis adjuncts, the central dynamic of both discourses being words and their effect on the interlocutor.[16] If, thus, we accept the imaginative writer as a 'dreamer in broad daylight', the poetic text assumes the psychoanalytical model of the Freudian 'dream-work'. It is precisely the displacement of latent psychical trauma into manifest poetic images that is of note, and particular attention should be paid to the emergence of an iconic discourse and the presentation of symbols in composite and hallucinatory form.

In his memoirs Alberti recalls, '¿Qué hacer, cómo hablar, cómo gritar, cómo dar forma a esa maraña en que me debatía? Sumergiéndome, enterrándome cada vez más en mis propias ruinas'

[What was I to do, to say, to shout in order to give shape to this mire in which I found myself? Sinking ever further into the rubble of myself] (*AP I/II*, 264). The poet's attempt to articulate abstract emotions through the orthodox means of language is facilitated by the highly visual nature of the psychical motifs that present themselves, and it is these images that are more fitting as a register of the abstract and imprecise contours of mental disturbance. As we shall see, Alberti's creative experience in *Sobre los ángeles* is similar to that of Francisco de Goya almost a hundred and fifty years earlier, given that in both cases artistic expression is informed by the closed world of illness. As Alberti recalled, each disturbed episode frequently produced a poem: 'Huésped de las nieblas, llegué a escribir a tientas, sin encender la luz, a cualquier hora de la noche, con un automatismo no buscado, un empuje espontáneo, tembloroso, febril, que hacía que los versos se taparan los unos a los otros, siéndome a veces imposible descifrarlos en el día' [Lodger of the fog, forced to write blindly, without light, at anytime of the night, with an unintentional automatism, a spontaneous, trembling and feverish thrust which made the verses overwrite each other, sometimes making it impossible for me to decode them in the morning] (*AP I/II*, 265).

Relevant to this essay are those poems that attempt to articulate Alberti's inner torment, in particular poems from the first section of *Sobre los ángeles*, as these are texts that tell of the crisis immediately after it happened and are thus more unexpected and impressionistic. Alberti's state of mind is frequently depicted as a desolate and sterile landscape, a post-nuclear panorama comprised of composite and fragmented images: 'Ciudades sin respuesta, / ríos sin habla, cumbres / sin eco, mares mudos' [Cities without reply, / mute rivers, peaks / without echoes and dumb seas] ('Paraíso perdido'). This apocalyptic world is temporally and spatially fragmented and cannot be viewed logically: 'Atrás, montes y mares, / nubes, picos y alas, / los ocasos, las albas' [beyond, mountains and seas, / clouds, beaks and wings, / sunsets and dawns] ('El ángel bueno (I)').

In this respect, these poetic texts represent 'una literaturización de la pintura' [a literary rendering of painting],[17] for, just as in Goya's *Caprichos* and *Pinturas negras* only a distant contact with external reality is maintained, here too the written word conveys 'disturbed spatial relations, obvious displacement and pictorial condensation. Reality and unreality lose their boundaries.'[18] Both Alberti and Goya give visible form to the irrational, be it through linguistic or pictorial imagery, in a dramatic and often disconcerting attempt at self-analysis. The imaginary theatre created by both artists is generated by isolation and illness, Goya's *Caprichos* and *Disparates* being attributed to any number of illnesses, ranging from syphilis to schizophrenia and lead-poisoning.[19] However, whilst in both cases personal suffering and psychic experience are articulated through the conventional forms of art and poetry, the implicit torment and anxiety are none the less formidable. Indeed, aesthetic formality appears to be the means through which both artists attempt to deal with their demons: 'That Goya escaped madness is due to the fact that in the midst of the terrible visions which weighed upon his soul he could still cling to the pattern of the human form.'[20]

Whilst for many years Alberti remained circumspect regarding the identity of 'el amor imposible, golpeado y traicionado' [impossible, beaten and deceitful love] (*AP I/II*, 264), regarded as one of the reasons for his crisis, both Geoffrey Connell's 1979 *viva voce* interview with the poet and a sequel to *La arboleda perdida* shed more light on the matter: 'Parte del drama de *Sobre los ángeles* es ella [Maruja Mallo]. Yo me separé de ella en la mitad de *Sobre los ángeles*, y entonces me enamoré de otra chica que no me fue bien.' [Part of the drama of *Sobre los ángeles* is [Maruja Mallo]. I split from her in the middle of writing *Sobre los ángeles*, and then I fell in love with another girl, which didn't work out.][21] Recent research undertaken by Robert Havard reveals a close link between Alberti's poetic texts and Mallo's paintings of the same period, described by Federico García Lorca as 'estampas de maniquí pintadas con ausencia de color, son noticias necrológicas' [prints of a mannequin painted with a total lack of colour; they are death announcements].[22]

What is more of note here, however, are the frequent journeys made by the young poet through the desolate outskirts of Madrid to visit Mallo in Vallecas, at the peak of his mental breakdown: 'Coincidiendo con el arrastrarme los ojos por los barrizales, los terrenos levantados, los paisajes de otoño, sumergidas hojas en los charcos, las humaredas de las neblinas, mi salud se resquebrajaba, y los insomnios y pesadillas me llevaban a amanecer a veces derribado en el suelo de la alcoba' [Dragging myself through the muddy autumnal countryscape, leaves submerged in puddles, the foggy mist, my health splintering with insomnia and nightmares causing me to wake prostrate on the bedroom floor] (*AP III/IV*, 29). Alberti even ventures to say, '"Los ángeles muertos", ese poema de mi libro, podría ser una transcripción de algún cuadro suyo' ['Los ángeles muertos', that poem from my collection, could be a transcription of one of [Mallo's] paintings] (*AP III/IV*, 29), a statement corroborated by Havard, who describes paintings such as 'Espantapájaros' (1929) and 'Tierra y excremento' (1932) as a 'fetid netherland [with] their aura of apocalypse and spiritual dilapidation'.[23]

In a curious visual premonition of Wim Wenders' 1987 film *Wings of Desire*, man is reduced to a static and impotent contemplation of his state, 'hombres / fijos, de pie, a la orilla / parada de las tumbas' [men / static and upright on the edge / of tombs] ('Paraíso perdido'). The precipice motif is employed to connote danger and infinity, 'solo, en el filo del mundo, / clavado ya, de yeso' [alone on the edge of the world, of plaster and already pierced through] ('El cuerpo deshabitado'), and again, 'ya en el fin de la Tierra, / sobre el último filo' [already on the edge of the earth, above the last row] ('Paraíso perdido'). The confusion experienced by Alberti during his neurotic episodes is translated with imprecise images and textures that serve to confuse rather than elucidate. Smoke and snow convey a diaphanous chaos, a smokescreen that prevents clarity of vision or perception and replicates the poet's total bewilderment at his state of mind. The descent of the unleashed snow in 'Juicio' is sudden and ferocious, accompanied by muffled voices, darkness and shadows suggestive of Goya's 1797 'El Hechizado por Fuerza':

> ¡Oh sorpresa de nieve desceñida,
>   vigilante, invasora!
> Voces veladas, por robar la aurora,
>   te llevan detenida.
>
> Ya el fallo de la luz hunde su grito,
>   juez de sombra, en tu nada.
> (Y en el mundo una estrella fue apagada.
>   Otra, en el infinito.)
>
> [What a suddenness of unleashed snow,
>   watchful, invasive!
> Hushed voices poised to snatch the dawn
>   carry you away prisoner.
>
> The lack of light now sinks its groans,
>   judge of shade, into your void.
> (And in the world a star is extinguished.
>   Another in infinity.)]

Just as Alberti's real visions had emerged from the shadows of a stairwell, so too the poetic angels make the transition from darkness to light through a monochrome wash, and a lyrical chiaroscuro is created with the constant interposition of nouns such as *ceniza* [ash], *ascua* [ember], *tinta negra* [black ink], *barro*, *fango* [mud] and *hollín* [soot]. An evanescent lack of definition blurs contours and lines, 'esas luces, espejos de ceniza' [those lights, mirrors of ash] ('Madrigal sin remedio'), attempting to present the irrational and supernatural dimension of the human psyche. The lyrical landscape with its palette of muddy browns and ochres is reminiscent of Goya's *Pinturas negras*, and the acutely visual dimension of the poetry cannot be overlooked, especially in the light of Alberti's statement: 'yo quería ofrecer una fotografía de mi alma en su estado de derrumbamiento' [My intention was to offer a photograph of my soul in its state of collapse].[24] Alberti had spent the winter of 1917 copying Goya's paintings in the Prado, which he describes as 'Un rayo de oscuridad mordiente partido con violencia en dos colores: negro y blanco. Blanco de sol y lozanía. Negro hondo de sombra, de negra sangre coagulada' [A ray of biting darkness split violently in two colours: black and white. White of sun and vigour. Deep black of shade, of black clotted blood] (*AP I/II*, 106).

In 1985, accompanied by Nuria Espert, Alberti attended the *Europalia* art exhibition in Belgium entitled 'Esplendor de España' and reflects, '¡Oh, Dios! ¿De dónde sacamos los españoles esa poderosa tristeza, esas aguas terribles del pozo de la muerte, ese vivo y lejano dolor que nos estremece?' [Oh God! Where do we Spaniards get this powerful sadness, these terrible waters from the well of death, this living and distant pain which sends shivers through us?]. In the context of an appreciation of the Spanish Masters, specifically Goya and Zurbarán, he continues, 'Yo escribí *Sobre los ángeles*, un libro descendidos muchos de sus peldaños en el infierno. Algunos de aquellos poemas míos están *vistos*, gráficamente, en estos ángeles, en esos que se abren en seis alas, y deben volar con un grave sonido de motor en sordina' [I wrote *Sobre los ángeles*, a book whose many stages are inspired by hell. Several of the poems are *seen*, graphically, through the angels, especially those that open in six wings and who should fly with the deep and muted sound of a motor engine'] (*AP III/IV*, 290–1). Both Goya and Alberti share an interest in capturing a sense of movement and dynamic power in their respective artistic disciplines and focus on images of ascent and elevation. Goya's neurotic episodes produced paintings such as the disturbing 'Flying Witches' (1797) and the supernatural *Caprichos* 'Subir y bajar', 'Buen viaje' and 'Allá va esa'. Just as Goya visually stressed dynamic power with a variety of movement such as 'escaping and writhing, dancing and whirling through the air, swinging and tumbling, climbing and flying',[25] so too Alberti attempts to convey his dramatic and frantic encounter with 'Los ángeles de la Prisa':

> Espíritus de seis alas,
> seis espíritus pajizos,
> me empujaban.
> [...]
> Acelerado aire era mi sueño
> por las aparecidas esperanzas
> de los rápidos giros de los cielos,
> de los veloces, espirales pueblos,
> rodadoras montañas,
> raudos mares, riberas, ríos, yermos.

> [Six-winged spirits,
> six straw spirits,
> were pushing me.
> [...]
> A speedy wind was my dream
> through the ongoing hopes
> of the rapidly spinning skies,
> of the swift, spiral towns,
> rolling mountains,
> stormy seas, shores, rivers, fallow lands.]

There can be no doubt that by writing the poems of *Sobre los ángeles*, Alberti was confronting his demons in an attempt to understand himself and his situation. In 'El angel bueno (I)' he tries to intellectualize and explain his neurosis:

> Un año, ya dormido,
> alguien que no esperaba
> se paró en mi ventana.

> —'¡Levántate!' Y mis ojos
> vieron plumas y espadas.

> [Asleep for one year,
> someone I was not expecting
> arrived at my window.

> 'Get up !' And my eyes
> saw feathers and swords.]

Alberti's initial encounter with the angel, agent of his chaos, is communicated through an indefinite collage of feathers and swords. The poet's eyes are filled with this overwhelming dramatic vision, the angel's wings creating both texture and spatial dynamism. The wings of angels frequently frame Mannerist paintings such as 'The Ascension of Christ' by Tintoretto (1576), connoting weightlessness and a heightened sense of drama. Just as El Greco's angels present the supernatural encounter between the spiritual world of angels and the physical one of humanity, Alberti's angels transcend the ego and the id and are the textual equivalents of the elongated angels in paintings such as 'Annunciation' and 'Agony in the Garden'. For just as Yolanda Pascual Solé observes that 'en *A la Pintura* Alberti parece efectivamente *traducir* en palabras el arte pictórico' [in *A la pintura* Alberti appears effectively to *translate* pictorial art into words],[26] here too as artist he attempts to delineate the impression and very essence of the angel's presence.

   In the poetic portrayal of his internalized trauma, Alberti has recourse to the rich religious imagery of his upbringing and education at the Jesuit Colegio de San Luis Gonzaga in El Puerto de Santa María, Cádiz. Several poems such as 'Desahucio' and 'El cuerpo deshabitado' are concerned with a pictorial and symbolic representation of the soul, doubtless inspired by the caustic harangues received as a boy: 'si te pudieras ver el alma, morirías de horror. La tienes sucia, lo mismo que un cendal manchado de barro' [if you could see your soul you would die of shame. It is filthy, the same as a piece of gauze smeared in mud] (*AP I/II*, 51). Father Lambertini's words reveal both an intransigent Jesuit rhetoric and, more importantly, a linguistic violence, a dialectic of mortal sin and the antithetical good–evil dynamic so central to the composition of *Sobre los ángeles*. In addition, it renders visible the abstract, transforming the soul into a besmirched gauze. Interestingly, twenty-first-century cultural discourse persists with traditional religious imagery to articulate mental health problems: 'I fragmented. *Dysfunctional* is a chic word used mainly by the cocktail set, but we all have our psycho-pathological baggage, some more disabling than others. Occasionally, I'd go back to my normal self and then I'd feel the hot breath of demons on the back of my neck, and they'd sink their teeth in.'[27] 'El angel Ceniciento' affirms Alberti's disengagement with reality and provides evidence of his psychosis:

> Precipitadas las luces
> por los derrumbos del cielo,
> en la barca de las nieblas
> bajaste tú, Ceniciento.
> [...]
> Dando bandazos el mundo,
> por la nada rodó, muerto.
> No se enteraron los hombres.
> Sólo tú y yo, Ceniciento.
>
> [The lights spilling over
> into the precipices of heaven,
> in a boat of mist
> you came down, Ceniciento.
> [...]
> Lurching the world
> rolled dead through the void.
> Mankind knew not.
> Only you and I, Ceniciento.]

1928 finds Alberti unable to relate to his surroundings, family or peers. As he put it, 'me empecé a aislar de todo; envidiaba y odiaba la posición de los demás' [I began to isolate myself from everything; I envied and hated the success of everyone else] (*AP I/II*, 265). The poetic texts reveal this dislocation from reality and serve to communicate the psychosis through the provision of poetic spaces that insulate the poet from an engagement with reality. If we apply the Freudian model elaborated in 'The Loss of Reality in Neurosis and Psychosis' (1924), we learn that in psychosis a piece of reality is remodelled: 'This is made possible by the existence of a *world of phantasy*, of a domain which became separated from the real external world at the time of the introduction of the reality principle. [The world of phantasy] is the storehouse from which the materials or the pattern for building the new reality are derived.'[28] Alberti's inability to relate to others and his complicity with the forces of his psyche are summed up in the last two lines of the poem. Equally his persecution complex and night terrors are represented by the image of the pillow in part III of 'El cuerpo deshabitado':

> ¿Quién sacude en mi almohada
> reinados de yel y sangre,
> cielos de azufre,
> mares de vinagre?

[...]
Contra mí, mundos enteros,
contra mí, dormido,
maniatado,
indefenso.

[Who is it that shakes in my pillow,
kingdoms of ice and blood,
heavens of sulphur,
seas of vinegar?
[...]
Against me, entire worlds,
Against me, asleep,
handcuffed,
defenceless.]

Sobre los ángeles has been described as one of the finest Spanish poetic collections of the twentieth century, not least on account of the vivid portrayal of the disintegration of the self. In addition, the work has provoked much debate regarding the precise nature of Spanish Surrealism. Alberti's constant denial of any contact with the Surrealist movement in France is emphasized in statements like the following: 'Sobre los ángeles es un libro profundamente español, producto de ciertas catástrofes internas que entonces sufrí' [Sobre los ángeles is a profoundly Spanish book, a product of certain personal crises that I suffered at the time].[29]

There is no doubt that Alberti's poetry is informed by his cultural heritage, both literary and pictorial. Alberti, like Goya, effectively invites us to reflect upon the human condition, in his case through a written word whose very composition, fragmentation and subversion replicates pictorial techniques. The intrinsically surrealist features of Spanish art and culture were not lost on the French Surrealists: 'Some Surrealists believed that Goya had intentionally exploited the world of dreams and a selection of the Caprichos was included in the "Fantastic Art" section of the International Surrealist exhibition in New York in 1936.'[30] This peculiar fusion of the Baroque and twentieth-century avant-garde is made all the more impressive given its transposition to poetic texts: 'Son muestras singulares de un arte entre barroco y superrealista, esperpéntico y desesperado, ya con todas las calidades que llegan a magnífica plenitud en Sobre los ángeles' [They are unique products of the fusion of Baroque and Surrealist art, grotesque and desperate, already possessing all the qualities that reach their

apotheosis in *Sobre los ángeles*].[31] Alberti's close knowledge and love of
painting lends his poetry a deeper dimension, transforming it, as
Carlos Areán says, into 'pintura de segundo grado' [a type of
secondary painting].[32] It would be fitting to leave the last word to
Alberti himself: 'Yo no hago ninguna distinción entre la poesía y
pintura, entre la palabra y la línea, entre la expresión gráfica y la
palabra' [I make no distinction between poetry and painting, between
words and brushstrokes, between the graphic and written idioms].[33]

Notes to Chapter 8

1. C. Brian Morris, *Rafael Alberti's 'Sobre los ángeles': Four Major Themes* (Hull: Hull
University Press, 1966), 11. All quotations from *Sobre los ángeles* itself refer to
Rafael Alberti, *Obras completas*, 3 vols. (Madrid: Aguilar, 1988), i. 377–445.
2. Judith Nantell, 'Irreconciliable Differences: Rafael Alberti's *Sobre los ángeles*', *The
Surrealist Adventure in Spain*, ed. C. Brian Morris (Ottawa Hispanic Studies 6;
Ottawa: Dovehouse, 1991), 145–65 at 146.
3. Vittorio Bodini, *I poeti surrealisti spagnoli* (Torino: Einaudi, 1963), p. cv.
4. C. M. Bowra, *The Creative Experiment* (London: Macmillan, 1949), 250.
5. Pedro Salinas, *Literatura española del siglo XX* (Madrid: Aguilar, 1961), 286–7.
6. Dylan Thomas, *Collected Poems* (London: Faber & Faber, 1965), 45.
7. See e.g. Rafael Alberti, *La arboleda perdida: Libros I y II de memorias* (Barcelona:
Seix Barral, 1975; first publ. 1938, 1959), 263–70; Manuel Bayo, *Sobre Alberti*
(Madrid: CUS, 1974); Vittorio Bodini, *Los poetas surrealistas españoles* (Barcelona:
Tusquets Editores, 1971), pp. civ–cv; Geoffrey Connell, '*Sobre los ángeles*: Form
and Theme', *Spanish Studies* 4 (1982), 1–14 at 9–10.
8. Rafael Alberti, 'Itinerarios jóvenes de España', originally publ. in *La Gaceta
Literaria* 49 (Jan. 1929, n.p.), and reproduced in Rafael Alberti, *Prosas encontradas
1924–1942* (Madrid: Ayuso, 1970), 25–6 at 25.
9. Alberti, *La arboleda perdida: Libros I y II de memorias*, 265. All references are to this
volume or to its companion, *La arboleda perdida: Libros III y IV de memorias*
(Barcelona: Seix Barral, 1987), indicated respectively in parentheses as *AP I/II*
and *AP III/IV*, followed by the page number(s).
10. Robert Havard, *The Crucified Mind: Rafael Alberti and the Surrealist Ethos in Spain*
(London: Tamesis, 2001), 73.
11. Ernesto Sábato, interview in *Diario 16* (8 July 1995), 21–2.
12. Bayo, *Sobre Alberti*, 28.
13. Vicente Aleixandre, 'Rafael Alberti, pintor', Alberti, *Obras completas*, ii. 269–70.
14. Bodini, *I poeti surrealisti spagnoli*, p. lviii.
15. Bowra, *The Creative Experiment*, 225.
16. 'Words were originally magic and to this day words have retained much of their
ancient magical power. Words provoke effects and are in general the means of
mutual influence among men. Thus we shall not depreciate the use of words in
psychotherapy and we shall be pleased if we can listen to the words that pass
between the analyst and his patient.' Sigmund Freud, *Introductory Lectures on*

Psychoanalysis, trans. James Strachey and Angela Richards (London: Penguin, 1991), 41–2.

17. Francis Cerdán, 'Rafael Alberti y la pintura de Antonio Saura: Visión memorable', *Dr Rafael Alberti: El poeta en Toulouse*, ed. Marie de Meñaca (Toulouse: Université de Toulouse – Le Mirail, 1984), 225–38 at 228.
18. Nigel Glendinning, *Goya and his Critics* (New Haven: Yale University Press, 1977), 169.
19. Ibid., chap. 8, 'Psychological and Pathological Interpretations', 165 –74.
20. Ibid., 164.
21. Connell, '*Sobre los ángeles*: Form and Theme', 10.
22. Quoted in Maruja Mallo, *59 grabados en negro y 9 láminas en color (1928–1942)*, introd. Ramón Gómez de la Serna (Buenos Aires: Losada, 1942), 8.
23. Havard, *The Crucified Mind*, 100.
24. Benjamin Prado, 'Rafael Alberti, entre el clavel y la espada', *Rafael Alberti: Premio de literatura en lengua castellana 'Miguel de Cervantes' 1983* (Barcelona: Anthropos, 1989), 71–103 at 83.
25. August L. Mayer, *Francisco de Goya*, trans. Robert West (London: J. M. Dent & Sons, 1924), 112.
26. Yolanda Pascual Solé, 'Estética impresionista en *A la pintura* de Rafael Alberti', *Bulletin of Hispanic Studies* [Liverpool] 74 (1997), 197–214 at 211.
27. Tony Slattery, interview in *The Independent* (9 Nov. 2001), 28.
28. Sigmund Freud, 'The Loss of Reality in Neurosis and Psychosis', idem, *On Psychopathology*, ed. James Strachey and Angela Richards (London: Pelican Freud Library, 1979), 225.
29. Bodini, *I poeti surrealisti spagnoli*, p. civ.
30. Glendinning, *Goya and his Critics*, 154.
31. Pedro Salinas, *Ensayos de literatura hispánica* (Madrid: Aguilar, 1961), 335.
32. Carlos Areán, 'La imágen pictórica en la poesía de Alberti', *Cuadernos hispanoamericanos* 289–90 (1974), 198–209 at 207.
33. Rafael Alberti, interview with Luis Pancorbo, *Gaceta del arte* (April 1974), 23.

CHAPTER 9

The Theory of Surrealist Collage through Image and Text: Àngel Planells and José María Hinojosa

Jacqueline Rattray

It is an evening in 1925 in the café 'La Rotonde', Paris. A group of artists—part of the 'Escuela española de París'—meet to talk. Joan Miró and Luis Buñuel are two of the more familiar faces in the 'Rotonde' group, amongst a number of other painters, sculptors, writers, musicians, filmmakers and intellectuals.[1] Sitting at one table, a poet and an artist are engaged in conversation. José María Hinojosa (1904–1936) is a writer from Málaga and an enthusiastic follower of Surrealist activity in Paris. Gregorio Prieto (1897–1992) is a neo-Cubist painter from Valdepeñas, who would later flirt with, although not be entirely seduced by, Surrealism.[2] During their conversation, Hinojosa presents the artist with an edition of his first book of poetry—a pre-Surrealist work entitled *Poema del campo* (1925).[3] Prieto accepts the gift, and afterwards, as was his custom of the time, writes his impressions on the last page of his copy.[4] In these notes Prieto also records the content of the conversation that passed between them in the café.

Of his recollections, two points in particular stand out in relation to artistic exchange. First, Prieto recalls the almost exclusive importance that Hinojosa seems to have attached to the nature of their friendship. In particular, he notes that Hinojosa made seemingly jealous remarks about two other poets—Rafael Alberti and Federico García Lorca—both of whom were mutual friends of theirs.

According to Prieto, Hinojosa 'me recriminaba mi gran amistad con Rafael' [he reproached me for my close friendship with Rafael] and then told him, on more than one occasion, that 'Tenemos que vernos más a menudo (y lograr un gran cariño) porque eres muy amigo de Federico y no mío.' [We must see each other more often (and reach a greater affection) because you are a good friend of Federico's and not mine.] Secondly, Prieto remarks upon the poet's eagerness to acquire an illustration from him for his next book of poetry. Hinojosa, otherwise known as the 'bohemio con cuenta corriente' [bohemian with a current account] to his friends, was an avid collector of contemporary art.[5] And, for many a struggling artist of the 'Rotonde' group—there were some fifty thousand painters in Paris at this time[6]—the wealthy poet's love of art brought them some form of financial support as well as artistic recognition.[7] But Prieto records with a note of irritation that 'me insistió tanto que en la mesa del café, para que se quedara tranquilo, le empecé unas líneas' [he insisted so much that, there at the coffee-table, so that he would quiet down, I began a sketch for him.][8]

Little is known of the friendship, if any, that was struck between the poet and the artist. The drawing Prieto sketched for Hinojosa never came to illustrate any of his books. And, unusually for any artist associated with him, no existing poem or Surrealist text of Hinojosa's is dedicated to Prieto. Nevertheless, Prieto's portrait of the poet still remains as a manifestation of a symbiotic relationship between the arts. The drawing Prieto began to sketch for Hinojosa in 'La Rotonde' captures the poet in a familiar pose, smoking his pipe. With ruffled hair and pensive look, this drawing also recalls certain portraits of Arthur Rimbaud, the French decadent poet whose 'long, prodigious and rational *disarrangement* of *all the senses*' so appealed to Surrealist aims.[9] The interaction between painting and poetry is evident in Prieto's view of Hinojosa in the café. The drawing is framed within a context of literal exchange—a book of poetry has changed hands for a drawing—and in literary intertext—Prieto draws on a poet whose work was shared round and read by many of the other 'Rotonde' artists. When Prieto's drawing is contrasted with the cover illustration for *Poema del campo* (1925)—the book Hinojosa gave him in the café—a physical change in the poet is captured. In the earlier portrait of the author, by Salvador Dalí—a later member of the 'Rotonde' group—Hinojosa is depicted in notably conservative, bourgeois attire, his hair neatly combed, again smoking a pipe.

Hinojosa's time in Paris is fundamental to an understanding of his bohemian transformation and of his adventure into Surrealism.[10] Like a form of biographical collage, the Parisian experience, and the new-found liberalism this entailed, can be seen in diametric opposition to the cultural conservatism of his rural Andalusia. Julio Neira has observed that 'Hinojosa vive en París la ruptura con su pasado poético y vitalmente conservador, y llega al surrealismo.' [In Paris, Hinojosa lives out the rupture with his poetic and vitally conservative past and arrives at Surrealism.][11] One particular aspect of Parisian life that highlights the cultural difference between France and Spain was noted by Buñuel, a friend of Hinojosa's since the 'Residencia' days and the founder of the 'Orden de Toledo.' For Buñuel, the sexual freedom of Paris was not only shocking to him personally but also carried a wider-reaching implication within society. Buñuel recalls how revolutionary it was to see couples kissing in the street and that 'Semejante comportamiento abría un abismo entre Francia y España, lo mismo que la posibilidad de que un hombre y una mujer vivieran juntos sin las bendiciones.' [Such behaviour opened up a chasm between France and Spain, as did the possibility of unmarried men and women living together.][12] This radical difference in lifestyle between Paris and Spain has a specific cultural relevance to the very etymology of collage, as one critic has noted: 'The very word "collage", from coller, to paste, has two meanings which are germane: technically, in the phrase "collage du papier", it describes the job of hanging wallpaper; as period slang, however, collage also refers to the unmarried cohabitation of two people and bore overtones of sexual impropriety.'[13] Collage is more than just a technique of Surrealist practice; it is one of the defining principles of the Surrealist revolt.

Interspersed throughout Hinojosa's book of poems, La sangre en libertad (1931), are four untitled collage-drawings—two framed and two free-floating—by the Catalan artist Àngel Planells (1901–1989).[14] Planells's collage-drawings illustrate several of the defining charac-teristics of Surrealist collage as set out by Max Ernst, the leading pioneer and theorist of Surrealist collage, whose work was brought to Spain through a chain of personal friendships as well as through contemporary reviews.[15] Planells first came into contact with Ernst's work through his friend Salvador Dalí, who brought back some of Ernst's collage-novels from Paris.[16] The critic Lucía García de Carpi suggests that Planells's collage experiments actually pre-dated his first encounter with Ernst's work (an uncanny example of the Surrealist fascination with premonition).[17] Looking at Planells's collage-drawings, the viewer is immediately aware that these are not collages in the conventional sense of the word—there are no pieces that have been literally cut and pasted. This general observation underscores one fundamental difference between the Surrealist use of collage and the Cubist *papier collé*.[18] The Surrealist collage can be defined more appropriately through anti-definition, as Ernst discovered when he played with etymology to conclude that 'it is not the glue (*colle*) that makes the collage'. By rejecting this one basic structural characteristic, the collage-process lends itself to all forms of Surrealist activity.

In keeping with Surrealism's political interests, there is a collective activity involved in Surrealist collage that rebels against individual claims to authorship and property.[19] The most obvious example of this collaborative authorship is seen in the production of the *cadavre exquis*, a practice based on the childhood game of 'consequences'. The *cadavre exquis* can be written or depicted pictorially, but, within this collectivity, each individual contribution is still acknowledged—a reminder that the Surrealist revolt does not subordinate the rights of the individual to the collective cause. Collective property is demonstrated in the selection and appropriation of ready-made materials. In the most famous examples, ready-mades come in the form of mass-produced objects, removed from context and put to subversive use in a Surrealist critique of capitalism. By using ready-mades, Surrealist collage becomes accessible to all. Anyone can make a Surrealist collage, regardless of artistic background or training, and this universalizing aspect of collage offers a challenge to the bourgeois distinction between high and low art.[20] Industrial objects are not the only ready-mades that are used. In painting, Surrealism cannibalizes references and styles from the past masters, and in Surrealist writing, language itself is exploited as a ready-made. Advertising slogans, proverbs and clichés, famous titles, well-known literary images and classical structures, all are used in Surrealist collage-poetry to challenge the reader's familiarity with language.[21]

Breaking boundaries between disciplines is one of the most obvious characteristics of Surrealist collage as anti-(art-)establishment.[22] By defying categorization, the Surrealist collage challenges the viewer's expectations and resists attempts to label and thus contain the work. During the actual process of collage production, individual Surrealists will frequently cross over into other disciplines (Planells, like many other Surrealist artists, also experimented in poetry).[23] His interest in language crosses over into pictorial representation in the collages that illustrate *La sangre en libertad*. These particular collages can be categorized as 'word-images'. They confuse the role of language by juxtaposing words with pictorial forms and by the pictorial depiction of language itself. The Surrealist collage appropriates and subverts the viewer's or reader's expectations by drawing attention to and then destroying the accustomed perception of the world. Playing upon conventional responses (whereby the spectator instinctively looks for a unified view of reality), Surrealism fragments this understanding to reveal that our perception of truth is fundamentally intertextual and interdisciplinary.

The first of Planells's collage-drawings in Hinojosa's *La sangre en libertad* makes explicit the challenge that confronts the viewer of the Surrealist collage.[24] This collage-drawing responds violently to the viewer's attempts to decode the picture, offering a literal defiance through the phrase that imposes itself upon the viewer-reader, 'la definición se impone'. Implicit in this phrase is a sense of clarity and of clarification, but because it is open to a number of inter-pretations—'the definition imposes itself', 'the definition is imposed', or even 'one imposes the definition'—any sense of clarification, or indeed, 'definition', soon disintegrates.

The whole picture is dominated by a mutilated and amputated fist, around which an incongruous assortment of images is brought together. The word-image element of Planells's collage is witnessed not only through the actual presence of words but through the inter-textual references within this composition. On top of the central arrangement, a fish dissolves into the shape of an eye, and this image touches upon a specific Surrealist ready-made: that collection of Surrealist texts by André Breton, *Soluble Fish*. The whole arrangement balances—'a filo de la navaja' [on a knife-edge]—on a cliché. There is an unspoken yet implicit connection between the knife, upon which the whole composition rests, and the various images of cutting in the collage itself—the severed thumb, the arm-substitute, the object that pierces the finger, the fish that stabs the hand. From the wound left by this surreal 'fish-knife', blood flows.

That all too familiar, self-contained paradox of blood, as symbol of both life and death, is emphasized in Planells's collage. On one side of the wound, drops of blood flow, and, on the other, these drops metamorphose into spermatozoa. The potential for life is implied although, being spilt, the spermatozoa are destined for death. The metamorphosis of familiar symbols is one of the ways in which this collage plays on the viewer's expectations. Another is through the Rimbaldian sensory disarrangement that is evident and adds another layer of confusion to the immediate visual response. The senses of sight and touch are clearly discerned through the hand and eye imagery. The gesture of the balloon-like figure, in the top left-hand corner, echoes the action of hearing. The senses of taste and smell are more tenuous links to make but they are implied through the food references of the fish and the knife.

The overall effect of Planells's collage is to create a tension, a general feeling of unease, through the violation of pictorial representation. The function of juxtaposition is central to the visual discomfort of this collage as it is to the whole range of Surrealist creations. The theory behind this particular form of image-production is explored by Breton in the 'First Manifesto of Surrealism'. Breton quotes the poet Pierre Reverdy:[25]

The image is a pure creation of the mind.

It cannot be born from a comparison but from a juxtaposition of two more or less distant realities.

The more the relationship between the two juxtaposed realities is distant and true, the stronger the image will be—the greater its emotional power and poetic reality ...

In general, Reverdy's theory is in agreement with Surrealist aims, even though Breton expresses a certain reservation—one that arises largely from a misreading of Reverdy and from taking this quotation out of context.[26] Both Reverdy and Breton highlight the power of juxtaposition in the production of the metaphor and discard the importance of simile, which imposes a hierarchy upon the literary image. Breton's concern is that Reverdy appears to be restraining language to its purely referential function, of depicting concrete 'realities' however far displaced from one another. Surrealism does not exclude abstract forms of expression, although it still remains rooted in some form of recognizable reality. This solidarity with the unreal is evident in Planells's collage. Recognizable objects—the hand, the knife, the script, the fish—are juxtaposed with amorphous forms. There are indecipherable shapes, such as the object that pierces the index finger, distorts like molten wax and then turns into hair. This object is connected through its hair-like strands to blood-vessels or nerves, which are left dangling from the severed thumb. There are also dissolving shapes such as the disappearing bird in the bottom left-hand corner of the fist, and the soluble fish–eye on the top.

An inversion of subject–object relations takes place in this collage, which causes the viewer to reflect upon the accustomed experience of responding to pictorial representation. This complicated experience of dual sensory response is succinctly represented in Planells's collage by the central image of the folded finger. This self-touching finger has become both the object and the subject of touch. Of the textual elements already highlighted in this collage, the scroll unfolding from the fish–eye, bearing the calligraphic words 'la definición se impone', is the most obvious one. In the act of reading this phrase, the viewer-reader's eye is carried along the scroll and away from the central arrangement of the collage. In responding to the statement, which is presented with an air of defiance, a direct self-questioning is provoked. Rather than being an object for mere aesthetic appreciation, Planells's collage now starts to look back at the viewer-reader. The eye has to switch between 'seeing' the picture to 'reading' the text, and this forces the viewer to respond to Planells's collage in a way that encapsulates both the passive and active roles of vision.

In responding to a poetic form of Surrealist collage, a process of fragmentation and reconstitution is similarly provoked. Hinojosa's poem 'Ya no me besas' from *La sangre en libertad* is not immediately obvious as a form of collage, as are those typographical collages that appear in Breton's 'First Manifesto of Surrealism'.[27] On a structural level, Hinojosa's poem, like Planells's collage-drawing, does not literally employ any other media—the only 'glue' used is metaphorical. There is no punctuation in 'Ya no me besas' other than a full stop at the end of each stanza. The overall effect is that visualized images appear juxtaposed and disjointed, or at times they dissolve into one another. The collage-process of this poem functions on an inner level, within the visualizing sphere of the reader. 'Ya no me besas' is a collage that draws on the reader's own intertextual resources to construct an inevitably personal response to the text. As will be witnessed, 'Ya no me besas' is a poem in which 'la definición se impone'.

Initially, the reader finds a frame of familiarity in this poem. The title, 'Ya no me besas', together with the regular verse structure of the poem situate this text within the familiar setting of love-poetry. But, as soon as the reader engages with the poem, the collage-process sets to work. A number of images, clichés and archetypal representations of love are seen ripped out of context and juxtaposed in an action that both appropriates and subverts established literary codes. The breaks between collage elements are not revealed through analysing the poem line by line. And, when seen in isolation, these individual images do not reveal anything particularly surreal about them in themselves. It is rather a question of how these images have been juxtaposed in the poem to create a visualizing tension for the reader. There is a visual violence in 'Ya no me besas' that is made explicit as well as mentally experienced. The familiar lovers' gaze is graphically violated in the poem, and overall the images resist visualization in purely ocularcentric terms.[28] A Rimbaldian disarrangement of all the senses confronts the reader to present a scene that is essentially unseen. The lack of visual coherence in the poem prevents the reader from merely observing the text from a distance and requires an interaction in the reading process.

The first stanza of 'Ya no me besas' introduces ready-made pieces of collage in terms of obvious intertexts as well as in the juxtaposition of sensory responses for the reader:

> Un viento inesperado hizo vibrar las puertas
> y nuestros labios eran de cristal en la noche
> empapados en sangre dejada por los besos
> de las bocas perdidas en medio de los bosques.

> [An unexpected wind rattled on all the doors
> and in the night our lips were of crystal
> soaked in the blood left by the kisses
> from our mouths lost in the midst of the woods.]

The poem opens with a familiar image of suspense and intrusion, which, when seen in isolation, echoes with that typically Gothic intertext of the haunted house. This image immediately shakes the reader out of conventional visual response by also appealing to the sense of hearing. Where a visual reaction is stimulated in the second line, sight is quickly negated, and a sensory disarrangement follows. The kisses in the night are described as a physical sensation rather than a physical encounter. The experience of these kisses, described over the remaining lines of this stanza, provokes an excess of sensory responses from the reader. The reader's view is suspended between seeing the lovers' lips as made of smooth and intact glass or of shattered crystal that has caused the bleeding. Like the knife upon which the amputated fist balances precariously in Planells's collage, in Hinojosa's description of the kisses, the act of cutting is always suggested but left unstated.

Initially the reader can see the 'crystal lips' in visual terms, but the reference to night immediately blinds the reader's view, and the other senses are brought into play. A tactile response can be evoked, as the kisses would feel cold and inanimate. A gustatory response is also implied by the taste as well as the smell of blood, which soaks the lips. The hard, impermeable and inanimate lips now dissolve into an image that brings together the fragility and the passionate intensity of the lovers' kisses. An almost cannibalistic urge is conveyed in the third line, which touches upon an intertextual reference from contemporary cinema. The Surrealist interest in vampire movies, most famously *Nosferatu*, is manifested here through a process of taking and adapting a ready-made image for its new Surrealist context. In the final line of this first stanza, the mouths are dismembered in an image that appropriates the well-known Surrealist obsession with images of body mutilation. Carried away by their kisses, the lovers are oblivious to the rest of the world and, in a familiar Hinojosian intertext, the mouths are lost in the fairy-tale image of enchanted woods.

The second stanza demonstrates a notable break in the logic of the poem. A metamorphosis has taken place, and the lips have been turned to stone. As before in response to the 'crystal lips', the reader is not confined to 'seeing' this image in purely visual terms:

> El fuego calcinaba nuestros labios de piedra
> y su ceniza roja cegaba nuestros ojos
> llenos de indiferencia entre cuatro murallas
> amasadas con cráneos y arena de los trópicos.

> [Fire incinerated our lips of stone
> and its red ashes blinded our eyes
> filled with indifference between four huge walls
> kneaded from skulls and sand from the tropics.]

Stone traditionally evokes a cold and sometimes rough stimulus to the touch. But this banal, everyday material is often given a new magical and mystical power within Surrealist art and thought. Searching for unusual stones was one cult activity of the French Surrealist group.[29] This practice was also followed by Hinojosa and the *Litoral* group in Málaga.[30]

The reference to fire in this second stanza offers an archetypal symbol for the burning passion of love. But, like the representation of blood in Planells's collage, as a predictable symbol of life and death, one ready-made meaning metamorphoses into another. Hinojosa's image moves from a symbolic rendering of fire as passion to the alternative, sterilizing meaning of fire in relation to death. This linguistic ready-made is then brought together with another; the cliché 'love is blind'. This cliché is depicted literally before it dissolves into another cliché, 'love hurts', when a visual violence is enacted upon the lovers. Thematically there is confusion between the acts of seeing and blinding in this stanza. The lovers witness the violent act of blinding upon each other whilst simultaneously undergoing the experience of blinding themselves. For the reader, the effect approaches the inversion of subject–object relations in Planells's collage-drawing, expressed through the self-touching finger or the ambiguous response to the phrase 'la definición se impone'.

In Hinojosa's poem, the loss of self during that lived moment of being in love is likened to death, when the lovers' eyes are described as being 'llenos de indiferencia entre cuatro murallas' [filled with indifference between four huge walls]. The reader can understand this image as denoting the ecstasy of their love or the oblivion of death. Whichever way this image is read, metaphorically or literally, an overwhelming feeling of being boxed in, or even imprisoned, is stimulated. There is an air of inescapability by the presence of the four huge walls in this scene, which are constructed out of skulls and sand from the tropics.

However, this image of insurmountability starts to disintegrate in the stanza's final line through the adjective 'amasadas'. At first, a reading of this signifier can link the building of the walls to the amassing of materials. But this same word also juxtaposes itself with the alternative signified to describe the walls as being doughy. Polysemy and clichés are two uses of literary ready-mades which are evident in this verse. A third is the use of intertext. In the background to this whole verse, the reader can discern a Catholic intertext that has a particular significance for Hinojosa's own spiritual torments at this time in his life. In Dante's *Purgatory* (Cantos XXVI–XXVII), the sin of lust is purged by the penitents' being forced to walk through a fire that purifies their lustful desires and keeps a tight rein on their wandering eyes.

The third stanza marks a break in the poem through the inter-jection of a narrator's voice and by moving into an air of reminiscence. The death-knell rung at the end of the second stanza is reinforced by the tone of this stanza. There is a strange dream-like atmosphere of peacefulness and acceptance, devoid of the unrestrained violence that was previously witnessed:

> Aquella fue la última vez que nos encontramos
> llevabas la cabeza de pájaros florida
> y de flores de almendro las sienes recubiertas
> entre lenguas de fuego y voces doloridas.

> [That was the last time that we ever met
> in your head you wore flowering birds
> and almond blossom covered your temples
> amidst tongues of fire and pain-stricken voices.]

There is an implication of departure here, which can be interpreted as the end of the lovers' relationship or their separation caused by death. The sense of loss, already introduced in the poem, continues when the narrator reminisces about the last appearance of the beloved, as if remembering their final good-bye. When this image is read as metaphor, the reader can draw on the obvious symbolism of the cycle of life and death, where the decaying corpse becomes fertilizer for new life from the earth.

A further reading can see the image of the lover's head covered with flowers as an intertextual ready-made taken from one well-known embodiment of literary mad-love: Ophelia. Of the various representations of Ophelia, one particular rendition that was amongst the texts shared around at the meetings in the 'Rotonde' café was a poem by Rimbaud.[31] In Hinojosa's rendition, the head of flowering birds also introduces a Surrealist prototype to the poem, which pre-dates the widespread use of this image in Surrealist circles.[32]

The final line of the third stanza juxtaposes a recognizable biblical ready-made within this Surrealist context. The language used causes the final two lines to overlap and the reader to join the two together through the connecting word 'entre' [amidst]. The biblical intertext of tongues of fire descending upon the disciples is taken to its literal extreme with the 'voces doloridas' [pain-stricken voices]. This depiction, however, remains suspended between the literal and the literary; between physical, oral pain and the wailing voices of grief-stricken mourners. The lack of punctuation in this whole stanza is particularly important for the way that the images are able to dissolve into one another. The reader feels compelled to impose a form of imaginary punctuation upon the stanza to separate out distinct images within the structure. The final line, however, presents clear difficulties to the reader trying to make grammatical sense of the whole. This final line tends to read like a juxtaposed collage-element, one that appears to have been metaphorically stuck on to the end of the stanza.

The collage effect in 'Ya no me besas' is particularly prominent in the fourth stanza. This stanza stands out like one of the dominant collage elements in Planells's collage: the amputated fist or the script with the probing phrase 'la definición se impone'. Once again, a ready-made intertext can be seen here, one taken from another poetic source that was shared by other members of the 'Rotonde' group: the Spanish mystic St John of the Cross.[33] The elements of Sanjuanist thought that are of particular concern here may be traced to St John's poem 'La noche oscura del alma' [The dark night of the soul]—the journeying in the dark without direction and the contrasting stages of water and aridity encountered by the lost souls en route. However, the mystical divine union at the end of the Sanjuanist journey becomes the lived reality of death and nothingness at the end of Hinojosa's use of this imagery:

> El rumbo de los barcos era desconocido
> y el de las caravanas que van por el desierto
> dejando sólo un rastro sobre el agua y la arena
> de mástiles heridos y de huesos sangrientos.
>
> [The route followed by the boats was unknown
> as was that of the caravans in the desert
> and they left only a trace on the water and sand
> of wounded masts and bleeding bones.]

This stanza narrates an alienating journey from the distance of a third-person observer. The reader is brought to 'view' this scene from an aerial perspective, which adds a sense of isolation on this lonely journey. There is a ghostly presence in this verse through the notable absence of any reference to the first or second person. Even the desert camels are only implied but never made explicit. Tension is created through the depiction of violence without any sign of an aggressor. The ships sailing across the seas and the caravans crossing the desert travel as if they were not being steered by anyone. Like death, this is a one-way journey with no way back, for they travel leaving 'sólo un rastro' [only a trace]. The trail that is left upon the waves and the desert sand is an ephemeral one, which will quickly fade away by a process of literal self-destruction. This self-inflicted violence is made explicit in the final line, which returns the reader to the opening images of the ships and caravan of camels on their journey.

The final stanza returns the reader's perspective to the overall collage process at work within this poem. The opening line cannibalizes a ready-made piece of collage from within Hinojosa's own collage. This is a self-referential instance of intratextuality rather than intertextuality:

> Aquella fue la última noche que nuestros labios
> de cristal y de sangre unieron nuestro aliento
> mientras la libertad desplegaba sus alas
> de nuestra nuca herida por el último beso.

> [That was the last ever night that our lips
> of crystal and blood united our breath
> while liberty unfurled her wings
> from the nape of our necks wounded by the last kiss.]

For the reader, a feeling of *déjà vu* is provoked through both the form and the content of this verse, through the repetitive use of language and the imagery evoked. Love and violence, intertwined thematically throughout the whole poem, now reach a climax. The depiction of the lips returns the reader to the image of the passionate, blood-soaked kisses in the opening stanza. Death, either as a literal depiction or as a ready-made euphemism, 'la petite mort', brings the poem to its conclusion in a final image of absolute liberty. The depiction of liberty unfolding her wings holds a classical significance of freedom personified as well as evoking the religious ready-made iconography of angels. The winged being also has a particularly Surrealist importance, one that has become closely associated with Ernst through his self-made mythological *alter ego* 'Loplop'. In 'Ya no me besas', while the figure of liberty unfolds her wings, the lovers unite in their final kiss. This kiss is planted on the nape of the neck, an erogenous zone that, paradoxically, is also the site for the *coup de grace*.

At this point, the reader becomes witness to an uncanny realization that the poet could never have lived to share. Shortly after the publication of *La sangre en libertad*, Hinojosa committed what has been termed—perhaps over-romantically—his 'literary suicide'. Turning his back on Surrealism, he dedicated himself to his love for a real woman. He rejected the revolutionary politics he once held and returned, full-circle, to his right-wing, bourgeois roots. This move would finally cost Hinojosa his life. Some seven years after writing 'Ya no me besas' Hinojosa was to meet his own death, executed by firing squad in Málaga on 22 August 1936, at the outset of the Spanish Civil War. This sense of premonition reveals itself through a reading of this as well as other poems from his ominously-titled last book, *La sangre en libertad*. The cover illustration to this book is a further prediction of the poet's tragic end. The drawing is by the artist-poet José Moreno Villa and depicts four overlapping profiles of Hinojosa, one of which shows the poet blindfolded, as if prepared for execution.

Going back, finally, to the café 'La Rotonde' in Paris and picking up on the dialogue between the poet and the painter, Hinojosa can be seen as enacting the collage process in his approach towards his friendship with Prieto. A process of selection and decontextualization is at work—Hinojosa chooses Prieto as his friend, and then tries to detach the artist from his already established poet-friends, Alberti and Lorca. Hinojosa's demands take the tone of a possessive lover and effectively constitute a violation of the boundaries of their friendship. Prieto's feelings of frustration and surprise with the poet are not only understandable, they are entirely in keeping with the unsettling effect of Surrealist collage.

Prieto was not alone in his irritation with the excitable Hinojosa. Benjamín Palencia, another artist from the 'Rotonde' group who provided the illustrations for a later book of Hinojosa's poetry, *Orillas de la luz* (1928), remarked in a letter to Lorca that 'Hinojosa desde que estuvo en París lo sabe todo y no se puede casi tolerar con las tonterías que hace y dice.' [Since he has been in Paris Hinojosa thinks he knows everything and he has become almost intolerable with all the nonsense that he does and says.][34] For Hinojosa, life in Paris was a lived collage-experience that sparked off an enthusiasm he came to live out through his poetry. However, for many of his contemporaries, this poetic infection with Surrealism was seen as merely literary affectation.

One participant of the 'Rotonde' group who was more sympathetic to Hinojosa's transformation was Buñuel. The same year that Lorca received Palencia's negative comments, Buñuel wrote the following positive comments about their mutual acquaintance: 'Hinojosa publica otro libro, mucho mejor que el primero. Lo ilustra Manolo [Ángeles Ortiz]. Allí tienes un caso. París ha convertido a don José María en otra persona muy diferente. Aquí se ha encontrado consigo mismo.' [Hinojosa is publishing another book, much better than his first one. Manolo Ángeles Ortiz is illustrating it. Now there's a case for you. Paris has converted Mr José María into a very different person. Here he has found himself.][35]

In his observations, Buñuel touches upon one fundamental attribute of Surrealist collage. More than being a purely visual process of assembling juxtaposed images, Surrealism is a lived reality whereby the banal is transformed into the magical by means of dismantling traditional hierarchies. In collage-production, this process involves going beyond artistic boundaries and employing material from everyday reality. In Hinojosa's life, as for many other members of the 'Rotonde' group, Paris was the locus of artistic inter-activity and, like the self-touching finger of Planells's collage, the moment of his self-realization. Looking back on 'Ya no me besas', the lover who is mysteriously present throughout this poem can now be seen in biographical terms as a reference to Hinojosa's own love-affair with Surrealism.

Notes to Chapter 9

1. For an overview of the three stages of the 'Escuela de París', see Gérard Xuriguera, *Pintores españoles de la Escuela de París*, trans. Antonio Urrutia (Madrid: Ibérico Europea, 1974), 9–18. For recollections of the 'Rotonde' group, see Mercedes Guillén, *Conversaciones con los artistas españoles de la Escuela de París* (Madrid: Taurus, 1960); Lluís Permanyer, *Los años difíciles de Miró, Llorens Artigas, Fenosa, Dalí, Clavé, Tàpies* (Barcelona: Lumen, 1975); Luis Buñuel, *Mi último suspiro* (Barcelona: Plaza & Janés, 1982), 79–91.

2. Lucía García de Carpi, *La pintura surrealista española (1924–1936)* (Madrid: Istmo, 1986), 255–6, has classified Prieto as a 'surrealista esporádico'.

3. During his lifetime, Hinojosa published six books of poetry and Surrealist texts. All references to his poetry are to the most recent edition of his *Obra completa (1923–1931)*, ed. Alfonso Sánchez Rodríguez (Seville: Fundación Genesian, 1998).

4. The dialogue between the two men is reproduced in Julio Neira, *José María Hinojosa: Vida y obra*, 2 vols. (PhD diss., Universidad de Extremadura, 1981), i. 79.

5. Hinojosa's sister Isabel remembers that 'José María era muy amigo de los pintores y tenía toda la casa de La Caleta llena de cuadros horribles: con ojos en la frente y cosas así.' Quoted in Alfonso Sánchez Rodríguez, *Una aproximación al 'Caso Hinojosa'* (PhD diss., Estudi General de Lleida, 1990), 47.

6. See Guillén, *Conversaciones*, 9–16, esp. 12; Buñuel, *Mi último suspiro*, 81.

7. Xuriguera, *Pintores españoles*, 68–75 at 72, records that, for Ortiz—who provided the illustrations for Hinojosa's second book, *Poesía de perfil*—'su vida, sin embargo, no es fácil. Hasta 1927 pinta con ardor y vende algunas telas de inspiración cubista, lo que le ayuda a no morir de hambre.'

8. Prieto's sketch of Hinojosa together with his notes regarding their conversation are currently held in the Fundación Gregorio Prieto, Valdepeñas. The drawing is reproduced in Hinojosa, *Obra completa*, 106.

9. For a discussion of Surrealism's interest in Rimbaud, see Gwendolyn M. Bays, 'Rimbaud: Father of Surrealism?', *Yale French Studies* 31 (1964), 45–51.

10. For Hinojosa's impressions of Paris, see his *Epistolario*, ed. Alfonso Sánchez Rodríguez and Julio Neira (Seville: Fundación Genesian, 1997).

11. Julio Neira, *Viajero de soledades* (Seville: Fundación Genesian, 1999), 46.

12. Buñuel, *Mi último suspiro*, 80.

13. Jeffrey Weiss, *The Popular Culture of Modern Art: Picasso, Duchamp and Avant-Gardism* (New Haven and London: Yale University Press, 1994), 29.

14. For further information on Planells, see García de Carpi, *La pintura surrealista española*, 82–93. More recent articles appear in *Revista Blanda* [Blanes], 3–5 (2000–2).

15. García de Carpi, *La pintura surrealista española*, 210, notes that 'Fue Luis Buñuel el que difundió [los] libros de collage [de Ernst] en España'. Some of Ernst's work is reproduced in E. Tériade's article on the Escuela de París, 'La pintura de los jóvenes en París', *La Gaceta Literaria* 24 (15 Dec. 1927), 149.

16. See García de Carpi, *La pintura surrealista esapñola*, 82–3.

17. 'Planells llega al surrealismo de una forma intuitiva. [...] Antes de conocer las obras de Max Ernst ya realizaba collages con grabados.' Ibid., 87.

18. For distinctions between Surrealist collage and *papier collé*, see Martin Jay, *Downcast Eyes: The Denigration of Sight in Twentieth Century Thought* (Berkeley: University of California Press, 1993), 247; Elza Adamowicz, *Surrealist Collage in Text and Image: Dissecting the Exquisite Corpse* (Cambridge: Cambridge University Press, 1998), 4.

19. See ibid., 131–2.

20. The English Surrealist David Gascoyne wrote in 1935: 'The most scandalous thing about surrealist art from the point of view of the reactionary critics is its tendency to do away with the old hierarchies of technical skill, "fine drawing", etc. [...] All that is needed to produce a surrealist picture is an unshackled imagination [...] and a few materials: paper or cardboard, pencil, scissors, paste, and an illustrated magazine, a catalogue or a newspaper. The marvellous is within everyone's reach.' Quoted by David Batchelor, 'From Littérature to La Révolution Surréaliste', Briony Fer, David Batchelor and Paul Wood, *Realism, Rationalism, Surrealism: Art between the Wars* (New Haven and London: Yale University Press, 1993), 47–61 at 61.

21. See Adamowicz, *Surrealist Collage*, 70, 75.

22. See García de Carpi, *La pintura surrealista española*, 46.

23. Ibid., 87.

24. Planells's collage is reproduced in José María Hinojosa, *Poesías completas: Facsímiles (1925–1931)*, introd. Julio Neira (Málaga: Litoral, 1987), 113.

25. Quoted in André Breton, *Manifestoes of Surrealism*, trans. Richard Seaver and Helen R. Lane (Ann Arbor: University of Michigan Press, 1969), 20.

26. For a discussion of the main points of contact and opposition between Reverdy's and Breton's perceptions of the poetic image, see Jacqueline Chénieux-Gendron, *Surrealism*, trans. Vivien Folkenflik (New York: Columbia University Press, 1990), 62–5.

27. Hinojosa originally published 'Ya no me besas' along with 'Campo de prisioneros' and 'Ascensión' under the collective title of 'Fuego granado, granadas de fuego', *Litoral* 8 (1929), 22–5 at 23–4. The poem is re-published in Hinojosa, *Obra completa*, 213.

28. The theory of ocularcentrism is discussed at length by Jay in *Downcast Eyes*.

29. See Sarane Alexandrian, *Surrealist Art* (London: Thames & Hudson, 1993; first pubd 1970), 141–2.

30. See Darío Carmona, 'Anedoctario', *Litoral* 29–30 (1972), n.p. [10].

31. The sculptor 'Fenosa nos ha confesado que había descubierto a Rimbaud, de quien le había impresionado profundamente la lectura de Ophélie.' Permanyer, *Los años difíciles*, 49–71 at 63.

32. At the opening of the International Surrealist Exhibition in London, 1936 (where Salvador Dalí gave a lecture wearing a diving suit) the guests were joined by a 'woman with a head of flowers, whose head was entirely hidden by a bouquet of roses'. See Alexandrian, *Surrealist Art*, 138. The flower-headed woman reappears throughout Dalí's paintings of the 1930s.

33. A literal dedication to St John of the Cross had already been made by Hinojosa in an earlier work, *Orillas de la luz*. Miró, like some of the other members of the 'Rotonde' group, cites St John of the Cross and St Teresa as major influences. See his interview with Rafael Santos Torroella in *Joan Miró, Selected Writings and Interviews*, ed. Margit Rowell (Boston: G. K. Hall, 1986; repr. New York: Da Capo Press, 1992), 226–7 at 227.

34. Letter dated Madrid, 1926, quoted in Sánchez Rodríguez, 'Una aproximación', 35–6.

35. Letter dated 2 Feb. 1926, reproduced in Agustín Sánchez Vidal, *El enigma sin fin* (Barcelona: Planeta, 1988), 155.

CHAPTER 10

The Cid Legend in Opera and Film: A Modern Afterlife for Epic and Ballad

Elizabeth Drayson

In the final scene of Samuel Bronston's epic film *El Cid* (1961), the hero is mortally wounded in battle against the Moorish army on the shore at Valencia. At the point of death, he insists that he must ride into battle with his loyal vassals the following day, and to fulfil his dying wish, his closest followers secretly strap his dead body onto his warhorse, which duly accompanies King Alfonso VI of Castile into the victorious fray, as Muslims scatter in terror at the sight of the seemingly immortal Cid leading his men. While the camera tracks the receding image of the corpse of Rodrigo Díaz mounted on his white horse Bavieca as it gallops along the shoreline, the final words of the narrator describe the Cid as riding 'out of the gates of history into legend'. The problem of the distinction between history and legend is crucial to the exploration of the modern afterlife of El Cid, traditionally Spain's greatest hero, who lived from about 1040 until 1099. The best-known account of his deeds appears in the early-thirteenth-century Castilian epic *Poema de mio Çid*, but stories of his life and exploits have been re-created in many different media and genres, including theatre, visual art, narrative poetry, modern novel, opera, film and even comic strips. This interrogation of two operatic and two film versions of the Cid tradition explores ways in which history and legend are presented in the form of a spectacle that revitalizes and manipulates the oldest stories according to the dictates of artistic medium and contemporary response.

The origins of the Cid legend are complex, for there exists no archetypal story upon which later reworkings are based, but many variant medieval story-lines. If history, in this context, can be understood as the official record or the chronicled facts of the Cid's life, the picture is quite detailed yet impersonal. Unlike many national and epic heroes, the Cid was a real historical figure. It is known roughly when he lived and died, that he was a member of the lesser nobility and came from the village of Vivar near Burgos, and that he worked as a kind of mercenary, fighting both Christian and Moorish sides during the eleventh-century struggles for supremacy. He had two daughters, María and Cristina, and a son Diego, who died in battle. It is also known that Rodrigo was banished from Castile by King Alfonso VI, later capturing Valencia and becoming its governor. By any standards, he was an exceptional man and an extraordinary soldier, revered for his uncanny military skills, legal expertise and powers of negotiation. The most historically accurate version of his life is recorded in the late-eleventh-century Latin work, the *Historia Roderici*.[1]

Yet it was not the official history but the stories, the narratives about the personal details of the Cid's life as an individual human being, that captured people's imagination and begot legends. In his study of the international reception of the Cid, Christoph Rodiek identifies four principal narrative strands, of which that in the *Poema de mio Çid* has attracted most scholarly attention.[2] It portrays the mature Cid as a loyal vassal who rises above banishment and dishonour to regain his king's favour and establish himself as a rich and powerful nobleman through his wisdom and moderation of character. The second narrative strand centres on the poem known as *Mocedades de Rodrigo*, written later than the *Poema de mio Çid*, which recounts stories of Rodrigo's early life, most notably depicting how he kills his future wife Jimena's father in order to avenge his own father's dishonour.

A third story-line relates to the death of King Fernando in 1065 and the subsequent siege of Zamora, where the Cid takes on a more secondary role as royal emissary to beleaguered Zamora and attempts to kill the traitorous knight Vellido Dolfos. This plot strand appears in many of the ballads of the Cid cycle, which also recount episodes from his early years. The fourth important storyline derives from a work commonly called the *Estoria del Çid,* written by a monk at the monastery of San Pedro de Cardeña in the mid thirteenth century, which centres on the hagiographical topos of the incorruptible corpse. This work is not extant, but Russell notes that it was certainly written in connection with the Cardeña cult of the Cid, and is known through its use by Alfonsine chroniclers in chapters 947–62 of the *Primera Cronica general.*[3] In this version, the self-embalmed Cid comes to life on various occasions, and the text also contains the legend of the Cid's corpse riding into battle that forms the climactic ending of Bronston's film.

In the Middle Ages as in later times, the legends of Spain's hero developed for different purposes, which mere historical records could not satisfy. These were variously for religious and political propaganda, as in the Cardeña monk's version and in the ballad cycle, to provide public entertainment, and also for the purpose of exemplarity, as in the epic texts. One of the most striking aspects of the different versions of Rodrigo Díaz's life and times is their powerful performance dimension. Both epic and ballad were performance texts, which exploited the action-filled narratives of war and personal conflict central to the Cid's life. While the *Estoria del Cid* was written in prose and not performed, it nevertheless presented an imaginative drama that lent itself to visual spectacle, as the 1961 film demonstrates. It is no chance that the majority of later re-creations of the Cid legends are in dramatic form, mainly as theatre, opera and later film. There are very few novels on this subject.

As epic and ballad were both sung and performed, they were, in this respect, natural forerunners of opera.[4] However, in what Jeremy Tambling describes as the 'quasi-aristocratic, stylized world of the opera house',[5] opera audiences for a long time remained elitist and therefore totally different from the popular audiences of epic and ballad, though these genres often lent plots and subjects to opera. So it may not be surprising that reformulations of the Cid legends as opera are abundant. At least twenty-six different operas have been written using the theme of the Cid, including works by Handel, Bizet and Debussy. Two of the most important Cid operas of the modern era are *Der Cid* (1865), by the German Peter Cornelius, and *Le Cid* (1885), by the Frenchman Jules Massenet.

The evolution of the Cid theme in these works is affected significantly by the dictates of the musical genre, while still showing creative growth and originality. The degree to which genre or medium defines plot development is significant, and these two versions were moulded by what is often considered as the most elaborate of art forms, in which the presence of music can strengthen, inflect or render words more subtle. Stanley Sadie points out in his history of opera that operatic action tends to move much more slowly than in spoken drama, which often means that source-material has to be severely cut for adaptation.[6] There is also the requirement for set pieces like arias or duets, which may be expanded at the expense of dramatic realism. In addition, Sadie notes the extent to which opera depends upon patrons, impresarios, promoters, commercial opera-houses and stage managers, whose machinery and costumes can also be central attractions to the public. Opera is dependent upon the singers too, since music has to be matched to the voices of the cast. The combination of these factors with the elitist image of the opera-house suggests that the response of the Establishment is a key factor in operatic success or failure.

In nineteenth-century France and Germany the Establishment liked grand opera, and the Cid theme fitted the bill perfectly. Grand opera usually had four or five acts, generally with a historical or quasi-historical background, and European settings from the Middle Ages to the early seventeenth century were favoured. Emphasis lay on colourful scenes and maximum scope for spectacle, and its subject-matter was 'a drama of passionate human relationships impinged upon, often with fatal results, by inexorable forces, usually involving the conflict of two peoples, religions or classes and having some relevance to contemporary conditions.'[7] This nexus of intense relationships between individual characters seemed to demand a historical dimension that was larger than life, again emphasizing the superiority of legend over chronicled history in its ability to engage interest. In an essay on French opera written about 1828, Jouy, an important French librettist, states that the proper concerns of serious opera were 'la fable, la féerie et l'histoire dans ce qu'elle a de plus héroïque'.[8] History had to verge on the fabulous, and grand opera did not seek to analyse historical forces like a historical drama, nor was there the scope to explore the psychology of its characters as in a tragedy. The dramatic conflict derived from the action of historical forces upon individual characters' psychologies, and this is exemplified in Cornelius' and Massenet's versions of the Cid theme.

Peter Cornelius wrote his own libretto for his three-act opera *Der Cid*, researching widely and drawing on Guillén de Castro's Golden-Age play *Las mocedades del Cid*, Corneille's drama *Le Cid* and Johann Herder's ballad-cycle *Der Cid*. It was first performed in Weimar in 1865, but it did not bring Cornelius the popular success he had hoped for, having only two performances in his lifetime. The historical dimension of the battles between Christian Spanish armies and the

Moors is the religious thematic backdrop to the personal story of Chimene's (Jimena's) desire for revenge for the Cid's murder of her father. The historical therefore takes second place to the psychological battle within Chimene herself. Cornelius was strongly influenced by Wagner, and just as Isolde loves Tristan, Chimene loves Rodrigo although he is the object of her vengeance, and she longs for her own death as well as his, because it is the only apparent solution to her conflicting emotions.

While Cornelius has been criticized for the failure of his music to match the dramatic tension of his subject-matter, his libretto seems modern and original in many respects. Rodiek comments that Cornelius moves away from the tendency to imitate Corneille's plot, developing a religious thematic strand.[9] It is striking that Cornelius is one of the few to incorporate material from the *Poema de mio Çid* in his version, rendering Jimena's prayer from the first *cantar* in German. The solution to Chimene's terrible dilemma is resolved through a dream sequence that reveals the repression of sexual love within a Christian context. In the first phase of the dream, Rodrigo, who is a murderer in his private life and a hero in his public one, is transfigured into the Archangel Michael. Cornelius may have been influenced by a similar type of episode in the Cardeña story, where Saint Peter appears to the Cid to announce his impending death. Chimene manages to control her warring passions by succumbing to the desire for death, sacrificing herself in the dream for Rodrigo/Michael.

In the second phase of the dream, Chimene justifies her love for the Cid by sublimating her desires through heavenly enlightenment, leading to forgiveness. Wakened from the dream, she bestows a Christian pardon upon Rodrigo, resolving the conflict in a way compatible with the lives of both protagonists, so that marriage to her father's killer becomes permissible. In his unusual use of Christian thematic elements and legend that have been on the whole avoided in the Cid's modern afterlife, such as Jimena's prayer and the Cardeña miracle, and by revealing psychic conflict through the narration of dream half a century before Freud, Cornelius makes one of the most original contributions to the evolution of the Cid story, and sets the female protagonist firmly on centre stage, rather than the male hero.

Jules Massenet's opera *Le Cid* shares important features with the German work, notably a religious and erotic slant and the foregrounding of the female protagonist. Yet, in contrast with *Der Cid*, Massenet's opera was an enormous success. It had four acts, with a libretto written by d'Ennery, Blau and Gallet that closely follows the plot of Corneille's play *Le Cid,* and it was first performed at the Paris Opera in November 1885. It confirmed Massenet's reputation as a successful opera composer, and the opera had been performed over 150 times by 1919, lapsing from the repertory after that until a notable performance at New York's Carnegie Hall in 1976, with Plácido Domingo as Rodrigo. Apparently such was the reputation of the opera that New Yorkers turned out en masse to hear it. Reviews describe it as a rediscovered masterpiece, and focus on the legendary nature of the Cid's life and its contemporary relevance. The critic from the New York *Post* wrote: 'He came out of history but in literature or in opera, he has become as much legend [...] Whatever the success of *Le Cid* in the past, it is certainly an opera for the present.'[10]

The legend Massenet put to music was once again the story from the *Mocedades de Rodrigo* plot-strand in which Rodrigo kills his intended wife's father to avenge the dishonour of his own father. *Le Cid* was Massenet's last attempt at a grand opera, and the libretto is poignant and powerful, especially in the agonized duets of Rodrigo and Chimène as they struggle with their feelings for each other and the seeming impossibility of reconciliation. In Act 1, scene 1, the rivalry for Rodrigo between Chimène and the Infanta Urraca picks up a theme from the early ballads of the Cid legend, and intensifies Chimène's jealousy and fear as well as Urraca's pain at the burden of being queen and therefore unable to choose whom she marries. Massenet was praised for his brilliant setting of Rodrigo's soliloquies. In Act 2, Scene 1, it is night at the Count's palace in Burgos where Chimène lives. Moonlight and a candle burning beside the Madonna illuminate Rodrigo's soul-searching as he formulates the crux of the drama:

> RODRIGUE (*s'avance lentement*)
>
> Percé jusqu'au fond du Cœur
> D'une atteinte imprévue aussi bien que mortelle,
> Par l'injuste rigueur d'une juste querelle
> Je deviens la victime, en étant le vengeur!
> O Dieu, l'étrange peine!
> Si près de voir l'amour récompensé,
> En cet affront, mon père est l'offensé,
> Et l'offenseur, le père de Chimène!
>
> [RODRIGO (moving forwards slowly)
>
> Pierced to the bottom of my heart

In an unexpected and deadly attack,
By the unjust severity of a just quarrel
I become the victim in being the avenger!
Oh God, what strange torment!
So close to seeing my love rewarded,
In this affront my father is the injured party,
The offender, the father of Chimène!]

Tragic external circumstances have caused his love to be constrained by the dictates of honour, and he is obliged to put the public righting of a wrong against his father before his personal joy in a way that might destroy it forever. Like Cornelius, Corneille and others before, Massenet's reworking of the Cid theme seems to challenge and question the very sources of human loyalty and love. The figure of the distraught and hopeless lover tortured by longing may have had great resonance for opera-goers even in the era of late Romanticism, yet the determined historicizing of these opera plots paradoxically removed them from contemporary concerns, creating a condensed, intense spectacle that offered both escapism and catharsis.

The stories and legends surrounding Rodrigo Díaz logically found further expression in twentieth-century film. Opera and film are considered together infrequently, but comparisons between them are illuminating. The exclusive, elitist, cultic associations of opera give way to a medium that is essentially democratizing, as Tambling remarks.[11] As the two Cid operas show, the genre provides little scope for character development and presents psychological states in a static form that permits few acting opportunities in comparison with film, which more often stresses the importance of narrative and shows character evolution in a detailed context inappropriate to opera. Also, the physical limitations of the opera-house are transcended in film, which benefits from choice of location and the ability to create visual spectacle on a much grander scale. These differences are important in filmic versions of the Cid theme, of which there are at least eight, beginning with the Italian production *Il Cid* in 1910. The best-known is Samuel Bronston's 1961 epic *El Cid*, starring Charlton Heston and Sophia Loren and hailed as 'one of the finest films of the entire epic genre'.[12] A striking comparison can be made with a little-known production that reworks a Cid legend, a film entitled *Las hijas del Cid* in Spanish or *La spada del Cid* in Italian, for it was a joint Spanish/Italian undertaking, made in 1962, just one year after Bronston's epic. It cannot currently be viewed, as it is undergoing conservation work at the Filmoteca in Madrid, but there is some valuable documentation available that is relevant to this discussion.

Las hijas del Cid presents two specific points of interest in terms of the development of the Cid theme in the twentieth century, and it is worthy of mention in any case as a bold European counter-attack on the Hollywood epic machine. The first point concerns the nature of the development of the legend, which bears upon the film's reception. Sadly, it was not a success, although newspaper reports during the shooting were extremely favourable. A year after it was made, in 1963, the *Primer plano* reviewer was enthusiastic: 'La película, rodada en brillantísimo eastmancolor, es una auténtica superproducción en cuanto a medios técnicos y artísticos empleados; pero sobre todo es una producción apasionante.'[13] However, it was not so well received elsewhere. A review in the German *Nachtausgabe* on 24 December 1963 compares it very unfavourably with the Hollywood version, describing it as 'läßt man es hier mit buntblutigen Gemetzel und einer mehr als grobschlächtigen Dramaturgie bewenden' [no more than a bloodbath of slaughter with very crude dramaturgy],[14] while the *Monthly Film Bulletin* review in the same year blames the plot: 'Fine pictorial qualities, soft colour, and an atmosphere of knightly conduct versus villainous skulduggery lift it from utter tedium, but the poverty of the plot is a serious handicap.'[15]

Miguel Iglesias, the director, had espoused a plot-strand that had not been reworked before by introducing the Cid's daughters, who are central to the epic *Poema de mio Çid,* in which they are beaten and left by their evil husbands to die in a lonely wood. This is an episode with enormous dramatic potential, one that turns the spotlight on two female characters, and which forms no part whatsoever of director Anthony Mann's plotting of the 1961 *El Cid.* However, instead of focusing on the two daughters, or upon their dishonoured father, the protagonist of Iglesias's film is Ramón, a young knight and the Cid's champion, who falls in love with María Sol, one of the Cid's daughters (he has three in this version). Heir to the Catalonian throne, Ramón is imprisoned, then rescued and crowned ruler of Catalonia, and is reunited with María. This potentially original manipulation of the Cid legend appears to have failed because of its lack of dramatic power and coherence and probably because of its marginal nature, which had no appeal for international audiences.

The second point of relevance relates to the presentation of history, which contrasts strongly with the historical dimensions of the operatic versions discussed. The invented love-story between Ramón and María Sol is enacted against a background described as portraying 'la más estricta verdad histórica', where ninety per cent of the scenes were claimed to have been shot in real locations.[16] While the two operatic contexts of the Cid legend already described laid no claim to historical authenticity but rather to moments of psychological authenticity, the medium of film seeks to provide 'an opportunity to see the past',[17] which raises the vexed question of exactly what a contemporary audience expects in terms of authenticity when viewing a medieval story.

The desire to create a visual spectacle of what actually happened underpins Anthony Mann's 1961 interpretation of the Cid theme, as it is encapsulated in that final scene of the film, when the Cid rode out of history and into legend. The implication is that what the viewer has seen up to this point has been a portrayal of historical reality, until the hero finally takes on apparently superhuman powers to defeat the Muslim enemy.[18] Great attention was paid to the question of historical authenticity in the making of *El Cid*, and Ramón Menéndez Pidal acted as consultant over matters of historical detail such as costume and methods of combat. The film has a veneer of historical verisimilitude that conforms, as David Williams explains in his essay on medieval movies, to our familiar expectations about what is medieval, while simultaneously presenting a feeling of oddness or strangeness that conveys a sense of the past. This is further illustrated by his point that the composer of the film music, Miklós Rózsa, researched extensively into religious and folk music of the eleventh century, yet what the viewer hears in the film was played by a full symphony orchestra. Beyond this visual and auditory veneer, there is a paucity of historical veracity as regards the creation of the plot. Contrary to the belief of some of the film's fiercest critics, the medieval sources used were not from the *Poema de mio Çid*, for the film reworks the plot strand from the *Mocedades de Rodrigo* used by Cornelius and Massenet, which also appears in certain ballads. The final scene is taken from the *Estoria del Cid* written in Cardeña. As Williams confirms, in this film as in other 'medieval' movies, narrative of real events is rare, with the preference being for legendary and imaginative sources.[19] However, this is not a feature peculiar to film versions alone, as the operatic tradition suggests.

Williams feels viewers should consider such films as modern imaginative responses to the history and literature of the past, and this seems especially apt in the case of the Hollywood *Cid*. A growing number of articles have appeared on this film recently, of which Mark Jancovich's essay on nation, history and representation in *El Cid* is highly relevant, for he interprets the film as expressing a central conflict between tolerance and intolerance, between acceptance of difference and desire to impose conformity and obedience.[20] One example he uses is when Rodrigo finds the Moor Moutamin a far more trustworthy ally than his Christian counterparts. Jancovich reads this central conflict in terms of the Cold War, as demonstrating its discourse while revealing its complexities. His interpretation is detailed and persuasive, though the frequent battle scenes in the epic film seem to undermine the idea that it parallels a conflict that was a war in every way except for actual fighting. Certainly Charlton Heston plays a Cid idealized, romanticized and modernized as never before, in order to appeal to an international audience in a way that *Las hijas del Cid* failed to do. However, the film's historical exactitude owes more to invention and fable than to chronicled records.

The four recreations of the Cid legends discussed here demonstrate a variable equilibrium between the influence of genre and medium on each version, and the ability to manipulate the old stories in a way that is fresh and topical. They exhibit similar purposes to the variant medieval portrayals of the Cid's life, in that they too serve to entertain or to exemplify and as political and religious propaganda. The technical resources of the cinema, which allow historical recreation on a huge scale, also highlight the dilemma inherent in distinguishing between fact and fiction that has characterized the depiction of Rodrigo Díaz since the twelfth and thirteenth centuries. This creative tension between history and legend is a defining aspect of another kind of history, that of the cumulative influences and reinventions of stories about Rodrigo, which effectively illustrate the nature of intertextuality. In the contexts of nineteenth-century Romanticism and nationalism, and twentieth-century Hollywood and Spain, these narratives are presented as spectacles within which the life and times of El Cid have been revitalized in a way relevant to contemporary audiences. The evidence in these cases indicates that what has been remembered and ascribed enduring cultural value is not exact and factual, but imaginative and mythical.

Notes to Chapter 10

1. See Ramón Menéndez Pidal, *La España del Cid*, 2 vols., 2nd edn. (Buenos Aires: Espasa-Calpe Argentina, 1943), ii.

2. See Christoph Rodiek, *La recepción internacional del Cid : Argumento recurrente – contexto – género*, trans. Lourdes Gómez de Olea (Madrid: Gredos, 1995; orig. pubd in German as *Sujet–Kontext–Gattung: Die internationale Cid-Rezeption*, Berlin: Walter de Gruyter, 1990).

3. See Peter Russell, 'San Pedro de Cardeña and the Heroic History of the Cid', *Medium Aevum* 27 (1958), 57–79 at 59.

4. See Susan Sutherland, *Opera* (London: Teach Yourself Books, 1997), 36.

5. Jeremy Tambling, *Opera, Ideology and Film* (Manchester: Manchester University Press, 1987), 13.

6. See Stanley Sadie (ed.), *History of Opera* (The New Grove Handbooks in Music; Basingstoke: Macmillan, 1980), 7.

7. Ibid., 204.

8. Quoted ibid., 204.

9. See Rodiek, *La recepción internacional del Cid*, 305–7.

10. Quoted by Gérard Condé, Commentary to *Le Cid: Opéra en quatre actes et dix tableaux; Livret intégral d'Adolphe d'Ennery, Louis Gallet et Edouard Blau* (Paris: Premières Loges, 1994), 1.

11. See Tambling, *Opera, Ideology and Film*, 3.

12. Gary A. Smith, *Epic Films: Casts, Credits and Commentary on over 250 Historical Spectacle Movies* (Jefferson, NC, and London: McFarland, 1991), 69.

13. *Primer plano* 1172 (1963), 3–4 at 3.

14. Quoted in Rodiek, *Die internationale Cid-Rezeption*, 307 n. 54.

15. *Monthly Film Bulletin* (Oct. 1963), 148.

16. Anon. review of *Las hijas del Cid* (*Primer plano*), 4.

17. David Williams, 'Medieval Movies', *The Yearbook of English Studies* 20 (1990), 1–32 at 3.

18. Intriguingly, the same desire to create authenticity led the author of the *Estoria del Çid* to describe in detail the complicated apparatus of boards, cards and painted cloth used to keep the dead hero upright in his saddle. See Russell, 'San Pedro de Cardeña', 62.

19. See Williams, 'Medieval Movies', 2.

20. See Mark Jancovich, '"The Purest Knight of All": Nation, History, and Representation in *El Cid* (1960)', *Cinema Journal* 40/1 (Fall 2000), 79–103.

❖

Impossible Love and Spanishness

Adventures of Don Juan (Sherman, 1949) and *Don Juan* (Sáenz de Heredia, 1950)

Jo Labanyi

It is well known that *Alba de América*, Juan de Orduña's 1951 patriotic epic produced for Cifesa, was a Spanish riposte to the 1949 Gainsborough production *Christopher Columbus*, directed by David MacDonald, which represented Fernando el Católico as a skirt-chasing idiot and stressed the Catholic Monarchs' ungrateful treatment of Columbus.[1] Another Cifesa 'superproduction', *Don Juan*, made the previous year (1950) by José Luis Sáenz de Heredia, is also a remake that attempts to correct the unacceptable representation of the Spanish monarchy in a recent English-language film: in this case, Vincent Sherman's Warner Brothers production *Adventures of Don Juan*, made in 1948 and released in 1949. Starring Errol Flynn in his last swashbuckling role, this film was shown in Spain under two titles,[2] which suggests that it caused the censors trouble. It was publicized under the title *El burlador de Castilla*: a title that acknowledges Tirso de Molina's original Don Juan play, *El burlador de Sevilla* (to which Sherman's completely free rendition makes no reference), but Castilianizing Tirso's Andalusian hero—the film's Spanish scenes take place at the Madrid court—in a way that undermines the early Francoist stress on Castilian austerity.

The dubbed version screened had the title *El capitán de Castilla*, which not only claims Don Juan for Castile but incorporates him into the State as a member of the military: he is in the film given the job of fencing-master to the cadets at Madrid's military academy, whom he rouses at the end to save Queen Margaret of Austria (wife of King Philip III) from the treacherous minister, the Count de Lorca, who seizes power, placing King and Queen under arrest. However, the title *El capitán de Castilla* (evoking the 1948 film *El capitán de Loyola*, directed by José Díaz Morales, a tedious biopic of St Ignatius of Loyola scripted by José María Pemán) is misleading for a film whose political intrigues are motivated by patriotism in the guise of Don Juan's love for the Queen, who, unlike the King, puts duty to the Spanish people before personal gratification (a duty which momentarily lapses towards the end as she and Don Juan lock in a classic Hollywood screen kiss).

This essay explores the ambivalence of Sáenz de Heredia's film, which attempts to have it both ways: that is, to draw on the pleasures of Hollywood spectacle while paying lip-service to Nationalist values. It ends by relating both films to Luisa Passerini's perception in her book, *Europe in Love, Love in Europe* (1999), that the discourse elaborated in Europe from the Enlightenment onwards on courtly and romantic love is a discourse on Europeanness, which supposes that only Europeans are capable of the emotional refinement enshrined in the traditions of courtly and romantic love. This effectively supposes that Europeanness is defined by a superior capacity for impossible love. The Romantic rereadings of Don Quixote and Don Juan are foundational texts in this modern European process, Zorrilla's redemptive version of the Don Juan story being a key example.

Passerini notes that, until the 1940s, it was common for Europeans to assert that North Americans were incapable of European emotional refinement—but that ironically it was Hollywood that, from the 1940s onwards, became responsible for disseminating the notion of romantic love worldwide.[3] It is arguably this tension between belief in the superiority of European to North-American ways of loving, on the one hand, and seduction by Hollywood's glamorization of romantic love, on the other, that underlies the relationship of Sáenz de Heredia's film to its Hollywood predecessor. This is a larger question than the issue of the film's positioning in relation to early Francoist Nationalist discourse.

Sáenz de Heredia's remake is much more complex in its engagement with its English-language predecessor than Orduña's *Alba de América*, for it attempts to produce a suitably 'Spanish' version of the Don Juan story precisely by co-opting Hollywood modes of representation. The result is a construction of 'Spanishness' that, despite its nods to patriotic and especially Catholic discourse, is far from orthodox. Above all, it is great fun: what little criticism there is on the film reads it as a straightforward exemplification of Nationalist values, failing to spot the ways in which these values are undermined by ironic repartee and a slick performance style.[4] For Sáenz de Heredia is drawing on popular cinematic conventions, which are notoriously ambivalent in their relation to dominant discourses.[5]

Critics of Sáenz de Heredia's films have become fixated on the fact that, as cousin of the founder of the Spanish Fascist Party, José Antonio Primo de Rivera, he was chosen by Franco to direct the horribly pious patriotic epic, *Raza* (1941), scripted by Franco himself under a pseudonym. It must be remembered that Sáenz de Heredia, although he fought for the Nationalists in the Civil War, received his training in film direction under Buñuel's tutelage, making popular comedies for the Republican production company Filmófono; and that, at the same time as he was filming *Raza*, he was writing the lyrics for the music-hall artist Celia Gámez. Although *Don Juan* was released by Cifesa, which by 1950 had come to be associated with the production of big-budget patriotic epics, it was actually (as the credits acknowledge) made by Sáenz de Heredia's own production company Chapalo Films, associated with more lightweight output.

Sáenz de Heredia's contribution to Spanish popular cinema remains undervalued. As an example of popular cinema, the qualities of *Don Juan* are measured in terms of audience pleasure, which necessarily works against the religious discourse of the original Tirso and Zorrilla versions, which Sáenz de Heredia reinstates into his version of the Don Juan story (Sherman's romp not only lacks any religious dimension but its plot owes nothing whatsoever to that of Tirso or Zorrilla).

Sherman's *Adventures of Don Juan* was bound to upset Spanish patriotic sensibilities in its dramatization of Don Juan's affair with a Spanish queen; that it was shown at all in Spain in 1949 is surprising, for Don Juan's courtship of Margaret of Austria occupies too much of the film for the censors to have been able to edit it out completely. Nevertheless, the film's representation of Spanish history is complex. On the one hand, it represents Don Juan as a patriot who saves the Spanish Crown from usurpation by a despotic minister: a frequent theme in Cifesa historical films of the time is the hero—or heroine, more usually—who rallies the people to support the Spanish Crown threatened by enemies. But these enemies were foreign (French or Habsburg); in Sherman's film, the 'good' Queen is a foreign

Habsburg, and the enemy is a Spaniard: the Count de Lorca, whose tyranny includes the use of Inquisition-type torture methods.

In practice, Sherman's Don Juan and Queen Margaret articulate the values of a very American-style concept of democracy through her declaration that the duty of a monarch is to make the people happy (a concept completely alien to Francoist populism, whose Catholic ethos of sacrifice had no place for happiness, not even for the victors), and through Don Juan's respect for the court dwarf, mocked by the King and Lorca and made by the narrative into the hero who saves the day, articulating belief in the rights of the (literal) 'little man'. The film's patriotic plot may thus have fuelled in Spanish spectators political beliefs that were inimical to Francoism, while ostensibly reinforcing patriotism—and claiming Don Juan as the greatest patriot of all. It is worth recalling that, in his 1932 political tract *Genio de España*, the Fascist apologist Ernesto Giménez Caballero had used the figure of Don Juan as an image of the Fascist messiah, who subjects the people to his will by force, through an ardent kiss[6]—it is impossible to read this without a Hollywood screen kiss coming to mind.

On the other hand, the film's treatment of patriotism and of liberal democratic values is undermined by a frivolous, almost postmodern undermining of belief in the notion of history as progress. The film opens by turning the pages of a pseudo-Renaissance illustrated book, to a mock documentary voice-over that appears to endorse a crassly naïve notion of Western historical development: 'In Europe, as the seventeenth century dawned, mankind was lifting itself from ignorance and superstition [...]. New books, new methods were aiding man in his climb towards knowledge and wisdom. In the laboratory, in the arts, in every field of endeavour, man was lifting himself, hand over hand, climbing onward, ever upward.' At this point the camera cuts to the exterior of a Renaissance mansion, as the voice-over continues: 'And, on the outskirts of London, on a summer night, another man was lifting himself, hand over hand, climbing upward, ever onward, toward his objective'—as the camera zooms in on Errol Flynn scaling the balcony, where a glamorous blonde called Catherine avidly envelops him in her arms.

This almost postmodern undermining of the Western belief in historical progress—shown to consist in war and violence, explicitly opposed to Don Juan's preference for love—is matched by Sherman's witty use of historical anachronism. Set at the time of Philip III (d. 1621), its representation of the Count de Lorca inevitably brings to mind the Conde-Duque de Olivares, the hated favourite minister of Philip IV till his fall in 1643. The first time we see Philip III, he is posing on a ridiculous dummy horse for his portrait. The scenario mimics Velázquez's *Las meninas*: we see the painter in the background in front of a large mirror. Velázquez did paint Philip III's portrait (on horseback), but in 1628, seven years after his death, for his patron Philip IV.[7] The film has evidently recreated Velázquez's likeness of Philip III, though emphasizing even more the King's short stature and making him completely ineffectual. The king calls the painter both 'Diego' (Velázquez's first name) and 'Pacheco' (surname of the painter of the reign of Philip III under whom Velázquez served his apprenticeship). There is another nod to Velázquez with the dwarf Sebastián, recalling Philip IV's dwarf Sebastián de Morra, whose presumed portrait by Velázquez is in the Prado.

Sáenz de Heredia's film—which has no historical figures as characters, though we are told at the start that Charles V has granted Don Juan a pardon and that the action takes place in Seville in 1553—plays in a similarly witty way with its intertextual references to Tirso's and Zorrilla's classic Don Juan plays, mixing scenes and characters from both works, but out of sequence, as Luis Miguel Fernández has shown.[8] Fernández fails to pick up the jokes at the expense of Charles V, intepreting them as signs of the film's patriotism. For example, when Don Juan enters the ship's cabin of the English female adventuress who is his sparring partner throughout the film, claiming to be the Emperor, she retorts that she does not believe he is 'ese viejo emperador acaparador de territorios' [that old territory-swallowing emperor] but she knows he's Spanish because of his 'altanería y presunción [...]: basta pisar para conquistar' [arrogance and presumption: one foot on land and conquest's done]—hardly a flattering reference to the imperial mission so much stressed in early Francoist ideology, quite apart from the risqué comparison of Charles V's imperial designs to the amorous designs of Don Juan. One is reminded here of Sherman's parodic prologue, whose leitmotif—'ever onward'—is a fair translation of Charles V's motto 'Plus ultra'.

Despite its intertextual nods to Tirso and Zorrilla and its reintro-duction of Don Juan's salvation through Inés's love, Sáenz de Heredia's version of the Don Juan story is almost as free as its Hollywood predecessor, as the opening disclaimer notes. Like Sherman's *Adventures of Don Juan*, this is an action-packed adventure story in the grand Hollywood tradition: the climax of both films is a spectacular duelling scene set on a monumental staircase, and Antonio Vilar's nonchalant duelling style is evidently modelled on that of Errol Flynn. Vilar—representing this Don Juan who dies instructing his servant to continue to announce him to the courts of Europe as 'Don Juan, español'—was of course Portuguese, and despite being a major star of early Francoist cinema had to be dubbed because of his foreign accent.

The film's female star, billed as such in the opening credits, where her name appears alongside that of Antonio Vilar, is not the Spanish actress who plays Doña Inés (María Rosa Salgado, whose name appears only later) but Annabella, the glamorous French star who plays the English female Don Juan, Lady Ontiveros, who teams up with Don Juan as his accomplice in seduction, outwitting him all the way and engineering his death by betraying him to the law (this is 'perfidious Albion' in a totally seductive guise). This subplot (Sáenz de Heredia co-wrote the script) turns the film into as much of a slick, Hollywood-style romp as Sherman's film. Indeed, moving from Venice to Seville at carnival time, the film's mode is the carnivalesque: in a cameo scene at the masked ball, Manolo Morán acts a cuckolded husband disguised as a Roman centaur, in what could be read as a jibe at the Roman imperial trappings that Spanish Fascism borrowed from Italy.

The sumptuous sets and costumes of Sáenz de Heredia's *Don Juan* are sixteenth-century Spain courtesy of Hollywood (Sherman's film had won an Oscar for its costume design), as is the performance style. In a classic Hollywood scene unparalleled in Spanish cinema of the time, Don Juan converses with Lady Ontiveros as she provocatively soaks herself in the bathtub, naked apart from turban and soapsuds; although Don Juan is speaking to her from behind a curtain, the use of shot/reverse shot allows us to see Annabella in the bathtub as if through Don Juan's desiring gaze. Lady Ontiveros had first en-countered Don Juan when emerging from the bathtub wrapped in towel and turban; this scene winks explicitly at Sherman's film when she asks Don Juan how he knew she was English and he replies, fingering the Hollywood-style négligée lying on a table, that he recognizes it as 'modelo inglés [...] ella se llamaba Catherine' [an English model [...] her name was Catherine]—the name of the English lover Don Juan seduces at the start of Sherman's film.

In fact, all the women in Sáenz de Heredia's film (as in Sherman's) respond with active pleasure to Don Juan's charms, including Doña Inés, played not as a victim but as a young woman who has enjoyed his embrace and wants him to go to heaven so they can be joined for eternity. Don Juan's initial embrace of Inés at the masked ball is the perfect Hollywood kiss, worthy of comparison with that between Don Juan and Queen Margaret in Sherman's film. Interestingly, both kisses are preceded by an unmasking, with Don Juan in Sáenz de Heredia's film lifting his carnival executioner's mask, and in Sherman's film pushing back Queen Margaret's hood. It seems that the kiss between Don Juan and Doña Inés in Sáenz de Heredia's film was not cut by the censorship office, nor indeed has it ever been suggested that the bathtub scene described above produced problems with the censors. (It is worth noting that the video version, released in a democratic Spain where 'anything goes', is still today classified as 'No recomendada para menores de 13 años' [Not recommended for those under 13]). On the contrary, the film received star billing in the press of the time, and was awarded the highest ranking 'De Interés Nacional' [In the National Interest], usually reserved for films with an evident patriotic content.

Why, then, was Sáenz de Heredia's film declared 'in the national interest'? Perhaps not so much because it 'corrected' Sherman's film as because it imitated its extravagant action and use of spectacle and glamour: that is, because it showed that a Spanish director and a Spanish production company could also do what Hollywood did well, and still end with Don Juan's salvation at the moment of death. The soft-focus lighting on Antonio Vilar's face at the moment of death does not mark a change from glamorous to pious mode, but rather reinforces Don Juan's role as object—and not only subject—of the gaze. This is not so much a sanctification as a feminization: something that Miriam Hansen has noted as characteristic of the cinematic representation of Rudolph Valentino and other 'Latin lovers' of the silent cinema. The same could be said of the close-ups in Sherman's film of Errol Flynn, who combines the appeal of the man of action (for example, Douglas Fairbanks who had starred in Korda's 1934 *The Private Life of Don Juan*) with the feminized glamour of the Latin lover.[9]

To conclude, what can the two Don Juan films discussed here tell us about the use of a discourse on romantic love to construct models of 'Europeanness'? In both films, as in most versions of his story, Don Juan's travels in Europe are stressed: he conquers women from various European countries at home and abroad. For he has become incorporated into the modern European imaginary as the incarnation of a superior restlessness that justifies conquest in the name of the pursuit of beauty. Sherman's rendering of the Don Juan story through the lens of Hollywood spectacle and glamour, making Don Juan and Queen Margaret the spokesmen for American democratic principles, allows him simultaneously to consecrate Europe as the historical site of romantic desire and to claim this desire for America. Or perhaps, given the camera's lingering on Errol Flynn's face and body, to represent America not just as subject but also as object of this utopian desire which puts beauty above ethics. Through Errol Flynn's seductive performance, Europe's desire becomes that of, and for, America.

Sáenz de Heredia's film uses similar tactics to achieve the reverse: the reclaiming of Don Juan as a Spanish desire. Sáenz de Heredia's film draws on the Hollywood conventions for the representation of romantic love utilized in Sherman's film, but replaces Sherman's comic ending—which sends Don Juan off in pursuit of yet another woman—with Zorrilla's tragic dénouement, in which Don Juan's desire is finally realized through death. In so doing, Sáenz de Heredia can be seen as complying with the stress on the redemption of sinners in National-Catholic rhetoric. But he can also be seen as rejecting a typically American optimism that refuses tragedy for a European tradition of impossible love, whose equation with death is the mark of its nobility. It is worth noting that, when Don Juan seduces Inés at the masked ball, her fancy-dress costume is that of a medieval lady, inscribing their love in the courtly love tradition—the classic tradition of impossible love—which, as Passerini notes, was constructed under modernity as the source of European civilization.[10]

Sáenz de Heredia's film is, of course, making the point that this European tradition of impossible love has a Spanish prototype in the story of Don Juan. It is crucial that his Don Juan should subject to his desire women from other European countries: Italy and England, not to mention the French star Annabella. It is also crucial that, at the end of the film, Don Juan should not just declare that he is a Spaniard—'Don Juan, español'—but should instruct his servant to proclaim this to the courts of Europe. Given that Don Juan is represented as the prototype of an originally Spanish desire that Europe makes its own, the casting of a Portuguese actor in the role of Don Juan is logical enough. By appropriating Hollywood conventions to tell this story of a Spanish desire which becomes European, Sáenz de Heredia is additionally claiming for Spain ownership of a desire that, thanks to Hollywood, has also become American.

Notes to Chapter 11

1. See Peter Evans, 'Cifesa: Cinema and Authoritarian Aesthetics', *Spanish Cultural Studies: An Introduction*, ed. Helen Graham and Jo Labanyi (Oxford: Oxford University Press, 1995), 215–22 at 217.

2. See Luis Miguel Fernández, *Don Juan en el cine español: Hacia una teoría de la recreación fílmica* (Santiago: Universidade de Santiago de Compostela, 2000), 59.

3. See Luisa Passerini, *Europe in Love, Love in Europe: Imagination and Politics in Britain between the Wars* (London: I. B. Tauris, 1999), 3. Passerini's insights in this book are currently being developed by her collaborative research project 'Europe: Emotions, Identities, Politics', funded by the Kulturwissenschaftliches Institut, Essen, in which I am participating.

4. See Luis Miguel Fernández, 'Don Juan en imágenes: Aproximación a la recreación cinematográfica del personaje', *Don Juan Tenorio en la España del siglo XX: Literatura y cine*, ed. Ana Sofía Bustamante (Madrid: Cátedra, 1998), 503–38 at 525–6; idem, *Don Juan en el cine español*, 173.

5. Fernández, 'Don Juan en imágenes', 527, notes the film's debt to the Hollywood adventure-story genre, but does not consider how this might work against the 'nationalist' values he sees enshrined in the film.

6. Ernesto Giménez Caballero, *Genio de España*, 8th edn. (Barcelona: Planeta, 1983; first pubd 1932).

7. See José López-Rey, *Velasquez* (London: Studio Vista, 1978), 92–3.

8. See Fernández, 'Don Juan en imágenes', 521–2.

9. Miriam Hansen, 'Pleasure, Ambivalence, Identification: Valentino and Female Spectatorship', *Stardom: Industry of Desire*, ed. Christine Gledhill (London: Routledge, 1991), 259–82 at 275, contrasts the 'feminine' appeal of Rudolph Valentino with that of action-movie stars such as Douglas Fairbanks, who she notes lacked social graces, especially towards women.

10. See Passerini, *Europe in Love, Love in Europe*, 2–4, 8–9, 15, 157–8, 188–221.

CHAPTER 12

❖

Why *Giselle*?
Tusquets's Use of the Ballet in
Siete miradas en un mismo paisaje

Abigail Lee Six

Esther Tusquets's *Siete miradas en un mismo paisaje* (1981) deals with seven variations on a certain Sara, during childhood and adolescence. The first in the book is called 'Giselle' and deals with this haute-bourgeoise Catalana's infatuation with a foreign ballerina whom she watches dance the eponymous role in the ballet. Sara starts taking her own ballet classes more seriously, now determined to become a ballerina too, and she also manages to make friends with the dancer and her husband and show them round Barcelona. In spite of these and other down-to-earth developments in the narrative (she goes with the ballerina to buy baby-clothes for her newborn grandchild, for example), the ballerina remains Giselle for her—we never even learn her real name or nationality—and it is to investigate what mystique that represents for Sara that this essay intends to try to clarify.

In order to do so, it will be necessary first to establish what the appeal of this particular ballet of the so-called *ballet blanc* repertoire could be. After all, Tusquets could have avoided specifying a particular ballet or could have chosen to specify a different one. Then, one must ask where the totally different ballet, *Scheherazade*, which plays a minor role in the story, fits in. That will enable us to make some hypotheses about Sara, which can then be tested by reference to some of the other *miradas* in Tusquets's text.[1]

Although *Giselle* might seem at first glance to be the epitome of conventional, romantic ballet, with the female dancers personifying nineteenth-century ideals of femininity (it premiered in 1841 in

Paris), these elements, as we shall see, are constantly undercut and problematized.[2] This is achieved by two different means, one that it has in common with all traditional ballets and another that is specific to *Giselle*. In common with mainstream classical ballets is the fact that the female dancers are given choreography that is designed to make them look delicate and graceful, the attributes of submissive, weak femininity; indeed the definitive centre-piece, the *pas de deux*, can be read as emphasizing this by showing the female dancer literally leaning on and being supported by the male partner. But at the same time, all audiences know that this appearance of fragility and dependency is achieved through hours of strenuous practice and are well aware of how much muscle power and gritty determination the illusion really rests on.[3] It is even possible to read the *pas de deux* as demonstrating the primary importance of the female dancer, relegating the male partner to secondary, supporting status. Indeed, *Giselle* happens to be credited with being the first ballet to give choreography to the male lead that placed him on a par with the starring ballerina; until this point in the history of ballet, it seems to have been taken for granted that he was second to the female lead.[4]

The description of the ballet in Tusquets's text, which expresses Sara's reception of it, articulates exactly these paradoxes, by its alternation between Sara's wonder at the dancer's strength and at her fragility: she is 'erguida con firmeza' [standing straight and strong], but also 'fragilísima' [extremely fragile],[5] for example, and when she falls during a *pas de deux* Sara cannot decide whether to suppose her responsible for the accident or to blame her partner, suggesting the ambivalence mentioned above about the male dancer's support as a dominant or a secondary role (*SM* 11): 'ella tropezó, o acaso la sostuvo mal su torpe príncipe encantador, lo cierto era que cayó' [she tripped, or perhaps her clumsy prince charming supported her wrongly, the fact is she fell over].

Not that any of this necessarily makes ballet an art-form attractive to feminist concerns; one could maintain that a reading that privileges the importance of the ballerina over the male principal dancer only serves to underline the idea of ballet parading women's bodies for the pleasure of the male-positioned, if not necessarily physiologically male, onlooker.[6] Even if one accepts the view that sees in *Giselle* the advent of the noticeable male dancer, this could be read as a development that increased the homoerotic attractions of the spectacle; male dancers, beautiful though they may be, never seem to have acquired matinee-idol status for heterosexual women ballet fans (just as Albrecht, the male lead of *Giselle,* signally fails to attract Sara's attention, let alone her desire). Be that as it may, it is possible to argue that classical, romantic ballet as a whole resides in a contrast between appearances and reality that is of the utmost relevance to gender theory: audiences know that it is the female dancer's strength and physical prowess that enable her to create an illusion of delicacy and fragility (the less accomplished the dancer, the beefier she looks); at the same time, the male lead's heterosexual acting role barely veils his homoerotic appeal. As we have seen, Sara's ambivalent response to *Giselle* seems to be sensitive (albeit unconsciously) to these issues.

The book of the ballet is attributed jointly to Jean Coralli (he had more to do with the choreography than the book, but it was customary to list the choreographer with the authors), Théophile Gautier and Vernoy de Saint-Georges.[7] It has two sharply contrasting acts. The first has a rustic setting and shows Giselle as a young peasant girl who loves to dance, too much so according to her mother, who warns her about the legend of the Wilis (of which more anon). Although she has a local suitor, Hilarion, she is uninterested in him because she is in love with another and he with her. She believes this man to be a peasant like herself, and they have already agreed to marry when, thanks to Hilarion's malevolent intervention, she discovers that in fact he is none other than a count, Albrecht, who is already betrothed to a duke's daughter. This discovery drives Giselle insane, and in that deranged state she commits suicide (in most versions) at the end of the first act.

The second act takes place at Giselle's burial site, a forest glade. Her tomb, marked with a cross bearing her name, is a prominent part of the set. Here is where the authors drew on Heinrich Heine's evocation of a Yugoslav folk-belief that betrothed virgins who die before their wedding day rise vampire-like in the hours of darkness and, led—or perhaps goaded—by their Queen Myrthe, dance men to death before they are forced to return to their graves at dawn.[8] These spectral creatures, traditionally costumed in identical long white tutus, are called Wilis, and the second act of the ballet shows Giselle being initiated into their ranks. In choreography described as 'Bacchanalian'[9] and 'suggesting anonymous promiscuous sex',[10] they collectively dance Hilarion to death. Then comes Albrecht's turn. Here Giselle challenges the authority of the Queen by trying to avoid killing him; although she is in the power of Myrthe, who forces her

to dance with Albrecht, Giselle successfully saves him by warning him
to cling to the cross on her tomb (strong resonances of vampire lore
here),[11] which he partially succeeds in doing, and perhaps also by the
tempo of the dancing, which includes slow passages as well as quick
ones and some spectacular lifts (particularly in the Russian version of
the choreography). At dawn, when the Wilis' power vanishes,
Albrecht is almost but not quite dead and finds the energy (in the
original version) to lay Giselle lovingly on a bed of flowers before
collapsing with exhaustion (other, more modern versions have her
simply sinking back into her grave).[12]

As even this brief summary demonstrates, *Giselle* is a ballet about
matriarchy at least as much as patriarchy. In the first act Giselle defies
her mother's authority only (no father or elder brother appears in the
cast-list), and in the second she is subjugated—albeit unsuccessfully—
by another woman, Myrthe, the Queen of the Wilis. The only
obvious gesture in the direction of patriarchy is in Act I, when the
noblewoman to whom Albrecht is betrothed asks her father's
permission to give Giselle a necklace. The hierarchy that is most
strongly stressed alongside the matriarchal, is a class- rather than
gender-based social structure.[13] When a noble hunting-party passes
through Giselle's village, the locals humbly accede to the request of its
members to provide them with refreshments and show suitable
servility towards them. When Giselle learns that her lover is in fact a
count, it is as much his higher social status as the fact that he is
betrothed to another that is presented as leading to her despair,
madness and finally suicide.

Thus, the question we must ask ourselves is this: has Tusquets's Sara
fallen in love with the pretty costumes and other accoutrements of
femininity at its most traditional or have the more sophisticated and
disquieting implications of the ballet captivated her—albeit
unconsciously—in all their paradoxicality? Here is where recourse to
the other stories of *Siete miradas* may help us. Certainly, the class issue
preoccupies the haute-bourgeoise Sara not only here but also elsewhere
in Tusquets's text.[14] In 'Giselle', she realizes that to become a ballerina
herself will be socially transgressive (rather than merely technically
demanding), using the vivid image of the footlights separating audience
and dancers for the class divide between them (*SM* 10):

Lo que habían sido hasta entonces las clases de danza de una muchachita
burguesa que completaban en cierto modo su cultura general [...] iban a
servir para algo muy distinto, iban a convertirse en el primer paso de aquella

radical transgresión que la situaría más allá de la línea divisoria de las candilejas, definitivamente al otro lado.

[what had been until then the dancing classes of a nice middle-class girl, which in a sense completed her general good breeding, were going to serve a very different purpose, were going to turn into the first step of that radical transgression that would place her beyond the dividing line of the footlights, definitively on the other side.]

In 'La casa oscura' she is troubled by the class difference between herself, her family and social circle on the one hand, and Ricardo, the poor boy that her family take on holiday with them on the other; after a brief period when he seems to have integrated with Sara's social milieu,

Ricardo [...] volvía a ser un muchacho pobre y feo y sin modales, al que se decía, eso sí, Dios sabía por qué, que llegaría a cualquier parte, y estaba allí como de prestado y fuera de lugar [...] y comentaría [...] mademoiselle lo tonto que había sido por parte del muchacho [...] no discernir sus límites y no saber mantenerse en su lugar.

[Ricardo was once more becoming a poor, ugly boy with no manners, of whom, granted, people did say, Heaven knew why, that he would go far, and he was there as if on loan and out of place; and Mademoiselle would comment on the silliness of the boy not to recognize his limitations and know his place.] (*SM* 232–3)

At an even younger age, she is traumatized in 'Orquesta de verano' by her family's refusal to grant admittance to her birthday party to a lower-class child (daughter of the hotel pianist) (*SM* 248–9). But most striking of all in this regard is the story entitled 'He besado tu boca, Yokanaán', in which she has a craze, not now on ballet but on acting, and falls in love with Ernesto, a working-class man whom she has met at her drama classes.

This affair across the class barrier echoes and in some senses provides a mirror image of the theme of *Giselle* (the ballet). There it was a peasant girl who fell in love with a nobleman. In Tusquets's story it is the girl who is from the higher class. In the supposedly unrealistic ballet, both Giselle and Albrecht recognize that their relationship is doomed, Giselle being slower to realize this only because he has tricked her into thinking he is a peasant like her. Their love can only be consummated in the spiritual domain in which the second act takes place. Sara also proposes a fairy-tale resolution to Ernesto—running away together to Italy to live happily ever after. Ernesto, who may seem more realistic because he rejects this idea and talks about needing to stay in Barcelona to further his career, is in fact revealed to be the one living in Cloud-cuckoo-land, because he entertains the possibility of Sara's family accepting him (*SM* 187–9): the equivalent of Giselle hoping—which she never does—that Albrecht would marry her even after she has discovered he is a count.

In other words, Sara, like the characters in *Giselle*, knows that love across the class divide can only be fulfilled if a fairy-tale denouement can be achieved: eloping to a distant utopia *para no volver* [*never to return*], to borrow the title Tusquets borrowed for her later novel from Darío and his love of fairy-tale resonances. In one sense, we could almost argue that the Sara in 'He besado tu boca' is as paradoxical as Giselle and in analogous ways: both understand the social status quo cannot be changed or disregarded and in that sense are conformists rather than rebels; and yet they seek a highly dramatic and socially transgressive way round this: suicide in Giselle's case followed by rebellious behaviour when she joins the new supernatural social hierarchy of the Wilis, elopement in Sara's plan (unrealized) and/or a stage career (abandoned). In one sense, then, we can understand Sara's admiration for Giselle as being for someone in a similar predicament who responds to it in a similar way, but the key difference is of course that whilst Giselle manages to prevail over her fate in some sense, thanks to a helpful dose of legend and fantasy, the prosaic limitations of real life defeat Sara.

Furthermore, Giselle remains pale, delicate and beautiful in the most conventional pattern of ideals of feminine beauty, yet her reward of spiritual consummation of her love rests upon her courageous challenge of two social systems: defying the prohibition to dance and to commit suicide on earth, and then beyond the grave, defying the authority of Queen Myrthe and the *raison d'être* of the whole community of Wilis beyond the grave.

For Sara, then, Giselle, the conformist yet defiant peasant and the subjugated yet rebel ghost, symbolizes the attractions of having one's cake and eating it: both physically and emotionally strong, yet ethereal and delicate; rising above the base qualities of revenge and vindictiveness associated with the negative images of femininity, she is rewarded by love fulfilled and ends in perfect eternal repose on a bed of flowers. For an adolescent girl from the haute bourgeoisie, troubled in equal measure by the classic concern of her age-group—finding true love—and her class—coming to terms with social privilege—it is, ironically, that most elitist of entertainments, the classical ballet, that provides her with the intoxicating possibility that she can have it all.

Interestingly, however, when Sara dances for 'Giselle' and her husband, she does not choose to attempt a passage from the eponymous ballet, but instead dances an extract from a very different work, the twentieth-century *Scheherazade,* with music by Rimsky-Korsakov and choreography by Fokine. Apart from the coincidence of the female lead's suicide in this ballet, the plot, style and atmosphere of it are entirely different from that of *Giselle.* Set in an Arabian harem, it portrays the infidelity of the King's concubines as they indulge in an orgy with his slaves as soon as he is out of the way. Instead of the sex being implicit and symbolic as Giselle and Albrecht dance together in Act II, we have undisguised sexual appetite from the women. But although so different in this way, *Scheherazade* does not lack its own paradoxical qualities. For example, the supremely patriarchal set-up of the harem is undercut by the matriarchal structure of the central scenes of the ballet, since the king is away and the concubines are in command over the male slaves who partner them for the orgy. The licentious and disloyal behaviour of the women, which could be read as giving a strongly negative, even mysogynistic image, is subverted by the devious and dog-in-the-manger behaviour of the king's brother and above all, by the terrible bloodshed at the end of the ballet, when, having discovered the concubines' treachery, the king and his brother kill all the slaves and the concubines barring the leading ballerina, who (as observed above) takes her own life.

As 'Giselle' points out to Sara, this is an erotic and sensual ballet, since, albeit rather naively, it expresses 'the Western myth about the languorous and voluptuous East'.[15] Even though Sara seems to have given an accomplished performance, 'Giselle' astonishes her by demonstrating how to give it a stronger erotic charge. This astonishment derives from the fact that Sara has type-cast her as the virginal Giselle character and is psychologically unprepared for her versatility as a dancer (*SM* 28–9): 'la tímida muchachita campesina enamorada primero y burlada luego por su príncipe encantador [...] era ahora una mujer en la fulgurante plenitud de su sexualidad y su belleza, una bacante que estallaba de lujuria y goce' [the shy little country girl in love at first and then jilted by her prince charming [...] was now a woman in the dazzling fullness of her sexuality and beauty, a Bacchante bursting with lust and pleasure].

This blatantly erotic ballet scene leads into the startling denouement of Tusquets's story, when the dancer's husband 'comforts' Sara
sexually for her sense of failure as a dancer and of despair at the immi-
nent departure of 'Giselle'. Although in one sense this is despicable
behaviour on his part for taking advantage of a vulnerable and naïve
young woman behind his wife's back, and although in another Sara
could be criticized for not putting up a fight and rebuffing him out of
loyalty towards the ballerina as well as general moral rectitude
(carrying on with a married man), the episode is not presented in this
way; one would most definitely be reading against the grain to
interpret it thus, since Sara explicitly considers these points, only to
find them inapplicable (*SM* 31):

Sara sabía que hubiera debido sentirse por fuerza asustada y ofendida,
escandalizada por el hombre y por sí misma y sobre todo por aquella Giselle
a la que estaban ambos [...] traicionando [...] pero [...] la fue invadiendo a
oleadas un extraño calor, un profundo bienestar. [...] Descubrió que le
gustaba demasiado [...] para poder creerse ante nadie culpable.

[Sara knew that she ought to have felt unavoidably frightened and offended,
scandalized by the man and by herself and above all because of the Giselle
whom they were both betraying, but a strange warmth, a profound sense of
well-being were coming over her in waves. She realized that she liked it too
much to be able to believe herself guilty before anyone.]

In fact, Tusquets makes it appear a positive development, which
somehow consummates Sara's love for the ballerina she thinks of as
'Giselle' (*SM* 32): 'advertía oscuramente que lo ocurrido aquí estaba de
modo confuso pero cierto relacionado con su amor por la bailarina'
[she was darkly aware that what had happened here was in a confused
but genuine way connected with her love for the ballerina].

If orgasm is the *petite mort*, there is an aesthetically satisfying echo
here of the ballets featured in Tusquets's text. From *Scheherazade* there
is the overtly sexual, promiscuous ambience, but the romantic ballet
Giselle provides the backbone of the whole plot and characterization
of the protagonist. Like Giselle, Sara falls in love with what she cannot
have: in her case a career in ballet that is virtually inaccessible to
someone of her age, class and background. This realization drives her
into a kind of madness, whereby she becomes infatuated with the idea
and the woman she sees as personifying it. The madness culminates in
a socially transgressive act—not suicide in Sara's case, but just *petite
mort* with a married man—which, however, simultaneously provides

her with some satisfaction of having achieved on a spiritual plane what was not possible in physical terms: a sense of consummation of her love for the ballet and the ballerina who incarnates it for her. Now she too can rest on a flowery bed (*SM* 29: 'un diván tapizado de satén negro con flores rojas' [a couch upholstered in black satin with red flowers] in a dressing-room, rather than Giselle's graveyard bed of flowers) in post-ecstatic repose.

Considered from a feminist viewpoint, this seemingly undemanding *ballet blanc* can be quite interestingly problematic. More importantly, Esther Tusquets's choice of *Giselle* as the intertext of her story thus entitled and as one ingredient of the seven that make up the whole of *Siete miradas en un mismo paisaje* provides much valuable information about Sara as well as an aesthetically elegant scaffolding around which to structure it.

Notes to Chapter 12

1. This essay treats the Saras in the text, who arguably are neither seven separate individuals nor a single character, as variations on a theme, so that findings coming out of one story can shed light on the characterization in another. See Abigail Lee Six, 'Protean Prose: Fluidity of Character and Genre in Esther Tusquets's *Siete miradas en un mismo paisaje*', *Changing Times in Hispanic Culture*, ed. Derek Harris (Aberdeen: Centre for the Study of the Hispanic Avant-Garde, University of Aberdeen, 1996), 177–86; Nina L. Molinaro, *Foucault, Feminism, and Power: Reading Esther Tusquets* (London and Toronto: Associated University Presses, 1991), 70–3.

2. Although Sally Banes, *Dancing Women: Female Bodies on Stage* (London and New York: Routledge, 1998), 3, rightly cautions against anachronistic readings of ballets, which should in fact be considered in the light of their historical and sociopolitical context, in order to study Tusquets's use of the ballet it will be necessary to take into account a different framework, namely its function in the text and in particular its function within the development of Sara's character. This essay will not, therefore, dwell on its reception and status in the nineteenth century, but limit itself to a study of what it appears to mean to Sara.

3. See ibid., 9.

4. See George Hall, *The Story of the Ballet 'Giselle'* (London: Ballet Books, 1961), 3, 8–9. Interestingly, Sandy Posner, *Giselle: The Story of the Ballet* (Leicester: Newman Wolsey, 1945), 23, who was no doubt comparing *Giselle* with a different range of predecessors, expressed an opposite view, asserting that *Giselle* 'enabled the ballerina to claim an equal share of the limelight and applause with her male partner who had hitherto gained the laurels by virtue of his superior physique'. More important than this disagreement is the consensus that male and female leads are equal in status in this ballet, a point also made by Arnold L. Haskell, *Ballet, a Complete Guide to Appreciation: History, Aesthetics, Ballets, Dancers* (Harmondsworth: Penguin, 1951), 139.

5. Esther Tusquets, *Siete miradas en un mimo paisaje* (Barcelona: Lumen, 1981), 9, 10; abbreviated to *SM* in text.

6. See E. Ann Kaplan, 'Is the Gaze Male?', *Desire: The Politics of Sexuality*, ed. Ann Snitow, Christine Stansell and Sharon Thompson (London: Virago, 1984), 321–8; Laura Mulvey, *Visual and Other Pleasures* (Basingstoke: Macmillan, 1989).

7. See Hall, *The Story of the Ballet 'Giselle'*, 3.

8. See Posner, *Giselle: The Story of the Ballet*, 27–8, for a fuller account of the legend. George Borodin, *This Thing Called Ballet* (London: Macdonald, 1945), 75, attributes the legend to Russia and refers to girls dying on—rather than before—their wedding day.

9. Hall, *The Story of the Ballet 'Giselle'*, 19.

10. Banes, *Dancing Women*, 28.

11. Ibid., 27, 29, expands on the resemblances with vampirism, noting that the Wilis are 'entrancing in the same way vampires are, for they evince a combination of attraction, especially sexual magnetism, and repulsion'. She goes on to point out that this is 'a variation with feminist significance on the vampire legend, where usually men prey on women'.

12. See ibid., 28 for more detail on the different endings. Walter Terry, *Ballet Guide: Background, Listings, Credits, and Descriptions of More than Five Hundred of the World's Major Ballets* (Newton Abbot and London: David & Charles, 1976), 165, also acknowledges the considerable degree of variation in the endings.

13. See Banes, *Dancing Women*, 16. Banes reads this preoccupation with class in the ballet as an example of how it embodies the concerns of its time, the 'bourgeois monarchy' of Louis-Philippe (ibid., 23).

14. For more on this, see Molinaro, *Foucault, Feminism, and Power*, 83–5.

15. Fernau Hall, *An Anatomy of Ballet* (London: Andrew Melrose, 1953), 279.

CHAPTER 13

Los dominios del lobo by Javier Marías: Hollywood and Anticasticismo Novísimo

Alexis Grohmann

'La familia Taeger, compuesta por tres hijos —Milton, Edward, Arthur—, una hija —Elaine—, el abuelo Rudolph, la tía Mansfield y el señor y la señora Taeger, empezó a derrumbarse en 1922, cuando vivía en Pittsburgh, Pennsylvania.' [The Taeger family, made up of three sons, Milton, Edward, Arthur, a daughter Elaine, Grandfather Rudolph, Aunt Mansfield and Mr and Mrs Taeger, began to collapse in 1922, while living in Pittsburgh, Pennsylvania.][1] So begins *Los dominios del lobo*, the first novel of the Spanish writer Javier Marías. It was written at the age of 17 and first published in 1971. The action of the novel, divided into eleven loosely interrelated episodes, consists of a series of stories and adventures that span the entire United States of America, from the East Coast (New York) to the West Coast (San Francisco, Los Angeles), from the far north (Minnesota) through the Midwest (Chicago) to the Deep South (Louisiana, Mississippi and Alabama). It is, it seems, the first ever 'foreign' Spanish novel, that is to say, one not set in Spain and not peopled by any Spanish characters (they are all American). This essay will attempt to shed some light on this radical 'non-Spanishness' in relation to collective literary phenomena of the early 1970s.[2]

Los dominios bears witness to a youthful fascination with adventures.[3] This explains in part why the instances of relative violence and cruelty of the action have playful and comic rather than serious effects. The author does not attempt to moralize, nor does he wish to impose a view or a 'message' on the reader.[4] The third-person semi-omniscient narrative is recounted from the point of view of the protagonists of the casually interrelated episodes that make up the narrative; it is replete with dialogue and devoid of any authorial commentary, thus avoiding any explicit authorial assessment of the action other than the characters's own. The reader is invited on a journey into another world, a 'jungla urbana que le permite al lector español no sentirse involucrado en ninguna situación concreta y gozar de un desarraigo ilusorio y aventurero' [urban jungle, which allows the Spanish reader not to feel implicated in any concrete situation and to take pleasure in an illusory and adventurous uprooting].[5]

However, this narrative of adventures also bespeaks an awareness of their fictional nature, as it accommodates an implicit metacommentary about the adventure of story-telling. *Los dominios* is a novel essentially imitating Hollywood films and film genres of the 1930s, '40s and '50s: the action-packed story-lines—involving playful, witty, and entertaining tales of gangsters and gangster warfare and rivalry, prisoners, hidden treasures, murder, blackmail, racketeering, corruption, double-crossing, friendship, love, sex and greed—are imitative of film comedies, melodramas and especially gangster movies and *films noirs* of those three decades. The USA which he set out to write about was, as he explains in the preface to the 1987 edition of the novel, not the 'real' one: in the tradition of imitative writing, it was a 'mediated' America, the America represented in 1930s, '40s and '50s Hollywood cinema. For that purpose, he went to Paris in June 1969 for a month and a half, because he was aware that there Henri Langlois's famous *Cinémathèque française* and a number of other cinemas or studios were dedicated to screening constantly what was to become his 'hypotext', American films of that era. Thus, Marías's literary flight from Spain was accompanied by a literal one. Paris was probably unique in the world at that time, since there, as was the case with the *nouvelle vague* filmmakers, one could be exposed to such films to that degree. Paradoxically, Marías's subject matter, his America, was most 'real' and alive in Paris, France, where he would develop what Genette calls the partial mastery required to imitate a text with the characteristics that have been chosen for imitation, in this case cinematic narratives.[6] Thus, the tale of the collapse of the Taeger family of Pittsburgh in episode 1, and the life of crime to which most of its members succumb, contains echoes of the unstable families in melodramas such as *The Magnificent Ambersons* (1942), *Cat on a Hot Tin Roof* (1942), *Written on the Wind* (1956), or the life of crime of family members or partners in gangster films like *The Brothers Rico* (1957) or *The Bonnie Parker Story* (1958), or even Hitchcock's

Shadow of a Doubt (1943), although the tone of Marías's narrative is lighter and mostly comical.

Episodes 2, 5, 9 and 10, the stories revolving around Osgood Perkins, his crime and time in prison and a hidden treasure, echo adventure films such as *The Treasure of the Sierra Madre* (1948) and *Rope of Sand* (1949), as well as the comedy *The Big Steal* (1949) and the melodrama *The Hustler* (1961). Episode 11, the melodramatic story of private investigator Andy Robbins and his attempt to save the sweetheart of the gangster Milt Taeger, imitates gangster films and murder mysteries such as Otto Preminger's elegant *Laura* (1944). Episode 4, which recounts Milt Taeger's arrival in Chicago in 1934, when he kills the second-in-command of one of the two rival gangsters vying for supremacy in the city during Prohibition, and episode 10, set in New York in 1936, where his eventual rise to gangster fame is confirmed, is a pastiche of gangster movies about public enemies of the Prohibition and Depression eras, such as *Little Caesar* (1930), *The Public Enemy* (1931), *Scarface* (1932), *White Heat* (1949) or *Baby Face Nelson* (1957).

White Heat (1949) is a gangster film that is also considered to be a prototypical *film noir*, and *Los dominios* also bears the marks of this other postwar American genre. So, for example, some of the women, such as Virginia Wainscott (episode 7) or Susan Bedford (episodes 6–7), are typical *femmes fatales*, cunning and sensuous women who seduce men for their own selfish ends, often leading them to distress or bringing about their downfall. The *femme fatale* was very prevalent in *films noirs* of the 1930s and '40s, which were pervaded by a mood of darkness, cynicism and often despair. Indeed, this dark atmosphere, the moral chaos and the corruption of all human values, is the main characteristic of *film noir*[7] and is also, albeit in a more playful and parodic tone, reflected in Marías's first novel, which is populated not only by *femmes fatales* but also by other *film noir* antiheroes, such as the down-at-the-heel private eye (Mike Robbins, episode 11), the ruthless blackmailer (Terence Barr, episode 3), the con-man (Wes McMullan, episode 7) and the racketeer and gangster (Milt Taeger, episodes 4 and 10).

The slightly 'dark' episode 7 in particular, with its tale of corruption, murder, false incrimination and duplicity perpetrated by an unfaithful wife and her lover, an ex-convict who joins the rural household as a handyman, with a view to appropriating the husband's fortune, is a very explicit and ironic imitation of two archetypal *films noirs*:

Double Indemnity (1944), in which an insurance agent connives with the glamorous wife of a client to kill her husband and collect, and, more especially, *The Postman Always Rings Twice* (1946), which tells the story of a guilty couple—the lover is a handyman—who murder the husband but get their 'come-uppance'. Indeed, like episode 7, most of the other episodes present us with characters who are most often villainous heroes or antiheroes, but who are nevertheless relatively likeable and with whom the reader is not discouraged to identify, introducing a moral ambiguity and chaos popularized by *film noir*.

The atmosphere of the novel as a whole also recalls other *films noirs* such as *The Big Sleep* (1946) or the suspenseful *Gaslight* (1944), as well as the melodramas *Rage in Heaven* (1941) or *This Gun for Hire* (1941). In fact, episode 3 contains an explicit intertextual reference to the embodiment of the cinematic gangster, James Cagney. When the composer Terence Barr, who has undertaken to blackmail his employer, is asked by the latter how much money he wants, his reaction is described as follows (*DL* 61): 'A Barr le encantó aquella pregunta. Se sentía importante y jamescagney. Intentó poner cara de duro y contestó secamente.' [Barr really liked that question. He felt important and James-Cagney-like. He tried putting on a tough guy's face and gave a brusque reply.] The adjective 'jamescagney' is a neologism and encapsulates the parodic and playful nature of the novel: Barr, evidently self-conscious about the acting he is doing in his newly-adopted role as blackmailer, emulates the archetypal tough guy and is described by way of a mediatory, cinematic and artificial adjective that draws attention to the intertextual or hypertextual nature of the text.

Marías's novel is thus an imitative recreation of such Hollywood narratives through a rewriting of these post-war genres, with which it enters into a 'dialogic' relationship.[8] The imitation is the result of identifying and generalizing the idiolect of these cinematic genres, borrowing their stylistic and thematic, that is their generic, language or code, which Genette explains is the reason why one can only speak of indirect, stylistic imitation.[9] The idiolect of those films becomes the somewhat indiscriminate matrix of imitation. Fiction is thus shown to be the result of an intertextual synthesis of texts. This highlights the text's literariness, the fact that it is a formal artifice, which Hutcheon has argued is one of the effects of imitative writing.[10] The other way for a text to point to its literariness is through precisely such meta-fictional elements as *mise-en-abîme*, and of this there are two concrete instances in *Los dominios*. Episode 7 of the novel, as is revealed in its last paragraph, suddenly turns out to be a film whose stars are the Hollywood actors who are the main characters of episodes 6 and 8. The reader is surprised and forced to recognize that the text read up to that point was not what it appeared to be. The story—episode 7— within the main narrative has suddenly become a film within the story about the two screen actors of the previous and subsequent episodes. This is taken even further in the last sentence of the narrative, when the entire novel is shown to have been a film.

Consequently, this final sentence introduces a new frame around the whole novel and an added distance between reader and text, making the reader very aware of the artificial nature of the fiction, as well as pointing to the hypotextual form—cinema—the novel reproduces. Episode 7 is a film framed by a narrative, which also turns out to be a film, which, in turn, is also a novel (*Los dominios*), in its turn imitating American films. (This chain of imitative writings could, of course, be extended to show that many of the films imitated are themselves reworkings of other texts, such as *Double Indemnity*, based on a script by the novelist Raymond Chandler that re-works James M. Cain's novel, written in the mode of the hard-boiled detective fiction pioneered by Dashiell Hammett and Chandler himself, and so on). The result of imitative writing is that 'narrative is presented as only narrative, as its own reality—that is, as artifice'.[11]

However, these features of Marías's first novel (his second one also shares all these elements, except that the hypotext imitated is not cinema but (British) Edwardian literature) are not really original. But, in the context of Spanish fiction written under Franco and in the late 1960s and early 1970s in particular, they are strikingly singular and significant. Present *en masse* in a novel, such elements will become commonplace in Spanish literature of the 1980s, but Marías's first two narratives stand in very stark contrast to other novels produced under Franco. Why is this the case?

To understand this, we ought perhaps to remind ourselves of the fact that, as is generally recognized, the dominant literary mode characterizing the majority of novels written under Franco and especially in the 1940s, '50s and early '60s is a realism that takes different forms.[12] Nora Catelli calls this an instance of 'la difícil, prolongada y fatídica relación de la narrativa española con el realismo' [Spanish fiction's difficult, prolonged and fateful relationship with realism].[13] Equally, it is worth highlighting that many novels were generally dominated by a tone of seriousness and a general lack of humour,[14] on which the opposition to Franco insisted, as the regime itself was promoting escapism and consumerist fun.[15] These writers could hence be described as *agelasts*, humourless or 'laughterless'.[16] Any novel that could be deemed to promote laughter or escapism was liable to be accused of promoting the regime's interests. In part, this explains why the range of genres was fairly restricted.[17] Furthermore, it is important to stress the fact that during this time most Spanish novels were firmly and more or less exclusively rooted in Spanish reality. Their realism, their attempts mimetically to reflect Spanish reality, their treatment of Spain as a problem and theme, meant that the novel became inextricably linked with Spain and notions of Spanishness, leaving itself open to the charge of parochialism and provincialism.[18]

Marías's first novel, as well as his second one, constitutes a rejection of the above and, as he has outlined more than once (not least in an essay entitled 'Desde una novela no necesariamente castiza'),[19] an attempt to break with Spanish literary tradition, Spain as theme, and more generally any form of Spanishness and *casticismo* (the quality of pure, traditional, essentialist Spanishness), because of what he and others perceived as a singularly unattractive realism dominating literature and a lack of interest in Spain as a theme. There were also extraliterary reasons for this break. First, Marías and many of his contemporaries felt that many of their elders were, politically and ideologically, profoundly unsympathetic and immoral figures (with Cela probably being the prime example). Secondly, having all been born after the end of the Civil War, not only had Marías and his contemporaries had no direct contact with a war that had stigmatized previous generations of writers and their work, but they had also not known a Spain other than Franco's. The dictatorial regime, in its efforts to construct a unity and supremacy of Spanish national identity, attempted to undertake an *españolización* based on patriotism and to instil a love for Spain informed by a grotesque triumphalism; 'to unify the nation by projecting difference outside its borders, or confining it to internal exclusion zones, in the form of otherness: *la anti-España* necessarily equated with foreign influence'.[20] This led Marías and other contemporary writers to the perhaps reductive yet under-standable equation of Spain and Spanishness with Francoism, so that the rebellion against Franco entailed an indissociable repudiation of Spain and of Spanishness and *casticismo* through a turn to the *anti-España*, its opposite other in the form of foreignness.

This is also why Marías and many of his contemporaries rejected realism and mimetic writing and opted for anti-realist and anti-mimetic forms, namely because realism and mimesis did not offer an escape from Spanishness. Realist writing under Franco remained closely associated with Spanishness and, by this circuitous route, Francoism. Indeed, these elements were seen as part of an interrelated web: Spain, Francoism, nation, patriotism, essentialism, Spanishness, *casticismo*, realism, mimesis and even *costumbrismo* (a Spanish prose form that emerged in the first part of the nineteenth century, characterized by detailed depictions of local customs and manners) formed the net from which they wanted to escape.[21] Furthermore, by breaking with tradition, Marías and his contemporaries had to start from scratch and invent their own 'tradition' or predecessors.[22]

Consequently, Javier Marías's novelistic development is defined—especially in the beginning—by running counter to the above inter-related chain of elements, and it can best be understood in the light of this. This is why his first novel is such an extravagantly cosmopolitan one, disengaged from Spain, its reality and any form of Spanishness, whose reflexive narrative is fragmentary and develops episodically and governed by chance, demands some reader-participation in constructing the story, is playful and eschews seriousness and moralizing, is devoid of any overarching 'message' and creates a mythical, mostly urban, America through its imitation of Hollywood cinema. Hence, not only does it partake in a tradition that sees imitation as a form of *protogymnasmata*, an initial step in an artist's literary formation, concomitantly demonstrating a very strong awareness of the importance of form and style, but it also gives rise to a 'second-degree' literature that according to Annick Bouillaguet represents another text *through* and *in* literature, thus pointing to the permanent presence of a mediatory element and asserting the autonomy of the work and its anti-realist form, in contrast with what she calls the 'first-degree' literature that strives to represent reality.[23]

Marías's contemporary writers are to a great extent those that became known as the *novísimos* poets. Together with Marías, it is they who best exemplify what constitutes this somewhat unjust, reductive, yet necessary rejection and the shared aesthetic, and who also foreshadow the shape of things to come, especially as regards novels of the 1980s.[24] As is well known, the *novísimos* are considered a not necessarily completely homogenous group of poets sharing an aesthetic most polemically, controversially and performatively exhibited in José María Castellet's famous anthology of 1970, *Nueve novísimos poetas españoles*, which became a sort of manifesto and has converted the adjective into the noun that has since been used to refer not only to those anthologized (including Pere Gimferrer, Félix de Azúa, Vicente Molina-Foix, Antonio Martínez Sarrión and Manuel Vázquez Montalbán), but also to all those partaking in equal measure in the rupture and aesthetic exemplified (such as Luis Antonio de Villena, Antonio Colinas, and Jaime Siles), as well as, in some instances, to novelists such as Marías.

Like Marías, none of the *novísimos* was born before 1939, and all rejected 'la noción dominante de un discurso' [the dominant notion of a discourse], that of social-realist poetry, attempting to break with Spanish culture under Franco and the 'trasnochado realismo que quería monopolizar la cultura de la oposición' [outdated realism that would monopolize the culture of the opposition] through anti-realism, whilst endeavouring to connect with Western culture.[25] Like Marías's first two novels, their work was characterized by strong metafictional (metapoetic) and intertextual elements, self-reflexive imitation of both popular culture (especially cinema, television, advertising and comic-strips) and high cultural forms (references, often esoteric, to primarily non-Spanish art), whose boundaries they blurred. Their work is further distinguished by exoticism, cosmopolitanism, a pronounced sense of humour and pleasure—indeed, they made pleasure part of what Chris Perriam calls the 'rebellion against the dreariness of Francoism and its domestic values as well as against the perceived prosaism of leftist social realism'[26]—an often camp sensibility, urban settings and a culturally constructed and mediated environment dominated by fragmentation and chaos, manifesting a scepticism and a loss of belief in rational, totalizing, causal systems (hence the use of ellipsis, collage, the episode or chance).[27] Finally, in their work, history and reality become unknowable except in mediated form.

Like the textually-mediated America in Marías's *Los dominios* or Pere Gimferrer's *Muerte en Beverly Hills*, or, indeed, the Venice so famously and frequently alluded to by the *novísimos*, the 'realities' referred to are thus elevated to the category of myth or reduced to text, 'la realidad significada pierde cualquier significado emotivo y todo valor referencial, quedando simplemente como texto' [the reality signified loses all emotive meaning and referential value and is reduced to mere text],[28] something very much akin to Barthes's 'healthy' sign in *Mythologies* that draws attention to the artificial process involved in constructing myth (which Barthes opposes to the 'unhealthy' realist and representational sign that effaces the involvement of mediation in representation).[29]

Therefore, probably the two most important features of the early Marías and the *novísimos* are, first, this resolute emphasis on mediation, which strongly attests to the belief, in Paul de Man's words, in literature's freedom from 'the fallacy of unmediated expression',[30] and, secondly, the consequent emphasis on the medium, on language and style, and the primacy of technique and form over content—'la forma del mensaje es su verdadero contenido' [the form of the message is its true content], Castellet famously wrote in the introduction to his anthology, paraphrasing Marshall McLuhan.[31] This displays the aestheticism of the belief in the self-sufficiency of the work, the autonomy of art.[32]

For all these reasons, the *novísimos* writers were given epithets as diverse as *venecianos* [Venetians], *extranjerizantes* [foreign-tending], *frívolos* [frivolous], *escuela del sándalo* [the sandal school] or the less imaginative *maricones* [queers] and, in Marías's case, also *angloaburrido* [Anglobore; *sic*] and *anglosajonijodido* [Anglosod; *sic*]. Many of them retaliated by christening their counterparts the *escuela de la berza* [cabbage school] and *manchegos* and, inverting Unamuno's 'Me duele España' [Spain pains me], one could say that, through their works they gave voice to a collective 'Me huele España' [Spain smells]. This new aesthetic, with all its features that many have called postmodern *avant la lettre*, foreshadowed developments in post-Franco literature and the novel in particular, something that has gone relatively unnoticed by those studying the post-Franco novel. Marías and the *novísimos* prefigured the shape of things to come. It could therefore be argued that, rather than 1975, the year of Franco's death and therefore the one normally posited as the turning point in most studies of the post-Franco Spanish novel, a more notable and emblematic year in which fruitfully to locate a beginning of post-Franco literature would be 1970.[33]

Notes to Chapter 13

1. Javier Marías, *Los dominios del lobo* (Barcelona: Anagrama, 1987; first pubd 1971), 17 (abbreviated *DL* in text).
2. For a more detailed discussion, see Alexis Grohmann, *Coming into One's Own: The Novelistic Development of Javier Marías* (Amsterdam and New York: Rodopi, 2002).

3. This is the same fascination that Marías' contemporary, Fernando Savater, displayed in 1976 in his book *La infancia recuperada* (Madrid: Taurus, 1994).

4. Eduardo Mendoza would later give voice to this shared view by saying that 'messages are good for answering machines'. In Marie-Lise Gazarián Gautier, *Interviews with Spanish Writers* (Elmwood Park, IL: Dalkey Archive Press, 1991), 205. Or, as the film producer Sam Goldwyn (1879–1974; MGM, 1924–59) put it: 'Pictures are for entertainment, messages should be delivered by [the telegraph agency] Western Union.'

5. Elide Pittarello, foreword 'Guardar la distancia' to Javier Marías, *El hombre que parecía no querer nada* (Madrid: Espasa-Calpe, 1996), 11–31.

6. See Gérard Genette, *Palimpsestes* (Paris: Le Seuil, 1982), 13.

7. See David Cook, *A History of Narrative Film* (New York: W. W. Norton, 1990), 467–71.

8. See Mikhail Bakhtin, 'From the Prehistory of Novelistic Discourse', *Modern Criticism and Theory: A Reader*, ed. David Lodge (London: Longman, 1988), 125–56.

9. See Genette, *Palimpsestes*, 90–1.

10. See Linda Hutcheon, *A Theory of Parody* (New York: Methuen, 1985), 31. Arguably all literature is to an extent imitative. The term 'imitative writing' here includes interrelated and overlapping concepts such as parody, pastiche, homage, collage, as well as the related carnivalization, metafiction, inter- and hypertextuality, comedy and *mise-en-abîme*. In addition to the three works last cited, see Wolfgang Karrer, *Parodie, Travestie, Pastiche* (Munich: Wilhelm Fink, 1977); Margaret Rose, *Parody/Metafiction* (London: Croom Helm, 1979); idem, *Parody: Ancient, Modern, and Post-modern* (Cambridge: Cambridge University Press, 1993); Julia Kristeva, 'Word, Dialogue and Novel', *The Kristeva Reader*, ed. Toril Moi (New York: Columbia University Press; London: Basil Blackwell, 1986), 34–61; Joseph Dane, *Parody* (Norman: University of Oklahoma Press, 1988); Annick Bouillaguet, *L'Écriture imitative* (Paris: Nathan, 1996).

11. See Hutcheon, *A Theory of Parody*, 31.

12. This is a point that is emphasized in studies of the Spanish novel under Franco. See e.g. Rafael Bosch and Manuel García Viñó, *El realismo y la novela actual* (Seville: Universidad de Sevilla, 1973); Juan Benet, 'Una época troyana', idem, *En ciernes* (Madrid: Taurus, 1976), 85–102; José María Castellet, *Literatura, ideología y política* (Barcelona: Anagrama, 1976); Robert C. Spires, *La novela española de posguerra: Creación artística y experiencia personal* (Madrid: Cupsa, 1978); Santos Sanz Villanueva, *Historia de la novela social española (1942–1975)* (Madrid: Alhambra, 1980); Margaret Jones, *The Contemporary Spanish Novel, 1939–1975* (Boston: Twayne, 1985); Barry Jordan, *Writing and Politics in Franco's Spain* (London: Routledge, 1990); Rafael Fuentes Molla, 'Novela española: Entre el testimonio y la experiencia', *España hoy II: Cultura*, ed. Antonio Ramos Gascón (Madrid: Cátedra, 1991), 109–49; Manuel Vázquez Montalbán, 'La novela española entre el posfranquismo y el posmodernismo', *La Rénovation du roman espagnol depuis 1975*, ed. Yvan Lissorgues (Toulouse: Presses Universitaires du Mirail, 1991), 13–25; José Carlos Mainer, *De postguerra (1951–1990)* (Barcelona: Crítica, 1994); Antonio Vilanova, *Novela y sociedad en la España de la posguerra* (Barcelona: Lumen, 1995); José María Martínez Cachero, *La novela española entre*

1936 y el fin de siglo: Historia de una aventura (Madrid: Castalia, 1997); Randolph D. Pope, 'Narrative in Culture, 1936–1975', *The Cambridge Companion to Modern Spanish Culture*, ed. David T. Gies (Cambridge: Cambridge University Press, 1999), 134–46; Chris Perriam et al., *A New History of Spanish Writing: 1939 to the 1990s* (Oxford: Oxford University Press, 2000).

13. Nora Catelli, 'Los rasgos de un mestizaje', *Revista de Occidente* 122–3 (July–Aug. 1991), 135–47 at 139.

14. See e.g. Juan Goytisolo, *El furgón de cola* (Paris: Ruedo Ibérico, 1967), 53; Gonzalo Sobejano, 'Ante la novela de los años setenta', *Ínsula* 396–7 (1979) [1], and 22 at 22; Félix de Azúa, 'Sobre el tiempo y las palabras: Los Novísimos', idem, *Lecturas compulsivas: Una invitación* (Barcelona: Anagrama, 1998), 201–9 at 206–7.

15. See Jo Labanyi, 'Literary experiment and cultural cannibalization', *Spanish Cultural Studies: An Introduction*, ed. Helen Graham and Jo Labanyi (London: Routledge, 1995), 295–9 at 298. As Azúa puts it in 'Sobre el tiempo', 207, 'el mundo literario hispano ha sido siempre de una seriedad, de una severidad, escurialense, fúnebre, de tanatorio'.

16. A Greek term used by Bakhtin, 'From the Prehistory of Novelistic Discourse', 138, to qualify those upon whom the transmission of the written heritage of ancient Rome rested and who 'elected the serious word and rejected its comic reflections as a profanation'.

17. As John Butt, *Writers and Politics in Modern Spain* (London: Hodder & Stoughton, 1978), 9, argues: 'In a situation in which all humane energies are devoted to attacking a particular regime, demands are put on literature which narrow its range [...] In the case of Spain, these demands unfortunately worked against the emancipation of language and imagination.'

18. See Robert C. Spires, *Post-Totalitarian Spanish Fiction* (Columbia: University of Missouri Press, 1996), 31; Labanyi, 'Literary experiment', 296.

19. In Javier Marías, *Literatura y fantasma* (Madrid: Siruela, 1993), 45–61.

20. Jo Labanyi, 'Postmodernity and the problem of cultural identity', *Spanish Cultural Studies*, ed. Graham and Labanyi, 396–406 at 397.

21. Or, as Catelli, 'Los rasgos de un mestizaje', 140, puts it, realism was equated with or connoted the other elements: 'Para los nuevos narradores el realismo es esencia, nación, casticismo, costumbrismo.'

22. The majority of the novelists among Marías's generation and their contemporaries of the 1970s and '80s have made this quite explicit. See e.g. the testimony of Juan José Millás, '¿De qué realidad me habla usted?', *Generación del 68*, ed. Santos Sanz Villanueva, *El Urogallo* (June 1988), 51–2: 'La mayoría de los autores españoles carecemos de tradición novelesca.' Antonio Muñoz Molina has devoted a whole essay to the subject, suitably entitled 'La invención de un pasado', idem, *Pura alegría* (Madrid: Alfaguara, 1998), 204–19.

23. Bouillaguet, *L'écriture imitative*, 19.

24. There are many links between the *novísimos* poets and post-Franco prose writing, such as the aesthetic 'manifesto', José de Azúa, Javier Marías and Vicente Molina-Foix, *Tres cuentos didácticos* (Barcelona: La Gaya Ciencia, 1975), which was meant to be the prose equivalent of Castellet's anthology of 1970 (see below), or the fact that many of the *novísimos* were or later became novelists (e.g. Gimferrer, Molina-Foix, Vázquez Montalbán, Azúa, Moix).

25. Jaime Siles, 'Los Novísimos: La tradición como ruptura, la ruptura como tradición', *Ínsula* 505 (Jan. 1989), 9–11 at 9, 10.

26. Perriam et al., *A New History of Spanish Writing*, 200.

27. 'Hay que escribir esbozos, ya que no hay explicación totalizadora. Lo que hay son atisbos, fragmentos, instantes'. Pere Gimferrer, quoted by Marta Beatriz Ferrari, 'Postismo/Novísimos: ¿La tradición de la ruptura?', *Letras de Deusto* 72/26 (July–Sep. 1996), 95–108.

28. Andrew P. Debicki, *Historia de la poesía española del siglo XX: Desde la modernidad hasta el presente* (Madrid: Gredos, 1994), 219.

29. See Roland Barthes, *Mythologies* (Paris: Le Seuil, 1957).

30. Paul de Man, *Blindness and Insight: Essays in the Rhetoric of Contemporary Criticism* (London: Routledge, 1983), 17.

31. José María Castellet, *Nueve novísimos poetas españoles* (Barcelona: Seix Barral, 1970), 31, 34. McLuhan's formula 'The medium is the message' comes from *The Gutenberg Galaxy: The Making of Typographic Man* (Toronto: Toronto University Press, 1962; often repr.).

32. See Debicki, *Historia de la poesía española*, 196, 199, 203, 219; Juan Cano Ballesta, *Las estrategias de la imaginación* (Madrid: Siglo XX, 1994), 169.

33. See the comments made to this effect by Debicki, *Historia de la poesía española*, 250–1; Labanyi's essays, 'Literary experiment' and 'Postmodernity and the problem of cultural identity'; eadem, 'Narrative in Culture, 1976–1996', *The Cambridge Companion to Modern Spanish Culture*, 147–62.

CHAPTER 14

From Brussels to Madrid: EU–US Audiovisual Relations and Spanish TV Production

Paul Julian Smith

Biotechnology, climate change, audiovisual industries: what do these three sectors have in common? They were all the subject of a major conference that drew Eurocrats, executives and the occasional academic to Brussels on 6 July 2000; and they are all examples of a newly complex global trade that is no longer a question of quotas and tariffs but of services and subsidies. In these areas, formerly domestic policies have spilled over frontiers and become flash points for international conflict. Transatlantic trade has become central to the world economy and is conducted between co-equals. But, asked the conference organizers, Have Cold War allies become millennial adversaries? Are European ethics incompatible with American economics?

The conference took place at a significant moment: news had just broken of the French company Vivendi's takeover of Hollywood's Universal. But opening positions remained as polarized as ever. In one corner was André Lange of the European Audiovisual Observatory, and in the other, Cindy Rose, Vice-President, Government Relations, Walt Disney Corporation, Brussels. Taking a historical perspective, Lange reminded the audience that Europe/US relations had always been adversarial. The brief European hegemony of the global film market before the First World War had given way to American expansionism between the wars and the post-war employment of trade relations as a tool of geopolitics. Most recently, US companies were continuing to increase market share in Europe and were aiming to control the end market by investing in multiplexes and thematic TV channels. EU companies, on the other hand, had no access to the US market.

In what was something of a Dutch auction, Disney's Rose (clearly anticipating criticism) claimed that US market share in Europe was down from 78 per cent in 1998 to 71 per cent in 1999, while EU market share in America had doubled to 6 per cent. Likewise, American feature production had fallen, while European production, no longer in crisis, had risen. But the EU problem, she said, was not production but distribution, with only 8 per cent of Euro features shown in European territories outside their home market. Rose recommended the EU learn from the US and make their films more 'commercially viable': they should involve distributors from the very beginning of the production process and increase marketing spend from the Euro average of 8–10 per cent of budget to the US average of 50 per cent.

Rose gave a stern warning that the progressive liberalization agreed by WTO accords made no provision for 'cultural exception' (a term frequently cited by the French). Predictably, this was resisted by Euro cultural protectionists. In a rare return to Cold-War rhetoric, one speaker denounced Hollywood's violent excesses as 'fascist'. More unexpected was Rose's admission that there was an overlap between culture, commerce and community. As the Disney Channel 'rolled out' over Europe, reported Rose, it hired a local team to make on-site production in each territory. Given the increasing demand for local product, now generally preferred to American imports, the dictates of the market-place thus coincided, fortuitously perhaps, with US companies' newly-discovered respect for cultural difference.

As discussion continued, it became clear that the integration of ethical concerns into what were previously economic debates was hampered by differing definitions of terms. American delegates spoke of 'consumers' and 'freedom of expression'. Europeans referred to 'public interest' and 'national identity'. For the French, we were reminded, film (like food and fashion) was not an economic commodity: it was a cultural icon. And while the representative from the Motion Picture Association of America hymned the internet, which, he predicted, would within two years bring the same universal distribution of film it had already brought to music, European broadcasters were sceptical that small territories such as Finland or Portugal could make much of an impact on the web. Indeed the one point on which all sides were agreed was that there could be no incentive to invest in innovative production unless digital pirating could be controlled. The vigorous enforcement of copyright was thus the unlikely bedfellow of the unlimited access of cybertopia.

Interdisciplinary discussions raise specific cross-sector analogies: if corporate polluters paid for environmental impact, could Hollywood majors be held responsible for 'cultural impact'? Was there an audiovisual equivalent of GM foods or global warming? But more generally, the meeting seemed to point the way to a new audiovisual order that consolidated the already existing codependence of the world's mightiest trading blocs. Two tendencies stood out. First, globalization can no longer be written off as Americanization. As the spokesman for the MPAA confirmed, the era of *Dallas* and *Dynasty* is over. Local markets require local products: regionalization is in, even if it is bankrolled by Hollywood. Secondly, media trends are no longer technologically driven. The business is not in the highways (multiplexes, digital TV, broadband streaming) but in the programming. It was Universal's library that made it so attractive to Vivendi; and, to quote the MPAA once more, 'content is king'. European culturalists, who see film as a vital resource for memory and democracy, may still mourn the hegemony they lost to Hollywood and see the Americans' turn to local production as a Trojan Horse. But with the Vivendi deal the clearest sign of Europe's co-operation with America, some feared that the biggest danger was one scarcely mentioned in Brussels: the exclusion of the developing world from a new audiovisual alliance in which convergence between the EU and US was ever accelerating.

Let us now explore these two themes of localization and the primacy of content in relation to an apparently marginal European case, that of Spain, and an apparently insignificant TV programme called *Cine de barrio* or 'Neighbourhood Cinema'. *Cine de barrio* is the state network Televisión Española's top-rated and long-running Saturday afternoon show. A generic hybrid, *Cine de barrio* book-ends the screening of an often obscure feature film of the Francoist period by studio talk with surviving stars and occasional documentary inserts, shot on location. Unashamedly trivial and parochial, *Cine de barrio* resists the trends for both quality production-values and transnational subject-matter visible elsewhere in the Spanish media.

What is the context of recent Spanish film and TV production and consumption? *Focus 2000,* the official statistical analysis produced by the European Audiovisual Observatory and distributed at each year's Cannes Film Festival, claims that '1999 was a year of maturity and success for the Spanish cinema'.[1] Local share in the domestic market was a high 17.2 per cent, with US market share 'exceptionally low' at 64.4 per cent. Interestingly, given that European films are generally thought not to travel outside their national territory, European non-Spanish films also achieved a 'no less exceptional' 19.2 per cent. Crucially, Spanish market share was not, as so often in Europe, dependent on only one or two titles; indeed, the Observatory notes that the highest profile release of the year, Almodóvar's *Todo sobre mi madre* [*All about my Mother*] 'only reaches 15th place in the national charts'. Benefiting from this group effort in production, then, 'Spain manages to place five films among the twenty five most popular European films in 1999 on the European Union market.' It is also worth noting that in line with the changing demographic of Spanish cinema audiences,[2] these films are mainly 'quality' productions, with high production values and relatively serious themes: outgrossing Almodóvar's uncharacteristically sombre study of the work of mourning is Fernando Trueba's *La niña de tus ojos* [*The Girl of Your Dreams*], a period picture focusing on a Spanish film star's experience in Nazi Germany.

It could be argued that the emphasis on quality and trans-nationalism in the film sector is also seen in Spanish television. Until recently, Spaniards dismissed their TV as trash.[3] And the institutional history is well known.[4] A statute of 1980 regulated the state-controlled Radio-Televisión Española, which remains accused of political bias and excessive commercialism. The Third Channel Law of 1984 set up essential local broadcasters in the self-governing areas of Catalonia, Galicia and the Basque Country. But the Private TV Law of 1988 unleashed a ratings war amongst new national channels such as Antena 3 and Telecinco. On one notorious occasion a chat-show host persuaded his entire audience to strip off for the camera.

Telecinco, a private network part-owned by the Italian mogul (and Prime Minister) Berlusconi, pioneered this shift down-market. With its majority foreign ownership it also operated on the fringes of illegality. But when audiences tired of trash and ratings fell, new executives were brought in from Italy who turned the channel around with a risky policy: quality in-house production.[5] National product now not only produces higher ratings than US imports; it is also initiated and fostered by cosmopolitan executives who fuse local issues with US formats: the successful series drama *Periodistas* and its many imitators are clearly based on US workplace dramas with their ensemble casts and concern for dramatizing social issues. Such shows stand in strong contest with the domestic settings and modest budgets of most previous Spanish TV production.

Which returns us to the continuing and anomalous success of *Cine de barrio*. Focusing as it does on the Francoist period, *Cine de barrio* at once transforms the tragedy of twentieth-century Spanish history into banality and shields its vulnerable audience from the equally menacing threat of modernity, so fully embraced by cosmopolitan Spanish media executives. While Spanish cinema and television aim primarily for the new quality demographic (young, single, urban and wealthy), *Cine de barrio* sets its sights on a neglected segment: old enough to remember its featured films (from the 1950s, 1960s or 1970s), sensitive to its recreation of a pseudo-familial space (the set mimics a traditional household), and nostalgic for a rural, preconsumerist economy.[6] It is not the least of its paradoxes that *Cine de barrio*, produced by public television, is shamelessly commercial: the show's oleaginous host, much ridiculed in the Spanish press, makes time for frequent asides to the camera in which he advertises box sets of videos by stars little known outside Spain, such as Sara Montiel, Lola Flores and Marisol, which are marketed in stores around the nation in special displays under the *Cine de barrio* brand-name.

Analysis of a four-minute sequence taken from a Christmas edition of *Cine de barrio* will give a taste of what it feels like to watch this curious programme. The sequence begins with location shots of minor celebrities (so called 'friends' of the programme and its host) singing traditional *villancicos* at a party. We then cut to the studio, where the host and his regular sidekicks (a male pianist and female companion) are festively dressed. Addressing the camera directly, the host pitches the boxed sets of videos marketed under the brand-name *Cine de barrio*. This sales pitch is illustrated by a clip from a feature starring the celebrated child star Marisol. The feature is not shown free to air, but is only available for payment. There then follows a clip from the featured film of the day, *El alegre divorciado*, starring the late Paco Martínez Soria, arch-*paleto*, and the vivacious, plump Florinda Chico: the latter is trying on a transparent negligée to the consternation of her husband. During an interview, shot on location at the now elderly Chico's home, the camera lingers on her memorabilia as our host flatters the star: surely she was as attractive as she was *simpática*? The collage effect of the editing suggests a free flow between past and present, harmless nostalgia and shameless commercialism.

Almost parodically parochial (as its name suggests), *Cine de barrio* also domesticates or banalizes Spanish history in a way that is disturbing to a foreign observer, frequently featuring clips from the notorious Francoist newsreel, the NoDo. Moreover, the films chosen for discussion are of the lowest possible quality, far inferior even to the videos marketed so insistently by the host. It seems clear that the success of the show cannot lie in these exceptionally cheap features: long-forgotten farces, musicals and sentimental religious pictures that at best raise faint memories of better-known films of the period. Rather, re-creating in phantom form the domestic milieu of the past, *Cine de barrio* could be seen as bearing out Slavoj Žižek's definition of nostalgia, purveying the pleasure of identification not with the past object but with the fantasized gaze of the past.[7]

Leaving aside such psychoanalytic speculation, the audiovisual context suggests that the immense popularity of *Cine de barrio* is a response to and a symptom of the neglect of a certain audience demographic by the national entertainment industry. If world film and television market trends suggest paradoxically that globalization may lead to increased domestic production, then the curious case of Spain reveals that a successful audiovisual sector may combine with equal ease transnational formats and those whose appeal is aggressively local, even parochial, by nature.

Notes to Chapter 14

1. *Focus 2000* (Strasbourg: European Audiovisual Observatory, 2000).
2. See *Informe 2000* (Madrid: Sociedad General de Autores y Editores, 2000).
3. This tendency continues in Lorenzo Díaz, *Informe sobre la televisión en España (1989–1998): La década abominable* (Barcelona: Zeta, 1999).
4. See Richard Maxwell, *The Spectacle of Democracy: Spanish Television, Nationalism, and Political Transition* (Minneapolis: University of Minnesota Press, 1995).
5. See Paul Julian Smith, 'Spanish Quality TV?', *Journal of Spanish Cultural Studies* 1 (2000), 173–92, on one of the most successful of these locally-produced serial dramas, entitled *Periodistas*.
6. Nathan E. Richardson discusses some of these films in *Postmodern Paletos: Immigration, Democracy, and Globalization in Spanish Narrative and Film, 1950–2000* (Lewisburg, PA: Bucknell University Press, 2002).
7. See Slavoj Žižek, 'Pornography, Nostalgia, Montage', idem, *Looking Awry: An Introduction to Jacques Lacan through Popular Culture* (Cambridge, MA: MIT Press, 1992), 107–22.

BIBLIOGRAPHY

ADAMOWICZ, ELZA, *Surrealist Collage in Text and Image: Dissecting the Exquisite Corpse* (Cambridge: Cambridge University Press, 1998).

ALARCÓN, P. A. DE, *Obras completas*, ed. Luis Martínez Kleiser (Madrid: Fax, 1954).

ALBERTI, RAFAEL, *Prosas encontradas 1924–1942* (Madrid: Ayuso, 1970).

—— interview with Luis Pancorbo, *Gaceta del arte* (April 1974), 23.

—— *La arboleda perdida: Libros I y II [III y IV] de memorias* (Barcelona: Seix Barral, 1975–87; I, II first publ. 1938, 1959).

—— *Obras completas*, 3 vols. (Madrid: Aguilar, 1988).

ALEXANDRIAN, SARANE, *Surrealist Art* (London: Thames & Hudson, 1993; first pubd 1970).

ALVAREZ JUNCO, JOSÉ, *Mater dolorosa* (Madrid: Taurus, 2001).

ANDERSON, ANDREW A., *Lorca's Late Poetry* (Leeds: Cairns, 1990).

AREÁN, CARLOS, 'La imágen pictórica en la poesía de Alberti', *Cuadernos hispanoamericanos* 289–90 (1974), 198–209.

ARNÁIZ, JOSÉ MANUEL, *Eugenio Lucas: Su vida y su obra* (Madrid: M. Montal, 1981).

ARTUNDO, PATRICIA, *La obra gráfica de Norah Borges, 1920–1930* (Buenos Aires: n.p., 1993).

AZÚA, FÉLIX DE, 'Sobre el tiempo y las palabras: Los Novísimos', idem, *Lecturas compulsivas: Una invitación* (Barcelona: Anagrama, 1998), 201–9.

——, MARÍAS, JAVIER, and MOLINA-FOIX, VICENTE, *Tres cuentos didácticos* (Barcelona: La Gaya Ciencia, 1975).

BAKHTIN, MIKHAIL, 'From the Prehistory of Novelistic Discourse', *Modern Criticism and Theory: A Reader*, ed. David Lodge (London: Longman, 1988), 125–56.

BANES, SALLY, *Dancing Women: Female Bodies on Stage* (London and New York: Routledge, 1998).

BARTHES, ROLAND, *Mythologies* (Paris: Le Seuil, 1957).

BATCHELOR, DAVID, 'From Littérature to La Révolution Surréaliste', Briony Fer, David Batchelor and Paul Wood, *Realism, Rationalism, Surrealism: Art between the Wars* (New Haven and London: Yale University Press, 1993), 47–61.

BAUR, SERGIO, 'Norah Borges, musa de las vanguardias', *Cuadernos hispanoamericanos* 610 (April 2001), 87–96.

BAYO, MANUEL, *Sobre Alberti* (Madrid: CUS, 1974).

BAYS, GWENDOLYN M., 'Rimbaud: Father of Surrealism?', *Yale French Studies* 31 (1964), 45–51.

BELLVER, CATHERINE, *Absence and Presence: Spanish Women Poets of the Twenties and Thirties* (Lewisburg, PA: Bucknell University Press, 2001).

BENET, JOSEP, and MARTI, CASIMIR, *Barcelona a mitjan segle XIX: El moviment obrer durant el bienni progressista (1854–1856)*, 2 vols. (Barcelona: Curial, 1976).

BENET, JUAN, 'Una época troyana', idem, *En ciernes* (Madrid: Taurus, 1976), 85–102.

BERGERO, ADRIANO, 'Science, Modern Art and Surrealism: The Representation of Imaginary Matter', *The Surrealist Adventure in Spain*, ed. C. Brian Morris (Ottowa Hispanic Studies 6; Ottowa: Dovehouse, 1991), 19–39.

BERGSON, HENRI, 'Bergson en la Residencia', *Residencia* 2 (1926), 174–6.

BODINI, VITTORIO, *I poeti surrealisti spagnoli* (Turin: Einaudi, 1963); trans. as *Los poetas surrealistas españoles* (Barcelona: Tusquets, 1971).

BONET, JUAN MANUEL, 'Hora y media con Norah Borges', *Renacimiento* [Seville] 8 (1992): 5–6.

BORGES, JOSÉ LUIS, 'Vertical', *Reflector* 1 (Dec.1920), repr. *El ultraísmo y las artes plásticas* [exhibition cat., 27 June – 8 Sept. 1996] (Valencia: IVAM, 1996), 150.

BORGES, NORAH, 'Nueve dibujos y una confesión: Lista de las obras de arte que prefiero', *La Nación* [Buenos Aires] (12 Aug. 1928), repr. Patricia Artundo, *La obra gráfica de Norah Borges, 1920–1930* (Buenos Aires: n.p., 1993), 157; also repr. Ramón Gómez de la Serna, *Norah Borges* (Buenos Aires: Losada, 1945), 25–6.

BORODIN, GEORGE, *This Thing Called Ballet* (London: Macdonald, 1945).

BOSCH, RAFAEL, and GARCÍA VIÑÓ, MANUEL, *El realismo y la novela actual* (Seville: Universidad de Sevilla, 1973).

BOUILLAGUET, ANNICK, *L'Écriture imitative* (Paris: Nathan, 1996).

BOURDIEU, PIERRE, *The Rules of Art: Genesis and Structure of the Literary Field*, trans. Susan Emanuel (Cambridge: Polity Press, 1996).

BOWRA, C. M., *The Creative Experiment* (London: Macmillan, 1949).

BRETON, ANDRÉ, *Manifestoes of Surrealism*, trans. Richard Seaver and Helen R. Lane (Ann Arbor: University of Michigan Press, 1969).

BROOKE, XANTHE, and CHERRY, PETER (eds.), *Murillo: Scenes of Childhood* (London: Merrell, 2000).

BROWN, JONATHAN, *Velázquez: Painter and Courtier* (New Haven and London: Yale University Press, 1986).

—— (ed.), *Picasso and the Spanish Tradition* (New Haven and London: Yale University Press, 1996).

—— and Garrido, Carmen, *Velázquez: The Technique of Genius* (New Haven and London: Yale University Press, 1998).

BUÑUEL, LUIS, *Mi último suspiro* (Barcelona: Plaza & Janés, 1982).

BUSTAMANTE, ANA SOFÍA (ed.), *Don Juan Tenorio en la España del siglo XX: Literatura y cine* (Madrid: Cátedra, 1998).

BUTT, JOHN, *Writers and Politics in Modern Spain* (London: Hodder & Stoughton, 1978).

CABANA, FRANCESC, *Història del Banc de Barcelona (1844–1920)* (Barcelona: Edicions 62, 1978).

CALVO SERRALLER, FRANCISCO, 'Eugenio Lucas Velázquez en la colección del Museo Nacional de la Habana', *Eugenio Lucas Velázquez en la Habana* [exhibition cat., Feb.–April 1996] (Madrid: Mapfre Vida, 1996), 25–65.

CAMACHO GUIZADO, EDUARDO, *La elegía funeral en la poesía española* (Madrid: Gredos, 1969).

CAÑELLAS, CÈLIA, and TORAN, ROSA, 'Ideologies i actituds professionals, criminologia i positivisme: El cas Wille', *L'Avenç: Història dels països catalans* 210 (1997): 12–16.

CANNON, CALVIN, 'Lorca's *Llanto por Ignacio Sánchez Mejías* and the Elegiac Tradition', *Hispanic Review* 31 (1963), 229–38.

CANO BALLESTA, JUAN, *Las estrategias de la imaginación* (Madrid: Siglo XX, 1994).

CARDWELL, RICHARD, 'Darío and *El arte puro*: The Enigma of Life and the Beguilement of Art', *Bulletin of Hispanic Studies* 48 (1970): 37–51.

—— '*Los raros* de Rubén Darío y los médicos chiflados finiseculares', *Rubén Darío y el arte de la prosa: Ensayo, retratos y alegorías*, ed. Cristóbal Cuevas, Actas del XI Congreso de literatura española contemporánea, 10–14 de noviembre de 1997 (Málaga: Publicaciones del Congreso de literatura española contemporánea, 1998), 55–77.

—— 'The War of the Wor(l)ds: Symbolist Decadent Literature and the Discourses of Power in Finisecular Spain', *Symbolism, Decadence and the Fin de Siècle: French and European Perspectives*, ed. Patrick McGuiness (Exeter: University of Exeter Press, 2000), 225–43.

CARMONA, DARÍO, 'Anedoctario', *Litoral* 29–30 (1972), n.p. [10].

CARMONA, EUGENIO, 'Bores ultraísta, clásico, nuevo, 1921–1925', *Francisco Bores: El ultraísmo y el ambiente literario madrileño* [exhibition cat., Sept.–Nov. 1999] (Madrid: Publicaciones de la Residencia de Estudiantes, 1999), 13–51.

CASTELLET, JOSÉ MARÍA, *Nueve novísimos poetas españoles* (Barcelona: Seix Barral, 1970).

—— *Literatura, ideología y política* (Barcelona: Anagrama, 1976).

CASTRO, ROSALÍA DE, *El caballero de las botas azules*, ed. Ana Rodríguez-Fisher (Madrid: Cátedra, 1995; first pubd 1867).

CATELLI, NORA, 'Los rasgos de un mestizaje', *Revista de Occidente* 122–3 (July–Aug. 1991), 135–47.

CAVANAUGH, CECILIA J., *Lorca's Drawings and Poems: Forming the Eye of the Reader* (London: Associated University Presses, 1995).

CERDÁN, FRANCIS, 'Rafael Alberti y la pintura de Antonio Saura: Visión memorable', *Dr Rafael Alberti: El poeta en Toulouse*, ed. Marie de Meñaca (Toulouse: Université de Toulouse – Le Mirail, 1984), 225–38.

CHARNON-DEUTSCH, LOU, *Narratives of Desire: Nineteenth-Century Spanish Fiction by Women* (University Park: Pennsylvania State University Press, 1994).

——, and LABANYI, JO (eds.), *Culture and Gender in Nineteenth-Century Spain* (Oxford: Clarendon Press, 1995).

CHÉNIEUX-GENDRON, JACQUELINE, *Surrealism*, trans. Vivien Folkenflik (New York: Columbia University Press, 1990).

CHERRY, PETER, 'Murillo's Genre Scenes and Their Context', *Murillo: Scenes of Childhood*, ed. Xanthe Brooke and Peter Cherry (London: Merrell, 2000), 9–41.

COCKBURN, JACQUELINE, 'Learning from the Master: Lorca's Homage to Picasso', *Fire, Blood and the Alphabet: One Hundred Years of Lorca*, ed. Sebastian Doggart and Michael Thompson (Durham: University of Durham, 1999), 123–42.

CONDE, CARMEN, *Júbilos: Poemas de niños, rosas, animales, máquinas y vientos*, prolog. Gabriela Mistral, illus. Norah Borges de Torre (Murcia: Sudeste, 1934).

CONDÉ, GÉRARD, Commentary to *Le Cid: Opéra en quatre actes et dix tableaux; livret intégral d'Adolphe d'Ennery, Louis Gallet et Edouard Blau* (Paris: Premières Loges, 1994).

CONNELL, GEOFFREY, '*Sobre los ángeles*: Form and Theme', *Spanish Studies* 4 (1982), 1–14.

COOK, DAVID, *A History of Narrative Film* (New York: W. W. Norton, 1990).

CRICHTON, RONALD, *Manuel de Falla: Descriptive Catalogue of his Works* (London: J. & W. Chester and Wilhelm Hansen, 1976).

CUEVAS, CRISTÓBAL (ed.), *Rubén Darío y el arte de la prosa: Ensayo, retratos y alegorías*, Actas del XI Congreso de literatura española contemporánea, 10–14 de noviembre de 1997 (Málaga: Publicaciones del Congreso de literatura española contemporánea, 1998).

DANE, JOSEPH, *Parody* (Norman: University of Oklahoma Press, 1988).

DARÍO, RUBÉN, *Obras completas*, 5 vols. (Madrid: Afrodisio Aguado, 1950).

—— *Cantos de vida y esperanza*, 12th edn. (Madrid: Espasa-Calpe, 1971).

DAVIES, CATHERINE, *Rosalía de Castro no seu tempo* (Vigo: Galaxia, 1987).

DAVIS, LISA E., 'Oscar Wilde in Spain', *Comparative Literature* 35 (1973), 136–52.

DEBICKI, ANDREW P., *Historia de la poesía española del siglo XX: Desde la modernidad hasta el presente* (Madrid: Gredos, 1994).

DELFINO, AUGUSTO MARIO, 'La exposición de Norah Borges en "Los Amigos del Arte"', *El Diario* [Buenos Aires] (23 Oct. 1926); repr. Patricia Artundo, *La obra gráfica de Norah Borges, 1920–1930* (Buenos Aires: n.p., 1993), 164.

DE MAN, PAUL, *Blindness and Insight: Essays in the Rhetoric of Contemporary Criticism* (London: Routledge, 1983).

DÍAZ, LORENZO, *Informe sobre la televisión en España (1989–1998): La década abominable* (Barcelona: Zeta, 1999).

DÍAZ-PLAJA, GUILLERMO, 'Tres discos románticos', *La Gaceta Literaria* 96 (15 Dec. 1930), 7.

DIEZ TABOADA, María Paz, *La elegía romántica española: Estudio y antologia* (Madrid: Instituto Miguel de Cervantes and CSIC, 1977).

DOGGART, SEBASTIAN, and THOMPSON, MICHAEL (eds.), *Fire, Blood and the Alphabet: One Hundred Years of Lorca* (Durham: University of Durham, 1999).

ELLMANN, RICHARD, *Oscar Wilde* (London: Hamish Hamilton, 1987).

Eugenio Lucas Velázquez en la Habana [exhibition cat., Feb.–April 1996] (Madrid: Mapfre Vida, 1996).

EVANS, PETER, 'Cifesa: Cinema and Authoritarian Aesthetics', *Spanish Cultural Studies: An Introduction*, ed. Helen Graham and Jo Labanyi (Oxford: Oxford University Press, 1995), 215–22.

FER, BRIONY, BATCHELOR, DAVID, and WOOD, PAUL, *Realism, Rationalism, Surrealism: Art between the Wars* (New Haven and London: Yale University Press, 1993).

FERNÁNDEZ, LUIS MIGUEL, 'Don Juan en imágenes: Aproximación a la recreación cinematográfica del personaje', *Don Juan Tenorio en la España del siglo XX: Literatura y cine*, ed. Ana Sofía Bustamante (Madrid: Cátedra, 1998), 503–38.

—— *Don Juan en el cine español: Hacia una teoría de la recreación fílmica* (Santiago: Universidade de Santiago de Compostela, 2000).

FERNÁNDEZ, PURA, *Eduardo López Bago y el Naturalismo radical: La novela y el mercado literario en el siglo XIX* (Amsterdam: Rodopi, 1995).

FERRARI, MARTA BEATRIZ, 'Postismo/Novísimos: ¿La tradición de la ruptura?', *Letras de Deusto* 72/26 (July–Sep. 1996), 95–108.

FERRATER, ESTEBAN DE, *Resumen del proceso original del estado civil de D. Claudio Fontanellas* (Madrid, Barcelona and Havana: Plus Ultra, 1865).

FERRER Y MINGUET, VICENTE, *La Causa Fontanellas justificada en la esencia de su procedimiento* (Madrid, Barcelona and Havana: Española and Plus Ultra, 1865).

Focus 2000 (Strasbourg: European Audiovisual Observatory, 2000).

FONTANA, JOSEPH, *La fi de l'antic règim i la industrialització (1787–1868)* (Barcelona: Edicions 62, 1998).

FOUCAULT, MICHEL, *Les Mots et les choses: Une archéologie des sciences humaines* (Paris: Gallimard, 1961).

FRADENBURG, LOUISE O., '"Voice Memorial": Loss and Reparation in Chaucer's Poetry', *Exemplaria* 2 (1990), 169–202.

FRADERA, JOSEP MARIA, *Cultura nacional en una societat dividida: Patriotisme i cultura a Catalunya (1838–1868)* (Barcelona: Curiel, 1992).

FREIRE LÓPEZ, ANA MARÍA, 'La fábula', *Historia de la literatura española*, dir. Víctor García de la Concha, viii: *Siglo XIX (I)*, co-ord. Guillermo Carnero (Madrid: Espasa-Calpe, 1997), 542–8.

Freud, Sigmund, *On Psychopathology*, ed. James Strachey and Angela Richards (London: Pelican Freud Library, 1979).
—— *Introductory Lectures on Psychoanalysis*, trans. James Strachey and Angela Richards (London: Penguin, 1991).
Frye, Northrop, *Anatomy of Criticism: Four Essays* (Princeton: Princeton University Press, 1957).
Fuentes Molla, Rafael, 'Novela española: Entre el testimonio y la experiencia', *España hoy II: Cultura*, ed. Antonio Ramos Gascón (Madrid: Cátedra, 1991), 109–149.
García de Carpi, Lucía, *La pintura surrealista española (1924–1936)* (Madrid: Istmo, 1986).
Gasch, Sebastià, 'Del Cubismo al Superrealismo', *La Gaceta Literaria* 20 (15 Oct. 1927), 121, cited in Juan Manuel Rozas, *La Generación del 27 desde dentro* (Madrid: Istmo, 1986), 144–53.
—— 'Lorca dibujante', *La gaceta literaria* 30 (15 Mar. 1928), 4.
—— Foreword 'Mi Federico García Lorca', Federico García Lorca, *Cartas a sus amigos*, ed. Sebastià Gasch (Barcelona: Cobalto, 1950), 7–14.
Gaya Nuño, Juan Antonio, 'En el centenario de Eugenio Lucas: El glorioso olvidado', *Goya* 98 (1970), 76–85.
Gazarián Gautier, Marie-Lise, *Interviews with Spanish Writers* (Elmwood Park, IL: Dalkey Archive Press, 1991).
Genette, Gérard, *Palimpsestes* (Paris: Le Seuil, 1982).
—— *Paratexts: Thresholds of Interpretation*, trans. Jane E. Lewin (Cambridge and London: Cambridge University Press, 1997).
Gibson, Ian, *Federico García Lorca: A Life* (London: Faber & Faber, 1989).
Gies, David T. (ed.), *The Cambridge Companion to Modern Spanish Culture* (Cambridge: Cambridge University Press, 1999).
Giménez Caballero, Ernesto, 'Itinerarios jóvenes de España: Guillermo de Torre', *La Gaceta Literaria* 44 (15 Oct. 1928), 7.
—— *Genio de España*, 8th edn. (Barcelona: Planeta, 1983; first pubd 1932).
Ginger, Andrew, *Antonio Ros de Olano's Experiments in Post-Romantic Prose (1857–1884): Between Romanticism and Modernism* (Lampeter: Edwin Mellen Press, 2000).
Ginzburg, Carlo, *I Benandanti: Stregoneria e culti agrari tra Cinquecento e Seicento* (Milan: Einaudi, 1966).
—— *Il formaggio e i vermi: Il cosmo di un mugnaio del '500* (Milan: Enaudi, 1976).
Gledhill, Christine (ed.), *Stardom: Industry of Desire* (London: Routledge, 1991).
Glendinning, Nigel, *Goya and his Critics* (New Haven: Yale University Press, 1977).
Gómez Carrillo, Enrique, *Sensaciones de arte* (Paris: G. Richard, 1891).
—— *Esquisses (siluetas de escritores y artistas): Oscar Wilde, Armand Silvestre, Charles Maurras, Paul Verlaine, etc.* (Madrid: Viuda de Hernández, 1892).
—— *Obras completas*, 20 vols. (Madrid: Mundo Latino, n.d. [1920?]).

GÓMEZ DE LA SERNA, RAMÓN, *Norah Borges* (Buenos Aires: Losada, 1945).

GOYTISOLO, JUAN, *El furgón de cola* (Paris: Ruedo Ibérico, 1967).

GRAHAM, HELEN, and LABANYI, JO (eds.), *Spanish Cultural Studies: An Introduction* (London: Routledge, 1995).

GROHMANN, ALEXIS, *Coming into One's Own: The Novelistic Development of Javier Marías* (Amsterdam and New York: Rodopi, 2002).

GUILLÉN, MERCEDES, *Conversaciones con los artistas españoles de la Escuela de París* (Madrid: Taurus, 1960).

HALL, FERNAU, *An Anatomy of Ballet* (London: Andrew Melrose, 1953).

HALL, GEORGE, *The Story of the Ballet 'Giselle'* (London: Ballet Books, 1961).

HANSEN, MIRIAM, 'Pleasure, Ambivalence, Identification: Valentino and Female Spectatorship', *Stardom: Industry of Desire*, ed. Christine Gledhill (London: Routledge, 1991), 259–82.

HARRIS, DEREK (ed.), *Changing Times in Hispanic Culture* (Aberdeen: Centre for the Study of the Hispanic Avant-Garde, University of Aberdeen, 1996).

HASKELL, ARNOLD L., *Ballet, a Complete Guide to Appreciation: History, Aesthetics, Ballets, Dancers* (Harmondsworth: Penguin, 1951).

HAVARD, ROBERT, *The Crucified Mind: Rafael Alberti and the Surrealist Ethos in Spain* (London: Tamesis, 2001).

HERNÁNDEZ, MARIO, 'El arte del dibujo en la creación de García Lorca', *Federico García Lorca: Saggi critici nel cinquantenario della morte*, ed. Gabriele Morelli (Rome: Schena, 1988), cited in Cecilia J. Cavanaugh, *Lorca's Drawings and Poems: Forming the Eye of the Reader* (London: Associated University Presses, 1995), 184.

—— *Libro de los dibujos de Federico García Lorca* (Madrid: Fundación Federico García Lorca, 1990).

HINOJOSA, JOSÉ MARÍA, 'Fuego granado, granadas de fuego', *Litoral* 8 (1929), 22–5.

—— *Poesías completas: Facsímiles (1925–1931)*, introd. Julio Neira (Málaga: Litoral, 1987).

—— *Epistolario*, ed. Alfonso Sánchez Rodríguez and Julio Neira (Seville: Fundación Genesian, 1997).

—— *Obra completa (1923–1931)*, ed. Alfonso Sánchez Rodríguez (Seville: Fundación Genesian, 1998).

Historia de la literatura española, dir. Víctor García de la Concha, viii: *Siglo XIX (I)*, co-ord. Guillermo Carnero (Madrid: Espasa-Calpe, 1997); ix: *Siglo XIX (II)*, co-ord. Leonardo Romero Tobar (Madrid: Espasa-Calpe, 1998).

HUTCHEON, LINDA, *A Theory of Parody* (New York: Methuen, 1985).

INDALECIO CASO, JOSÉ, *Exposición de hechos para la defensa de D. Claudio Fontanellas, hijo del primer Marques de Casa-Fontanellas, en causa pendiente contra el mismo por supuesta usurpación de estado civil* (Madrid: Luis Palacios, 1862).

—— *Nueva exposición de hechos para la defensa de D. Claudio Fontanellas y noticia de unos papeles falsos, agenciados en ideas para probar de nuevo que dicho procesado es Claudio Feliu: Opúsculo ameno y edificante* (Madrid: Santa Coloma, 1864).

—— *Discursos pronunciados en defensa de D. Claudio Fontanellas suplicando de la Real sentencia de vista de 31 de Diciembre de 1862 por lo que se condenó á dicho procesado á la pena de nueve años de presidio como usurpador de estado civil* (Barcelona: Luis Tasso, 1864–5).

Informe 2000 (Madrid: Sociedad General de Autores y Editores, 2000).

ITURBURU, CÓRDOVA, 'Definición de Norah Borges de Torre', *La Gaceta Literaria* 73 (1 Jan. 1930), 5–6.

JAMESON, FREDERIC, *The Political Unconscious: Narrative as a Socially Symbolic Act* (Ithaca, NY: Cornell University Press, 1981).

JANCOVICH, MARK, '"The Purest Knight of All": Nation, History, and Representation in *El Cid* (1960)', *Cinema Journal* 40/1 (Fall 2000), 79–103.

JARNÉS, BENJAMÍN, 'Los ángeles de Norah Borges', *La Gaceta Literaria* 7 (1 Apr. 1927), 2.

JAY, MARTIN, *Downcast Eyes: The Denigration of Sight in Twentieth Century Thought* (Berkeley: University of California Press, 1993).

JONES, MARGARET, *The Contemporary Spanish Novel, 1939–1975* (Boston: Twayne, 1985).

JONES, R. O., and SCANLON, GERALDINE M., 'Ignacio Sánchez Mejías: The "Mythic" Hero', *Studies in Modern Spanish Literature and Art, presented to Helen F. Grant*, ed. Nigel Glendinning (London: Tamesis, 1972), 97–108.

JORDAN, BARRY, *Writing and Politics in Franco's Spain* (London: Routledge, 1990).

JUTGLAR, ANTONI, *Historia crítica de la burguesía en Cataluña* (Barcelona: Anthropos, 1984).

KAPLAN, E. ANN, 'Is the Gaze Male?', *Desire: The Politics of Sexuality*, ed. Ann Snitow, Christine Stansell and Sharon Thompson (London: Virago, 1984), 321–8.

KARRER, WOLFGANG, *Parodie, Travestie, Pastiche* (Munich: Wilhelm Fink, 1977).

KIRKPATRICK, SUSAN, 'Fantasy, Seduction, and the Woman Reader: Rosalía de Castro's Novels', *Culture and Gender in Nineteenth-Century Spain*, ed. Lou Charnon-Deutsch and Jo Labanyi (Oxford: Clarendon Press, 1995), 74–97.

KRISTEVA, JULIA, 'Word, dialogue and novel', *The Kristeva Reader*, ed. Toril Moi (New York: Columbia University Press; London: Basil Blackwell, 1986), 34–61.

KRONIK, J. W., 'Enrique Gómez Carrillo, Francophile Propagandist', *Symposium* 21 (1967), 50–60.

LABANYI, JO, 'Literary experiment and cultural cannibalization', *Spanish Cultural Studies: An Introduction*, ed. Helen Graham and Jo Labanyi (London: Routledge, 1995), 295–9.

—— 'Postmodernity and the problem of cultural identity', ibid., 396–406.

—— 'Narrative in Culture, 1976–1996', *The Cambridge Companion to Modern*

Spanish Culture, ed. David T. Gies (Cambridge: Cambridge University Press, 1999), 147–62.

LARRA, MARIANO JOSÉ DE, *Artículos*, ed. Carlos Seco Serrano (Barcelona: Planeta, 1990).

LEÓN, MARÍA TERESA, 'La narradora', *La Gaceta Literaria* 85 (1 Jul. 1930), 8.

LE ROY LADURIE, EMMANUEL, *Montaillou: Village occitan de 1294 à 1324* (Paris: Gallimard, 1975)

—— *Le Carnival de Romans* (Paris: Gallimard, 1979)

LISSORGUES, YVAN (ed.), *La Rénovation du roman espagnol depuis 1975* (Toulouse: Presses Universitaires du Mirail, 1991).

LIVERMORE, ANN, *A Short History of Spanish Music* (London: Duckworth, 1972).

LODGE, DAVID (ed.), *Modern Criticism and Theory: A Reader* (London: Longman, 1988).

LOMBROSO, CESARE, *Genio e follia: Prelezione al corso di clinica-psychiatrica* (Milan: Chiusi, 1864).

—— *L'uomo delinquente* (Milan: Hoepli, 1876).

—— *L'Homme criminel* (Paris: Alcan, 1887).

LOMBROSO-FERRERO, GINA, *Criminal Man according to the Classification of Cesare Lombroso* (New York: G. Putnam's Sons, 1911).

LÓPEZ-REY, JOSÉ, *Velasquez* (London: Studio Vista, 1978).

LORCA, FEDERICO GARCÍA, *The Selected Poems of Federico García Lorca*, ed. Francisco García Lorca and Donald M. Allen (New York: New Directions, 1961).

—— *Obras completas*, ed. Arturo del Hoyo (Madrid: Aguilar, 5th edn. 1967; 22nd edn. 1986).

—— *Deep Song and Other Prose*, ed. and trans. Christopher Maurer (London and New York: Marion Boyars, 1982).

—— *Epistolario*, 2 vols., ed. Christopher Maurer (Madrid: Alianza, 1983).

—— *Poema del cante jondo; Romancero gitano*, ed. Allen Josephs and Juan Caballero, 8th edn. (Madrid: Cátedra, 1985).

—— *Primer romancero gitano; Llanto por Ignacio Sánchez Mejías; Romance de la corrida de toros en Ronda; y otros textos taurinos*, ed. Miguel Ángel García Posada (Madrid: Castalia, 1988).

—— *Poet in New York*, trans. Greg Simon and Steven F. White, ed. and introd. Christopher Maurer (Harmondsworth: Viking Penguin, 1989).

—— *Romancero gitano; Poeta en Nueva York; El público*, ed. Derek Harris (Madrid: Taurus, 1993).

—— *Poesía inédita de juventud*, ed. Christian de Paepe (Madrid: Cátedra, 1994).

—— *Epistolario completo*, ed. Christopher Maurer and Andrew A. Anderson (Madrid: Cátedra, 1997).

LORENZO ALCALÁ, MAY, 'Norah Borges, illustradora', *Noticias: Voz e imagen de Oaxaca* [digital edn.] (11 Mar. 2001), (accessed 21 Feb. 2002, no longer available); first publ. in *La Nación* [Buenos Aires], Cultura (18 Feb. 2001), 1, 8.

'Los estetas', *Vida Nueva* 21 (1898), n.p.

LUKÁCS, GEORG, *The Theory of the Novel: A Historico-philosophical Essay on the Forms of Great Epic Literature*, trans. Anna Bostock (London: Merlin Press, 1978; first pubd 1916).

MCDONOGH, GARY WRAY, *Good Families of Barcelona: A Social History of Power in the Industrial Era* (Princeton: Princeton University Press, 1986).

MCGUINNESS, PATRICK (ed.), *Symbolism, Decadence and the Fin de Siècle: French and European Perspectives* (Exeter: University of Exeter Press, 2000).

MACHADO, MANUEL, *Antología*, 6th edn. (Madrid: Espasa-Calpe, 1959).

MAINER, JOSÉ CARLOS, *De postguerra (1951–1990)* (Barcelona: Crítica, 1994).

MALCHOW, HOWARD, *Gentlemen Capitalists: The Social and Political World of the Victorian Businessmen* (London: Macmillan, 1991).

MALLARMÉ, STÉPHANE, *Œuvres complètes*, ed. H. Mondor and G. Jean Aubry (Paris: Pléiade and Gallimard, 1945).

MALLO, MARUJA, *59 grabados en negro y 9 láminas en color (1928–1942)*, introd. Ramón Gómez de la Serna (Buenos Aires: Losada, 1942).

MALUQUER I VILADOT, JOAN, *Teatre català: Estudi històrich-crítich* (Barcelona: Renaixença, 1878).

MANNHEIM, HERMANN (ed.), *Pioneers in Criminology* (London:Stevens, 1960).

MARFANY, JOAN-LLUÍS, *Aspectes del modernisme* (Barcelona: Curial, 1990).

MARÍAS, JAVIER, *Los dominios del lobo* (Barcelona: Anagrama, 1987; first pubd 1971).

—— *Literatura y fantasma* (Madrid: Siruela, 1993).

—— *El hombre que parecía no querer nada* (Madrid: Espasa-Calpe, 1996).

MARISTANY, LUIS, *El gabinete del doctor Lombroso (Delincuencia y fin de siglo en España)* (Barcelona: Anagrama, 1973).

MARRAST, ROBERT (ed.), *Poesías líricas y fragmentos épicos* (Madrid: Castalia, 1970).

MARTÍNEZ CACHERO, JOSÉ MARÍA, *La novela española entre 1936 y el fin de siglo: Historia de una aventura* (Madrid: Castalia, 1997).

MAXWELL, RICHARD, *The Spectacle of Democracy: Spanish Television, Nationalism, and Political Transition* (Minneapolis: University of Minnesota Press, 1995).

MAYER, AUGUST L., *Francisco de Goya*, trans. Robert West (London: J. M. Dent & Sons, 1924).

MAYR-HARTING, HENRY, *Perceptions of Angels in History* (Oxford: Clarendon Press, 1997).

MAZA, SARAH, *Private Lives and Public Affairs: The Causes Célèbres of Prerevolutionary France* (Berkeley: University of California Press, 1993).

MEÑACA, MARIE DE (ed.), *Dr Rafael Alberti: El poeta en Toulouse* (Toulouse: Université de Toulouse – Le Mirail, 1984).

MÉNDEZ CUESTA, CONCHA, *Canciones de mar y tierra,* foreword by Consuelo Berges (Buenos Aires: n.p., 1930); reviewed anonymously *Sudeste* 4 (1931), 4.

MENÉNDEZ PELAYO, MARCELINO, *Obras completas,* ed. Ángel González Palencia (Madrid: CSIC, 1948).

MENÉNDEZ PIDAL, RAMÓN, *La España del Cid,* 2 vols., 2nd edn. (Buenos Aires: Espasa-Calpe Argentina, 1943).

MILLÁS, JUAN JOSÉ, '¿De qué realidad me habla usted?', *Generación del 68,* ed. Santos Sanz Villanueva, *El Urogallo* (June 1988), 51–2.

MIRÓ, JOAN, *Selected Writings and Interviews,* ed. Margit Rowell (Boston: G. K. Hall, 1986; repr. New York: Da Capo Press, 1992).

MOLINARO, NINA L., *Foucault, Feminism, and Power: Reading Esther Tusquets* (London and Toronto: Associated University Presses, 1991).

MORELLI, GABRIELE, *Federico García Lorca: Saggi critici nel cinquantenario della morte* (Rome: Schena, 1988).

MORRIS, C. BRIAN, *Rafael Alberti's 'Sobre los ángeles': Four Major Themes* (Hull: Hull University Press, 1966).

—— (ed.), *The Surrealist Adventure in Spain* (Ottawa Hispanic Studies 6; Ottawa: Dovehouse, 1991).

MULVEY, LAURA, *Visual and Other Pleasures* (Basingstoke: Macmillan, 1989).

MUÑOZ MOLINA, ANTONIO, *Pura alegría* (Madrid: Alfaguara, 1998).

MURGÍA, MANUEL, 'Exposición de bellas artes 1858 (I)', *Museo universal* (1858), 153–4.

NANTELL, JUDITH, 'Irreconciliable Differences: Rafael Alberti's *Sobre los ángeles*', *The Surrealist Adventure in Spain,* ed. C. Brian Morris (Ottawa Hispanic Studies 6; Ottawa: Dovehouse, 1991), 145–65.

NEIRA, JULIO, *José María Hinojosa: Vida y obra,* 2 vols. (PhD diss., Universidad de Extremadura, 1981).

—— *Viajero de soledades* (Seville: Fundación Genesian, 1999).

NIETZSCHE, FRIEDRICH, *The Birth of Tragedy,* trans. Douglas Smith (Oxford: Oxford University Press, 2000; first pubd 1872).

Norah Borges, casi un siglo de pintura [exhibition cat., July–Aug. 1996] (Buenos Aires: Centro Cultural Borges, 1996).

NORDAU, MAX, *Degeneration,* trans. G. L. Mosse (New York: Howard Fertig, 1968).

ORTEGA Y GASSET, JOSÉ, *La deshumanización del arte* (Madrid: Revista de Occidente en Alianza Editorial, 1998; first pubd 1925).

PASCUAL SOLÉ, YOLANDA, 'Estética impresionista en *A la pintura* de Rafael Alberti', *Bulletin of Hispanic Studies* [Liverpool] 74 (1997), 197–214.

PASSERINI, LUISA, *Europe in Love, Love in Europe: Imagination and Politics in Britain between the Wars* (London: I. B. Tauris, 1999).

PÉREZ DE AYALA, RAMÓN, *Obras completas,* ed. José Garcia Mercadal (Madrid: Aguilar, 1963).

PERMANYER, LLUÍS, *Los años difíciles de Miró, Llorens Artigas, Fenosa, Dalí, Clavé, Tàpies* (Barcelona: Lumen, 1975).

PERRIAM, CHRIS, ET AL., *A New History of Spanish Writing: 1939 to the 1990s* (Oxford: Oxford University Press, 2000).

Pintura española de la Era Industrial, 1800–1900 (Madrid: Fundación de Arte y Tecnología, 1998).

PITTARELLO, ELIDE, foreword 'Guardar la distancia' to Javier Marías, *El hombre que parecía no querer nada* (Madrid: Espasa-Calpe, 1996), 11–31.

POPE, RANDOLPH D., 'Narrative in Culture, 1936–1975', *The Cambridge Companion to Modern Spanish Culture*, ed. David T. Gies (Cambridge: Cambridge University Press, 1999), 134–46.

POSNER, SANDY, *Giselle: The Story of the Ballet* (Leicester: Newman Wolsey, 1945).

POTTER, HELEN, *Impersonations* (New York: Edgar S. Werner, 1891).

PRADO, BENJAMIN, 'Rafael Alberti, entre el clavel y la espada', *Rafael Alberti: Premio de literatura en lengua castellana 'Miguel de Cervantes' 1983* (Barcelona: Anthropos, 1989), 71–103.

PREBISCH, ALBERTO, 'Los dibujos de Norah Borges', *Martín Fierro* 36 (1926), 1; repr. Patricia Artundo, *La obra gráfica de Norah Borges, 1920–1930* (Buenos Aires: n.p., 1993), 165.

QUANCE, ROBERTA, 'Un espejo vacío: Sobre una ilustración de Norah Borges para el ultraísmo', *La revista de Occidente* 239 (2001), 134–47.

QUINN, PATRICK F., *The French Face of Edgar Poe* (Carbondale: Southern Illinois University Press, 1957).

RABASSÓ, CARLOS A., and RABASSÓ, FCO. JAVIER, *Federico García Lorca entre el flamenco, el jazz y el afrocubanismo* (Madrid: Libertarias, 1998).

Rafael Alberti: Premio de literatura en lengua castellana 'Miguel de Cervantes' 1983 (Barcelona: Anthropos, 1989).

RAMAZANI, JAHAN, *Poetry of Mourning: The Modern Elegy from Hardy to Heaney* (London and Chicago: University of Chicago Press, 1994).

RAMOS GASCÓN, ANTONIO (ed.), *España hoy II: Cultura* (Madrid: Cátedra, 1991).

Reviews of film *Las hijas del Cid, Primer plano* 1172 (1963), 3–4; *Monthly Film Bulletin* (Oct. 1963), 148.

Revista Blanda 3–5 (Blanes, 2000–2).

RICHARDSON, NATHAN E., *Postmodern Paletos: Immigration, Democracy, and Globalization in Spanish Narrative and Film, 1950–2000* (Lewisburg, PA: Bucknell University Press, 2002).

RÍOS-FONT, WADDA, 'From Romantic Irony to Romantic Grotesque: Mariano José de Larra and Rosalía de Castro's Self-Conscious Novels', *Hispanic Review* 65 (1997), 177–98.

RISCO, ANTONIO, '*El caballero de las botas azules* de Rosalía, una obra abierta', *Papeles de Son Armadans* 71 (1975), 113–30.

RODIEK, CHRISTOPH, *La recepción internacional del Cid : Argumento recurrente – contexto – género*, trans. Lourdes Gómez de Olea (Madrid: Gredos,1995; orig. pubd. as *Sujet – Kontext – Gattung: die internationale Cid-Rezeption*, Berlin: Walter de Gruyter, 1990).

RODRIGO, ANTONINA, *Lorca–Dalí: Una amistad traicionada* (Barcelona: Planeta, 1981).

ROJAS SILVEYRA, MANUEL, 'La exposición de Norah Borges', *La Prensa* [Buenos Aires] (n.d.); repr. Patricia Artundo, *La obra gráfica de Norah Borges, 1920–1930* (Buenos Aires: n.p., 1993), 162–4.

ROS, XON DE, 'Science and Myth in *Llanto por Ignacio Sánchez Mejías*', *The Modern Language Review* 95 (2000), 114–26.

ROS DE OLANO, ANTONIO, *El doctor Lañuela: Episodio sacado de las memorias de un tal Josef* (Madrid: Manuel Galiano, 1863).

ROSE, MARGARET, *Parody/Metafiction* (London: Croom Helm, 1979).

—— *Parody: Ancient, Modern, and Post-modern* (Cambridge: Cambridge University Press, 1993).

ROSENBLUM, ROBERT, 'The Spanishness of Picasso's Still Lifes', *Picasso and the Spanish Tradition*, ed. Jonathan Brown (New Haven and London: Yale University Press, 1996), 61–93.

ROURE, CONRADO, *Recuerdos de mi larga vida: Costumbres, anécdotas, aconteci-mientos y sucesos acaecidos en la ciudad de Barcelona, desde el 1850 hasta el 1900* (Barcelona: El Diluvio, 1925–7).

ROZAS, JUAN MANUEL, *La Generación del 27 desde dentro* (Madrid: Istmo, 1986).

RUSSELL, PETER, 'San Pedro de Cardeña and the Heroic History of the Cid', *Medium Aevum* 27 (1958), 57–79.

SÁBATO, ERNESTO, interview in *Diario 16* (8 July 1995), 21–2.

SACKS, PETER M., *The English Elegy from Spenser to Yeats* (Baltimore and London: Johns Hopkins University Press, 1985).

SADIE, STANLEY (ed.), *History of Opera* (The New Grove Handbooks in Music; Basingstoke: Macmillan, 1989).

Sagasta y el liberalismo español [exhibition cat., 2000] (Madrid: Fundación Argentaria, 2000).

SALINAS, PEDRO, *Literatura española del siglo XX* (Madrid: Aguilar, 1961).

—— *Ensayos de literatura hispánica* (Madrid: Aguilar, 1961).

SÁNCHEZ, L. ALBERTO, 'Enrique Gómez Carrillo y el modernismo', *Atenea* [Chile] 117/299 (1950), 185–205.

SÁNCHEZ RODRÍGUEZ, ALFONSO, *Una aproximación al 'Caso Hinojosa'* (PhD diss., Estudi General de Lleida, 1990).

—— 'Concha Méndez y la vanguardia: Apuntes para un retrato de mujer moderna', *Una mujer moderna: Concha Méndez en su mundo (1898–1936)*, ed. James Valender (Madrid: Publicaciones de la Residencia de Estudiantes, 2001), 115–33.

SÁNCHEZ VIDAL, AGUSTÍN, *El enigma sin fin* (Barcelona: Planeta, 1988).

SANTOS TORROELLA, RAFAEL, 'Alenza, Lucas, Lameyer', *Goya* 104 (1971), 78–89.

—— *Salvador Dalí escribe a Federico García Lorca (1925–1936)* (Madrid: Ministerio de Cultura, 1987).

SANZ VILLANUEVA, SANTOS, *Historia de la novela social española (1942–1975)* (Madrid: Alhambra, 1980).

SAVATER, FERNANDO, *La infancia recuperada* (Madrid: Taurus, 1994; first pubd 1976).

SCHIESARI, JULIANA, *The Gendering of Melancholia: Feminism, Psychoanalysis and the Symbolics of Loss in Renaissance Literature* (Ithaca, NY, and London: Cornell University Press, 1992).

SEGAL, CHARLES, *Orpheus: The Myth of the Poet* (Baltimore and London: Johns Hopkins University Press, 1993).

SHAW-MILLER, SIMON, *Visible Deeds of Music* (New Haven and London: Yale University Press, 2002).

SILES, JAIME, 'Los novísimos: La tradición como ruptura, la ruptura como tradición', *Ínsula* 505 (Jan. 1989), 9–11.

SIX, ABIGAIL LEE, 'Protean Prose: Fluidity of Character and Genre in Esther Tusquets's *Siete miradas en un mismo paisaje*', *Changing Times in Hispanic Culture*, ed. Derek Harris (Aberdeen: Centre for the Study of the Hispanic Avant-Garde, University of Aberdeen, 1996), 177–86.

SLATTERY, TONY, interview in *The Independent* (9 Nov. 2001), 28.

SMITH, GARY A., *Epic Films; Casts, Credits and Commentary on over 250 Historical Spectacle Movies* (Jefferson, NC, and London: McFarland, 1991).

SMITH, PAUL JULIAN, 'Spanish Quality TV?', *Journal of Spanish Cultural Studies* 1 (2000), 173–92.

SNITOW, ANN, STANSELL, CHRISTINE, and THOMPSON, SHARON (eds.), *Desire: The Politics of Sexuality* (London: Virago, 1984).

SOBEJANO, GONZALO, 'Ante la novela de los años setenta', *Ínsula* 396–7 (1979), 1 and 22.

SPIRES, ROBERT C., *La novela española de posguerra: Creación artística y experiencia personal* (Madrid: Cupsa, 1978).

—— *Post-Totalitarian Spanish Fiction* (Columbia: University of Missouri Press, 1996).

SUTHERLAND, SUSAN, *Opera* (London: Teach Yourself Books, 1997).

SYMMONS, SARAH, *Goya* (London: Phaidon, 1998).

TAMBLING, JEREMY, *Opera, Ideology and Film* (Manchester: Manchester University Press, 1987).

TÉRIADE, E., 'La pintura de los jóvenes en París', *La gaceta literaria* 24 (15 Dec. 1927), 149.

TERRY, WALTER, *Ballet Guide: Background, Listings, Credits, and Descriptions of More than Five Hundred of the World's Major Ballets* (Newton Abbot and London: David & Charles, 1976).

THOMAS, DYLAN, *Collected Poems* (London: Faber & Faber, 1965).

TORRE, GUILLERMO DE, 'Manifiesto Vertical', *Grecia* (1 Nov. 1920), Suppl., repr. *El ultraísmo y las artes plásticas* [exhibition cat., 27 June – 8 Sept. 1996] (Valencia: IVAM, 1996), 140–1.

—— 'El renacimiento xilográfico: Tres grabadores ultraístas', *Nosotros* [Buenos Aires] 161 (1924), 274–6.

TUSQUETS, ESTHER, *Siete miradas en un mimo paisaje* (Barcelona: Lumen, 1981).

ULACIA ALTOLAGUIRRE, PALOMA, *Concha Méndez: Memorias habladas, memorias armadas*, foreword by María Zambrano (Madrid: Mondadori, 1990).

El ultraísmo y las artes plásticas [exhibition cat., 27 June – 8 Sept. 1996] (Valencia: IVAM, 1996).

VALENDER, JAMES (ed.), *Una mujer moderna: Concha Méndez en su mundo (1898–1936)* (Madrid: Publicaciones de la Residencia de Estudiantes, 2001).

—— 'Concha Méndez en el Río de la Plata (1929–1930)', ibid., 149–63.

VÁZQUEZ MONTALBÁN, MANUEL, 'La novela española entre el posfranquismo y el posmodernismo', *La Rénovation du roman espagnol depuis 1975*, ed. Yvan Lissorgues (Toulouse: Presses Universitaires du Mirail, 1991), 13–25.

VEGA ARMENTERO, REMIGIO, *¿Loco o delincuente? Novela social contemporánea (1890)*, ed. Pura Fernández (Madrid: Celeste, 2001).

VENTOSA, RICARDO, and VILLALAZ, DEMETRIO DE, *Acusaciones pronunciadas en la causa criminal seguida contra Claudio Feliu y Fontanills sobre usurpación del estado civil de D. Claudio de Fontanellas ante la Excma. Sala Tercera de la Audiencia de Barcelona en grado de Revista seguidas por la sentencia ejecutoria dictada por la misma Real Sala* (Barcelona: Ramírez y Rialp, 1865).

VICENS I VIVES, JAUME, and LLORENS, MONTSERRAT, *Industrials i politics: Segle XIX* (Barcelona: Vicens-Vives, 1991; first pubd 1958).

VILANOVA, ANTONIO, *Novela y sociedad en la España de la posguerra* (Barcelona: Lumen, 1995).

VILLAMIL, FERMÍN, *Historia justificativa de la defensa en el proceso Fontanellas con las biografías y retratos de las personas interesadas en la causa, de la parte que en ella tomaron, papel que hicieron, y refutación de la obra que sobre lo mismo publica D. Estevan Ferrater, relator de la Audiencia de Barcelona* (Barcelona: Oliveres, 1865).

WARDROPPER, BRUCE W., *Poesía elegíaca española* (Salamanca: Anaya, 1967).

WEISS, JEFFREY, *The Popular Culture of Modern Art: Picasso, Duchamp and Avant-Gardism* (New Haven and London: Yale University Press, 1994).

WHITE, HAYDEN, *Metahistory: The Historical Imagination in Nineteenth-Century Europe* (Baltimore: Johns Hopkins University Press, 1975).

—— 'Getting Out of History: Jameson's Redemption of Narrative', *Diacritics* 12 (1982); 2–13, repr. *The Content and the Form* (Baltimore: Johns Hopkins University Press, 1987), 142–68.

WIENER, MARTIN J., *English Culture and the Decline of the Industrial Spirit, 1850–1980* (Harmondsworth: Penguin, 1992).

WILCOX, John C., *Women Poets of Spain, 1860–1990* (Urbana and Chicago: University of Illinois Press, 1997).

WILLIAMS, DAVID, 'Medieval Movies', *The Yearbook of English Studies* 20 (1990), 1–32.

WOLFGANG, M. E., 'Cesare Lombroso', *Pioneers in Criminology*, ed. Hermann Mannheim (London: Stevens, 1960), 168–277.

XURIGUERA, GÉRARD, *Pintores españoles de la Escuela de París*, trans. Antonio Urrutia (Madrid: Ibérico Europea, 1974).

ZEIGER, MELISSA F., *Beyond Consolation: Death, Sexuality and the Changing Shapes of Elegy* (Ithaca, NY, and London: Cornell University Press, 1997).

ZEMON DAVIS, NATHALIE, *The Return of Martin Guerre* (Cambridge, MA: Harvard University Press, 1983).

ŽIŽEK, SLAVOJ, *Looking Awry: An Introduction to Jacques Lacan through Popular Culture* (Cambridge, MA: MIT Press, 1992).

INDEX

Instituto Cervantes

The Instituto Cervantes, the only official Spanish Government Language Centre, is a public institution founded in 1991 to promote Spanish language teaching and knowledge of the cultures of Spanish speaking countries throughout the world.

It is the largest Spanish teaching organisation worldwide, with 50 branches in four continents.

In the last academic year 3500 students in London came to the Instituto Cervantes to share the Spanish experience.

For further information, visit

http://londres.cervantes.es

call 0207 235 0353 or email: cenlon@cervantes.es

Instituto Cervantes
102 Eaton Square
London SW1 W9AN